Knowing the Heart of God

Knowing the Heart of God

GEORGE MACDONALD

BETHANY HOUSE PUBLISHERS
MINNEAPOLIS, MINNESOTA 55438

Published by Bethany House Publishers
A Ministry of Bethany Fellowship, Inc.
6820 Auto Club Road, Minneapolis, Minnesota 55438

Printed in the United States of America

Library of Congress Cataloging-in-Publication Data

MacDonald, George, 1824–1905.
  Knowing the heart of God / George MacDonald : compiled,
arranged, and edited by Michael R. Phillips.
     p.   cm.

  1. Christian life. 2. God—Knowableness. 3. Obedience—Religious as-
pects—Christianity. I. Phillips, Michael R. , 1946–
II. Title.
BV4501.M3384   1990
242—dc20
ISBN 1–55661–131–5

89–49343
CIP

Men would *understand*; they do not care to *obey*. They try to understand where it is impossible they should understand except by obeying. They would search into the work of the Lord instead of doing their part in it . . . It is on them that *do* his will that the day dawns. To them the day star arises in their hearts. Obedience is the soul of knowledge.

George MacDonald
The Hope of the Gospel

CONTENTS

${\rm I}$NTRODUCTION

To George MacDonald, all of life's truth could be discovered as part of an extremely simple, two-step process: realizing who God is, then obeying him.

Finding agreement, however, about what comprise the two elements of that process is not an easy task. For most men and women major stumbling blocks sit squarely in the middle of the road, which hinder them at each point. Both Christians and non-Christians alike are shackled by deeply entrenched false notions about God. We do not realize it, of course, because our misconceptions are much more subtle and less glaring to our eyes than those of our Victorian predecessors, to whom MacDonald wrote. Similarly, we are not aware of our distorted mental pictures of God, because the teachings Christians have received and the general prevalent views of our culture at large are so deeply ingrained that we scarcely pause to question them.

We might expect non-Christians or inactive churchgoers who rarely give their beliefs much thought to hold inaccurate viewpoints about God. Because they have not searched for truth, they can hardly be blamed for not finding it. If blame is to be laid at their door, it is for not caring enough about truth to seek it out.

A much more serious charge could be leveled at the Christian community of the twentieth century—those considering themselves enlightened, actively growing, energetic Christians who pray and attempt to apply biblical principles in their relationships and everyday dealings, and whose faith is a vital part of daily existence. For even the majority of those individuals largely mistake much in the divine character of the God whom they worship and serve. To a large extent, therefore, they misinterpret the primary focus of what God desires from them as followers of his Son. Not grasping the true essence of God's character, they also misunderstand Jesus—his person, his message, and his mission on earth—thinking he came to save them *from* God, rather than to lead them home *to* our Father.

From such historically embedded false concepts of God, George

MacDonald sought to free his readers. His writings picture the Father warmly and wonderfully full of love for his creatures. Coming to know this God in the true fullness of his being is, according to MacDonald, a process of discovery. Such it was in his own life, and into such a discovery of the character of God he leads us in his writings.

Once people begin to acquaint themselves with their Maker—once they begin to discover the *who* of God—then the question changes to one of *how*: how do we come to know him on a deeper level? Though many of us have been Christians for years, we find ourselves meeting our heavenly Father seemingly for the first time. Now we want to reallly *know* him! We want to probe the depths of God's character; we want to understand more of his ways; we want to draw close to his heart.

At this point, according to MacDonald, everything changes. No longer is the spiritual path one of discovery, but rather—to put it simply—one of hard work. Once we know who God is, the quest to *know* him intimately—as our Creator, our Father, our friend, our co-worker—becomes a probing, pursuing, active process of diligent application on our part. We then move out of the realm of the divine character to initiating our own growth by the efforts we make to draw close to the heart of God.

In MacDonald's view, there is but one path, but one way to draw intimately close to our Father: through the door of obedience. God became a man in the person of Jesus Christ in order to teach us of God's character and to show us how to obey. Thus, to acquaint ourselves with the Father, we must obey the Son. There is no other way to truly know God. MacDonald even goes so far as to say that without such obedience, notwithstanding what a person may think he "believes," one cannot be considered a Christian at all.

In the same way that we misunderstand God's character, so also do we misunderstand what is involved in knowing him. The very word "know" is part of our difficulty. We mistakenly assume "knowledge" is what it takes to know God. Thus, belief for many Christians is viewed as having to do with a mental assent to certain basic doctrines about Christ, and we attempt to strengthen our so-called belief by learning more and more about God and the Bible and Jesus, and by becoming more and more involved in a variety of church and other Christian activities that are intended to bolster this "faith" of ours. We expend enormous energy increasing our mental knowledge—reading, studying, discussing, analyzing the Scriptures—thinking this is helping us to "know" God more fully. We read books, watch Christian television, vocalize spiritual slogans, listen to Christian music, display Christian paraphernalia, tell people about Jesus—give them books and tracts and

pamphlets and New Testaments, explain to them many scriptural principles, and make every attempt to convince others of the truth of the
Gospel. All the while, however, these efforts have to do with the *ideas*
of Christianity. But there is no salvation in being mentally convinced
of the Gospel's truth, nor in possessing a huge repository of biblical
wisdom. None of these things will deepen intimacy with our Father.
Knowing God can never come from studying and gathering knowledge
about him, not from convincing others of truth, not from knowing truth
yourself.

MacDonald says: "Men would understand, they do not care to *obey*.
They try to understand where it is impossible they should understand
except by obeying. There is no salvation in correct opinions. A man's
real *belief* is that by which he lives. To *do* his works is to enter into a
vital relationship with Jesus, to obey him is the *only* way to be one with
him. The relation between him and us is an absolute one; it can begin
to *live* in no other way but in obedience: it *is* obedience."

This second volume in the *Discovering God* series, therefore, is not
a book from which you will merely increase your knowledge *of* or *about*
God. Contained herein are George MacDonald's words of truth not to
help you understand God more fully but rather to help you in your
desire to obey him. If obeying the Son is not the desire of your heart,
then this book will have little to offer you. But if obeying the words of
Jesus is the hunger of your being, your intimacy with God will increase,
not from any words you read here, but from your own willing attempts
to do what God—not George MacDonald, not your friends, not your
pastor—tells you.

If you have not previously read a great deal of George MacDonald,
you are in for a mind- and heart-expanding experience, and more than
likely the upsetting of many traditionally held views. You may find
yourself doubting MacDonald's wisdom at points, arguing in your
mind against issues he raises, even getting angry with him. But if you
find yourself thinking, praying, and probing the depths of your faith
from new vantage points, George MacDonald will have succeeded in
widening your spiritual horizons.

George MacDonald was no teacher of "theology" in the usual sense
of the word. His writing was varied. Among his 53 published books
are included more than 400 poems, 25 short stories, a dozen literary
essays, 50 sermons (some ranging more than 50 pages in length), a
number of book-length fairy tales, several fantasies, as well as some 30
realistic novels of between 300 and 800 pages each. And on nearly every
page, in nearly every poem, and certainly in every sermon, the two
things George MacDonald cared most about—the character of God,

and obedience to his commands—were clearly visible.

Thus, the attempt has been made here, as in the previous volume, *Discovering the Character of God*, to offer a rounded sampling of George MacDonald's thought from multiple sources—his poems, his sermons, and his fiction. You will undoubtedly find yourself enjoying certain of the genres more fully, and may even skip selections here and there. This is not intended as a book to read straight through, but one to be digested slowly. Though the chapters average eight to ten pages in length, they are divided into many smaller sections in order that you may read brief portions at a time and perhaps use the book devotionally for daily readings. But to accurately represent MacDonald's thought and to adequately convey his approach as a writer, selections from all these various genres are necessary.

There are those who voice concern about the spiritual implications of fiction, thinking that the novel is somehow less "real" than a more didactic book. The reality of fiction, however, lies on a deeper plane than mere "factness." Reality is a function of truth. And truth—however conveyed—*is* real. There is, therefore, a reality pervading the novels of George MacDonald, because the situations and characters point toward truth, and toward the One in whom is contained all truth.

By communicating his message in such a fashion, George Mac-Donald was following the example of his Lord. For fiction was frequently the vehicle Jesus used in order to best convey principles of life in God's kingdom. As Jesus spoke to ordinary people, he found that telling them stories through nonfactual characters was the *best* means to express realities and truths they might not have grasped so deeply in any other way.

"Pure theology, as it happens, figures much less prominently in Holy Scripture than might be expected, suggesting that God the Author is not so much a theologian as He is a writer of *literature* in the broadest sense of that word. And similarly, when the Son of God came into the world, He came as a storyteller as much as a preacher.

"In fact, in Matthew 13:34 we are told that 'Jesus spoke all these things to the crowd in parables; He did not say anything to them without using a parable.' This is a startling verse. Paraphrased, it might read: 'Jesus didn't preach to the people. Instead He just told them stories all day long.'

"What this means, in effect, is that a great deal of what Jesus said is *not literally true*. The parables are *fiction*, works of the imagination that Jesus made up . . . and the truth they contain is an imaginative or spiritual truth . . . and often enough the only explanation He deigned to offer was, 'He who has ears, let him hear.' . . . For it is not just that fiction . . . can occasionally be a useful channel for presenting the gospel or can provide colorful 'illustrations.' Far more than that, there are times and places when *fiction alone* can effectively communicate the truth."[1]

"Do good to your neighbor" was not a teaching that originated with Jesus; it had been set forth by hundreds of great men before. But it was Jesus who penetrated clearly and incisively to the very heart of the matter with his parable of the Good Samaritan, immortalizing the truth as no one before or since has ever done. In fictional form, the truth came alive for all time. Through the nonfactual, but highly *real*, genre of the parable—of fiction—Jesus brought spiritual principles to life.

Christian fiction is nothing new. George MacDonald is not the first to weave spiritual truth through imaginative, poetic, and fictional formats, but he is the greatest such writer I know. What some point to as defects in his novels—the fact that they are interspersed with comments, observations, and digressions—I view as the feature that so elevates his writing above the norm as a medium for communicating spiritual truth. For George MacDonald neither the pure didactic nor the pure story was sufficient: the principles must be stated; then they must be lived. Thus, following God's example in the Bible, MacDonald made full use of many forms of writing: poetry, teaching, history, long fiction, short fiction, and parable.

MacDonald's priorities are reflected in these topical readings. His homiletic principles are stated from his sermons, followed by passages from his novels that exemplify those same truths. The fictional selections are an intrinsic part of the process: how the truths are *lived* was a question always at the forefront of MacDonald's mind. The fictional readings here provide the practical illustration to undergird the teaching. They are not mere additions to the meaty sections of the text; they are equally vital to the reader who would learn from MacDonald how to practically obey the Lord.

This is but a scant sampling of MacDonald's thought on knowing the heart of God through obedience to Jesus. His writings include more than 1000 pages of sermon material, and some 12,000 to 14,000 pages of fiction. This compilation of a mere 300 pages of selections is only a tip of the iceberg. The sermons are fairly thoroughly reproduced in edited form. But for deeper treatment, especially from the novels, I would urge your reading of the stories in their entirety—either in edited format, or in their originals (the availability of both is given in the appendix).

For those interested in further background about MacDonald himself, his life, his theological bent, his impact in his own day, and/or studies and analyses of his books, I would point you to two sources: one, the biography of MacDonald, *George MacDonald: Scotland's Beloved Storyteller*; and secondly, one or more of the volumes of "The Masterline Series"—articles and essays about the person and work of George MacDonald by various authors who have studied his work in depth. Information on both of these can also be found in the appendix.

I would like to express my appreciation to those few intrepid souls over the years whose dedication to MacDonald helped keep him faintly in the public eye until the reawakening of interest in his works began in more earnest. Foremost among those is Bethany House Publishers, whom I once more salute—not only for their excellence and integrity as a publishing house in today's environment, where compromise of values is all too common, but for their commitment to make George MacDonald's work available. Bethany House, along with Sunrise Books, is preserving the works of George MacDonald for future generations, for which our children and grandchildren always will be grateful.

Michael Phillips
Eureka, California

At My Window
After Sunset—

Heaven and the sea attend the dying day,
And in their sadness overflow and blend—
Faint gold, and windy blue, and green and gray:
Far out amid them my pale soul I send.

For, as they mingle, so mix life and death;
An hour draws near when my day too will die;
Already I forecast unheaving breath,
Eviction on the moorland of yon sky.

Coldly and sadly lone, unhoused, alone,
Twixt wind-broke wave and heaven's uncaring space!
At board and hearth from this time forth unknown!
Refuge no more in wife or daughter's face!

Cold, cold and sad, lone as that desert sea!
Sad, lonely, as that hopeless, patient sky!
Forward I cannot go, nor backward flee!
I am not dead; I live, and cannot die!

Where are ye, loved ones, hither come before?
Did you fare thus when first ye came this way?
Somewhere there must be yet another door!—
A door in somewhere from this dreary gray!

Come walking over watery hill and glen,
Or stoop your faces through yon cloud perplext;
Come, any one of dearest, sacred ten,
And bring me patient hoping for the next.

Maker of heaven and earth, father of me,
My words are but a weak, fantastic moan!
Were I a land-leaf drifting on the sea,
Thou still wert with me; I were not alone!

I am in thee, O father, lord of sky,
And lord of waves, and lord of human souls!
In thee all precious ones to me more nigh
Than if they rushing came in radiant shoals!

I shall not be alone although I die,
And loved ones should delay their coming long;
Though I saw round me nought but sea and sky,
Bare sea and sky would wake a holy song.

They are thy garments; thou art near within,
Father of fathers, friend-creating friend!
Thou art for ever, therefore I begin;
Thou lov'st, therefore my love shall never end!

Let loose thy giving, father, on thy child;
I pray thee, father, give me everything;
Give me the joy that makes the children wild;
Give throat and heart an old new song to sing.

Ye are my joy, great father, perfect Christ,
And humble men of heart, oh, everywhere!
With all the true I keep a hoping tryst;
Eternal love is my eternal prayer.

WRONGLY KNOWING CHRIST

But ye did not so learn Christ; if so be that ye heard him, and were taught in him, even as truth is in Jesus: that ye . . . be renewed in the spirit of your mind.

Ephesians 4:20–23 (RV)

How do we come to know Christ? How have we learned of him? It ought to be a startling thought that we may have learned wrongly of him. To wrongly know him must be even worse than not to know him at all. The question we have to ask ourselves is this: have we learned Christ as he taught himself, or as men have taught him who *thought* they understood, but did not understand him? Do we know Christ merely according to low, fleshly, human fancies and explanations, or do we indeed know him as God knows him?

Throughout its history, the Christian religion, because it is higher and wider and larger in scope, has been more open to corruption and misrepresentation than any other religion. As a result, have we learned Christ from false statements and corrupted lessons about him, or have we learned *himself*? Is only our brain full of things *about* him, or does he himself dwell in our hearts, the power of our life?

How Theology Turns Many Away From the Gospel

I have been led to what I am about to say by a certain statement from a man in the front ranks of those who reject Christianity on the basis of their perception of it, and who thus claims we can know nothing of the infinite God. The statement is this:

> The visiting on Adam's descendants through hundreds of gen-

erations dreadful penalties for a small transgression which they did not commit; the damning of all men who do not avail themselves of an alleged mode of obtaining forgiveness, which most men have never heard of; and the effecting a reconciliation by sacrificing a son who was perfectly innocent, to satisfy the assumed necessity for a propitiatory victim; are modes of action which, ascribed to a human ruler, would call forth expressions of abhorrence; and the ascription of them to the Ultimate Cause of things, even now felt to be full of difficulties, must become impossible.

I do not quote this passage in order to oppose it, for notwithstanding that its author is not a Christian, I entirely agree with it. One of my earliest recollections as a child is of beginning to be at strife with the false system here assailed. I would sooner join the ranks of those who "know nothing," and thus weigh my heart down with hopelessness, than I would believe a single point of this low so-called Christian theology.

Neither will I inquire why the writer of this passage puts forward these so-called beliefs as representing Christianity, when so many wise and knowledgeable people who believe in Christ with true hearts, some of them of higher rank in literature than himself, believe not one of such things as he has set down.

He would probably answer that despite the few who do not believe them, such remain the things held by the bulk of both educated and uneducated who call themselves Christians. Alas, I am unable to deny that he would be right! Many Christians vainly think that with an explanatory clause here and there they can turn away the disgracefulness of this false theology. It helps nothing that many Christians, not thinking through the implications in any depth, use *quasi* mitigated forms to express their tenets, and imagine that so they indicate a different class of ideas: it would require but a brief examination to be convinced that they are ultimately identical.

No Salvation in Opinion

But if I did have to do with the writer of the above passage, I would ask him why it is that, refusing these dogmas as abominable, yet knowing they are attributed to men whose teaching has done more to civilize the world than that of any other—why is it he has not taken the pains to inquire how it could be so? He is a thinking man. How can he be satisfied without looking into the matter? Surely even he would see that this could not possibly be the foundation of such a powerful religion, and that it must indeed be so different, and so good, that even the forced companionship of such lies as those he has recounted has been unable to destroy its regenerative power.

I hardly know which error is worse—the untruth of Christians who have erected a false system of doctrines to explain a God whose heart they have not sought to know, or the untruth of non-Christians who foolishly do not look beyond such flimsy fabrications. Neither side, it seems, is hungry to find the *real* truth, but only to build up or tear down something that is not even there!

Surely the author who has prompted my remarks will allow that there was a man named Jesus, who died for the truth he taught. Can the author believe Jesus died for such an alleged truth as the author has outlined?

Would it not be wise for the man to find out what Jesus really did teach, according to the primary sources of our knowledge of him?[1] For certainly until we see God as he is, and are changed into his likeness, all our beliefs must partake more or less of superstition. But if there be a God, the greatest superstition of all will be found to have consisted in denying him. Of all useless things a merely speculative theology is of the least value.[2]

In actual fact, however, I am not now speaking to this man. I have only been making reference to him with the object of making my position plain to those who call themselves Christians. They are those to whom I would now speak.

To Christians, therefore, I ask: "How do you come to hold such opinions concerning our Holy God as the above author set forth?[3] Would you, like him, imagine justice and love dwelling in eternal opposition in the bosom of the eternal unity and thus have us love Christ to protect us from God—the one home of safety—in whom alone is bliss, away from whom all is darkness and misery? If so, you have not a glimmer of the truth, and know next to nothing about God, and misrepresent him hideously every Sunday. If God were such, it would indeed be the worst possible misfortune to have been created, or have anything to do with God at all."[4]

Most would answer, "Those are the things he tells us himself in his Word; we have learned them from the Scriptures." Others would give long explanations that seem to them to explain the various points satisfactorily so that they are no longer repugnant.

Of those whose presentation of Christian doctrine is represented in the quotation above, there are two classes of people: those who are content it should be so, and those to whom those things are grievous, but who do not see how to get rid of them. To the latter, it may be some little comfort to have one who has studied the New Testament for many years and loves it beyond the power of speech, to declare to them his conviction that there is not an atom of such teaching in the whole, lovely, divine utterance. That I do now declare. Such things are altogether of human invention—honest invention, in part at least, I grant, but still not true. Thank God, we are in no way bound to accept any man's explanation of God's ways and God's doings, however good the man may be, if his explanation does not commend itself to our conscience. The man's conscience may be a better conscience than ours, and his judgment clearer. But still we cannot accept something we do not see as good.

But it is by no means my object to set forth what I believe or do not believe. A time may come for that. But my design now is very different indeed. I desire to address those who call themselves Christians.

Is it right that your beliefs on the greatest of all subjects should stem from your opinions? I ask further: is Christianity even capable of being represented by opinion, even the very best of opinions? If you answer, "The opinions I hold, and by which I represent Christianity, are those of the Bible," I reply by asking: "Who can perfectly understand, still less perfectly represent, the whole mind, scope, and intent of thought of the writers in the Bible?"

Is Christianity a system of articles of belief? Never. It would be better for a man to hold the most obnoxious untruths, opinions the most irreverent, if at the same time he *lived* in the faith of the Son of God, that is trusted in God as the Son of God trusted in him, than for him to hold every formula of belief perfectly true, and yet know nothing of a daily life and walk with God. The one, holding doctrines of devils, is yet a child of God. The other, holding the doctrines of Christ, is of the world—yes, of the devil.

To hold to a doctrine or an opinion with the intellect alone is not to believe it. A man's *real* belief is that which he lives by. If a man lives by the love of God, and obedience to God's law, as far as he has recognized it, then whatever wrong opinions the man holds are outside of him. They are not true, and they cannot really be inside any good man. At the same time, no matter how many correct opinions another man holds, if he does not order his life by the law of God's love, he is not a child of God. What a man believes is the thing he does, not the thing he thinks.[5]

A man will be judged by his faithfulness to what he professes to believe. How many men would be immeasurably better, if they would but truly believe, that is, act upon, the smallest part of what they profess to believe, even if they cast aside all the rest. If there be a God and one has never sought him, it will be small consolation to remember that one could not get proof of his existence.[6]

There is no salvation in correct opinions, neither is there damnation in wrong opinions. Suppose your theories right, suppose they contain all that is to be believed. Those theories are not what makes you a Christian, if a Christian you indeed are. On the contrary, in many cases they are just what keeps you from being a Christian. For when you say that, to be saved, one must hold to this or that notion, you are putting your trust in some idea *about* God, rather than in the living God and his will.[7]

It is one thing to believe in *a* god: it is quite another to believe in God! One of four gates stands open to us: to deny the existence of God; to acknowledge his existence but say he is not good; to say, "I wish there was a God," and be miserable because there is none; or to say, "There is a God, and he must be perfect in goodness or he could not be," and thus give ourselves to him heart and soul.[8]

We Are Not Saved by the Atonement, We Are Saved by Jesus

Some of you say we must trust in the finished work of Christ. Or that our faith must be in the merits of Christ, or in the atonement he has made, or in the blood he has shed.

All these statements deny the *living* Lord, *in whom* we are told to believe, who, by his presence with and in us, and our obedience to him, lifts us out of darkness into light, leads us from the kingdom of Satan into the glorious liberty of the children of God.

No manner or amount of belief *about* Christ is the faith of the New Testament. No opinion, I repeat, is Christianity, and no preaching of any plan of salvation is the preaching of the glorious gospel of the living God. Even if your plan, your theories, were absolutely true, the holding of them with sincerity, the trusting in this or that about Christ, or in anything he did or could do, the trusting in anything but himself, his own *living* self, is a delusion.

Many will agree with me heartily. Yet the moment you come to talk with them, you find they insist that to believe in Christ is to believe in the atonement, meaning by that only their special theory about the atonement. And if you say we must believe in the atoning Christ, but not in any *theory* concerning the atonement, they go away and denounce you, saying, "He does not believe in the atonement!"

If I explain the atonement otherwise than they explain it, they claim that I deny the atonement. They consider it of no consequence that I believe in the Atoner with my whole heart, soul, mind, and strength.

Because I refuse to accept an explanation that is not in the New Testament, though they believe it is, they would brand me as a heretic and no Christian!

Is it any wonder men such as he whom I quoted earlier refuse the Christianity they suppose such "believers" to represent!

I do not say that with this sad folly over opinions there does not mingle a genuine faith in the Lord himself. But I do say that the *importance* they place on theory is even more sadly obstructive to true faith than such theories themselves. While the mind is occupied with the question, "Do I believe or feel this thing right?" the *true* question is forgotten: "Have I left all to follow him?"[9] The important thing is whether we are letting God have His own way with us, following where he leads, learning the lessons he gives us.[10] We can never be at peace until we have performed the highest duty of all—until we have arisen, and gone to our Father."[11]

Religion is simply the way home to the Father. Because of our unchildlikeness, the true way is difficult enough—uphill, steep, but there is fresh life with every surmounted height, a purer air gained, more life for more climbing. But the path that is not the true one is not therefore an easy one. Uphill work is hard walking, but through a bog is worse. Those who seek God with their faces hardly turned toward him—who, instead of beholding the Father in the Son, take the most ridiculous opinions concerning him and his ways from those who, if they have themselves ever known God, have never taught him from their own knowledge of him, but from the dogmas of others—go wandering about in dark mountains, or through marsh, spending their strength in avoiding precipices and bog-holes, sighing and mourning over their sins instead of leaving them behind and fleeing to the Father, whom to know is eternal life. If they set themselves to find out what Christ thought and knew and meant, and to do it, they would soon forget their false teachers, and find it a good riddance. But alas! they go on bowing before long-faced, big-worded authority, the more fatally when it is embodied in a good man who, himself a victim to faith in men, sees the Son of God only through the theories of others, and not with the clear sight of his own spiritual eyes.[12]

To the man or woman who gives himself to the living Lord, every belief will necessarily come at the right time. The Lord himself will see that his disciple believes aright concerning him. If a man cannot trust God for this, what claim can he make to faith in God? It is because he has little or no faith, that such a man is left clinging to preposterous and dishonoring ideas, human traditions concerning the Father, neither the teaching of Jesus nor that of his apostles. The living Christ is to them but a shadow, the all-but-obliterated Christ of their theories that no soul can thoroughly believe in.[13]

Is It Bad Not to Believe in God?

A Fictional Selection from *The Baron's Apprenticeship*

D o you think it very bad of a man not to believe in a God?"
  "That depends on the sort of God he imagines that he either does or does not believe in. Most people have totally wrong conceptions of God. A thousand times would I rather see a man not believe in God at all than believe in an evil god that could cause suffering and misery as if he were a devil. But if a man had the same notion of God that I have—a God who is even now doing his best to take all men and women and beasts out of the misery in which they find themselves—and did not at least desire that there might be such a God, then I confess I would have difficulty in understanding how he could be good. When one looks at the gods that have been offered though the years who are not worth believing in, it might be an act of virtue not to believe in them."

  "One thing more, Mr. Wingfold—and you must not think I am arguing against you or against God, I just want to understand—might not a man think the idea of God such as you believe in too good to be true?"

  "Why should he be able to think anything too good to be true? Badness itself can have no life in it. If a thing be bad, it cannot possibly be true. But if the man really thought as you suggest, I would ask him, 'If such a being did exist, would you be content never to find him, but to go on forever saying, *He can't be. He can't be! He's so good he can't be!*? Supposing one day you find him, will you say to him: *If you had not been so good, if you had been just a little bad, then I would have believed in you'*?"

  "But if the man could not believe there was any such being,

what could be done for him to give him the heart to look for him?"

"God knows—God *does* know. It all depends on whether such a man had been doing what he knew he ought to do, living as he knew he ought to live, or whether he had by wrong-doing injured his deepest faculty of understanding."

"And if the man was one who sought to do right, who tried to help his neighbor—yet still denied the God that most people seem to believe in? What would you say then?"

"I would say, 'Have patience. If there be a good God, he cannot be altogether dissatisfied with such a man. I do not know when any man or woman has arrived at the point of development where he is capable of really believing in God: the innocent child who has never heard of Jesus may be capable, and a gray-haired intelligent man of science incapable. If he be such a person as you have described, I believe that, no matter how uninteresting he may say the question of a God is to him, the God of patience is taking care of him, and the time must come when something will make him want to know whether there be a God, and whether he can get near to him.' I should say, 'He is in God's school; don't be too troubled about him, as if God might overlook and forget him. He will see to all that concerns him. He has made him, and he loves him, and he is doing and will do his very best for him.' "[14]

Jesus Thinks About Us

A Fictional Selection from *A Daughter's Devotion*

Everyone knows I am very ill. Sit down there, on the foot of the bed, only take care you don't shake it. I want to talk to you. People nowadays, you know, say there isn't any hell—or perhaps none to speak of?"

"I should think the former more likely than the latter," said Mary.

"You don't believe there is a hell then? I am glad of that! for you are a good girl and ought to know."

"You mistake me, sir. How can I imagine there is no hell when he said there was?"

"Who's *he*?"

"The man who knows all about it, and means to keep you out of it."

"Oh yes, I see!—But I don't for the life of me see what a fellow is to make of all that—don't you know? Those parsons! They all insist there's no way but theirs, and I never could see a handle anywhere to that door!"

"I don't see what the parsons have got to do with it, or what you have got to do with the parsons. If the thing is true, you have as much to do with it as any parson in England. If it is not true, neither you nor they have anything to do with it."

"But I tell you, if it be all true that—that we are all sinners, I don't know what to do."

"It seems to me a very simple thing. *He* as much as said he knew all about it, and came to find men that were lost, and take them home."

"He can't well find one more lost than I am! But how am I to believe it? How *can* it be true? It's ages since he was here, if he ever was at all, and there hasn't been a sign of him ever since the whole time!"

"There you may be quite wrong. I think I could find you some who believe him just as near them now as he was to his own brothers and disciples—who believe that he hears them when they speak to him, and heeds what they say."

"That's bosh! You would have me believe contrary to what my good senses tell me!"

"You must have strange senses, Mr. Redmain, that give you evidence where they can't possibly know anything. If that man spoke the truth when he was in the world, he *is* near us now. And if he is not near us and did not speak the truth, that is the end of it all."

"The nearer he is, the worse for me!" sighed Mr. Redmain.

"The nearer he is, the better for the worst man that ever breathed."

"That's an odd doctrine! It seems a cowardly thing to go asking him to save you, after you've all your life been doing what ought to damn you—if there be a hell, mind you, that is."

"But think," said Mary, "if that should be your only chance of being able to make up for the mischief you have done? No punishment you can have will do anything for that. No suffering of yours will do anything for those you have made to suffer. But it is so much harder to leave the old way than to go on and let things take their chance."

"There may be something in what you say. But still I can't see it any better than sneaking—to do a world of mischief, and then slink away into heaven, leaving all the poor wretches to look after themselves."

"I don't think Jesus Christ is worse pleased with you for feeling like that," said Mary.

"What? What's that you say?—Jesus Christ worse pleased with me? That's a good one! As if he ever thought about a fellow like me!"

"If he did not think about you, you would not be thinking about him just this minute, I suspect. He said himself he didn't come to call the righteous, but sinners to repentance."

"I wish I could repent."

"You can, if you will."

"I can't make myself sorry for what's gone and done with."

"No, you need him to do that. But you can turn from your old ways and ask him to have you for a pupil. Aren't you willing to learn, if he is willing to teach you?"

"I don't know. It's all so dull! I never could bear going to church."

"I said nothing about church. It's not one bit like that! It's like going to your mother and saying you're going to try to be a good boy, and not disobey her any more."

"Well, I've had as much of it as I can stand for now."[15]

The Lost House

Out of thy door I run to do the thing
    That calls upon me. Straight the wind of words
Whoops from mine ears the sounds of them that sing
About their work, "My God, my father-king!"

I turn in haste to see thy blessed door,
    But, lo, a cloud of flies and bats and birds,
    And stalking vapors, and vague monster-herds
        Have risen and lighted, rushed and swollen between!

Ah me! the house of peace is there no more.
Was it a dream then?—Walls, fireside, and floor,
    And sweet obedience, loving, calm, and free,
        Are vanished—gone as they had never been!

    I labour groaning. Comes a sudden sheen!—
And I am kneeling at my father's knee,
Sighing with joy, and hoping utterly.

KNOWING CHRIST ARIGHT

I count all things but loss for the excellency of the knowledge of Christ Jesus my Lord.

Philippians 3:8

If ye be willing and obedient, ye shall eat the good of the land.

Isaiah 1:19

Doing As He Says

We can never come to know Jesus as he is by believing any theory *about* him. What I would point people to is a faith in the living, loving, ruling, helping Christ. It is not faith that Christ did this, or that his work wrought that which will save us. Rather, it is faith in the man *himself* who did and is doing everything for us.

Do you ask, "What is faith in him?"

I answer, the leaving of your way, your objects, your self, and the taking of his and him; the leaving of your trust in men, in money, in opinion, in character, in religious doctrines and opinions, *and then doing as Christ tells you.*

I can find no words strong enough to serve for the weight of this necessity—this obedience.

It is the one terrible heresy of the church that it has always been presenting something else than obedience as faith in Christ. The work of Christ is not the Working Christ, any more than the clothing of Christ is the Body of Christ. If the woman who touched the hem of his garment had trusted in the garment and not in him who wore it, would she have been healed?[1]

It is the vile falsehood and miserable unreality of Christians—their faithlessness to their Master, their love of their own wretched sects, their worldliness and unchristianity, their talking and not doing—that has to answer, I suspect, for the greater part of the world's atheism. It is better to be an atheist who does the will of God, than a so-called Christian who does not. The atheist will not be dismissed because he said "Lord, Lord," and did not obey. The thing that God loves is the only lovely thing, and he who does it, does well, and is upon the way to discover that he does it very badly. When he comes to do it as the will of the perfect Good, then is he on the road to do it perfectly.[2]

The reason that so many who believe *about* Christ rather than in him get the comfort they do is that, touching the mere hem of his garment, they cannot help believing a little in the live man inside the garment. But, alas, their comfort is too little. It is hardly to be wondered at that such believers should often be miserable. They lay themselves down to sleep with nothing but the skirt of his robe in their hand—a robe, in actual fact, that never was his, only by them is supposed his— when they might sleep in peace with the living Lord in their hearts. Instead of knowing Christ, they lie wasting away in self-examination as to whether they are believers, whether they are really trusting in the atonement, whether they are truly sorry for their sins—a sure way to madness of the brain and despair of the heart.

Some even ponder the imponderable—whether they are of the elect, whether theirs is a saving faith—when all the time the man who died for them is waiting to begin to save them. He will set them free and take them home to the bosom of the Father—if only they will listen to what he says to them, which is the beginning, middle, and end of faith. If they would but awake and arise from the dead of their theories and come out into the light that Christ is waiting to give them, he would begin at once to fill them with the fullness of God.

Obedience Is *the Only Faith*

Do you want to live by faith? Do you want to know Christ aright? Do you want to awake and arise and *live*, but do not know how?

I will tell you:

Get up, and do something the master tells you. The moment you do, you instantly make yourself his disciple.

Instead of asking yourself whether you believe or not, ask yourself whether you have this day done one single thing because he said, "Do it," or once abstained because he said, "Do not do it." I do not say that you will not have, as a matter of course, done this or that good thing that fell into harmony with the words of Jesus. But have you done or not done any act, as a conscious decision made *because* he said to do it or not?

It is simply absurd to say you believe, or even want to believe in him, if you do not do anything he tells you. If you can think of nothing he ever said as having consciously influenced your doing or not doing, you have no ground to consider yourself his disciple. To such he says, "Why did you not do the things I told you? Depart from me. I do not know you!"

Yet you can at once begin to be a disciple of the Living One—by obeying him in the first thing you can think of in which you are not obeying him.

We must learn to obey him in everything, and so must begin somewhere. Let it be at once, and in the very next thing that lies at the door of our conscience!

Oh, do not be as the fools who think of nothing but Christ as a theological person to be discussed, and do not set themselves to do his words! What will they have to answer for, such teachers who have turned the regard of their listeners away from the direct words of the Lord himself, which are spirit and life, to contemplate instead various plans of salvation that they twist out of the words of his apostles!

There is but one plan of salvation, and that is to believe in the Lord Jesus Christ! And that *belief* is no mere mental acknowledgment *about* him, but involves nothing more, nothing less than to take him for what he is—our Master, and to take his words as if he meant them, which he did.

To *do* his words is to enter into vital relation with Jesus; to obey him is the *only* way to be one with him. The relationship between him and us is an absolute one; it can begin to *live* in no other way but in obedience: it *is* obedience. There can be no truth, no reality, in any initiation of at-one-ment with him, that is not obedience.

It is eternally absurd to think of entering into a relationship with God, the very first of which is not founded on doing what he says. I know what the father of lies whispers to those to whom such teaching as this is distasteful: "It is the doctrine of works!" But one word of the Lord humbly heard and received will suffice to send all the demons of false theology into the abyss. Jesus said that the man that does not do the things he tells him, builds his house to fall in utter ruin. Jesus instructs his messengers to go and baptize all nations, "teaching them to observe all things whatsoever I have commanded you."

Do you say it is faith Jesus requires, not works?

Heartily I agree! Is not faith the highest act of which the human mind is capable? But faith in what? Faith in what Jesus is, in what he says—a faith that can have no existence except in obedience—a faith which *is* obedience. To do what Jesus wishes *is* to put forth faith in him.

But instead of this, human teaching has substituted this or that belief *about* Jesus, faith in this or that supposed design of his manifestation in the flesh. They make *true* faith in him and his Father secondary to the acceptance of the paltry contrivance of a juggling morality, which they attribute to God and his Christ, imagining it the atonement and the so-called plan of salvation.

So I ask again: "Do you put your faith in Christ, or in human doctrines and commandments?" If it is in Christ, do you see that above all things and all thoughts, you are bound to obey him? Do you find it hard to trust him? Hard it will remain, while the things he tells you to do, things you can do, you will not try. How will you grow capable of trusting him to do his part by you, as long as you do not do your part by him? True faith, true belief, is not possible where there is not a daily doing of the things he says. They are what make faith take root and spring to life.

How else can you be made capable of trusting him? The very thing that makes you able to trust in him, and so receive all provision from him, is obedience to him. Neglecting the things he says, there is no soil in which your faith can grow.

Thus again comes the question: what have you done this day *because* it was the will of Christ? What have *I* done? If we chance to do his will because it falls in with our own designs, that may be a good thing. But it is not obedience. Obedience comes when, as a conscious act, we lay aside the appetite, the desire, the inclination of our flesh, our self, the tendency in which our human soul would go if left to itself, and instead do what *he* tells us, subduing our own will, mastering it, subjugating it, and bringing it into submission to *his*.

Have you or I *today* dismissed, even once, an anxious thought for tomorrow, because Jesus told us to?

Have you ministered to any needy soul or body, and kept your right hand from knowing what your left hand did, telling no one of your action?

Have you, this day, begun to leave all and follow him?

Did you set yourself not to criticize, talk against, or judge others? Did you bring fair and righteous judgment to your decisions?

Are you wary of covetousness?

Did you forgive your enemy and do him good or show him kindness?

Are you seeking the kingdom of God and his righteousness before all other things? Are you hungering and thirsting after righteousness?

Have you this day given, of money, of time, of possessions, of skill, or of compassion, to someone who asked of you?

Have you shown consideration, done good, returned kindness for a wrong done you, extended patience, been a servant, rejoiced in adversity, taken the role of humility before others, prayed for someone you don't like, trusted God to supply a pressing need? Have you done any of these things, suppressing your natural tendency to the contrary, and done them with rejoicing *because* Jesus said to do them?

Tell me something that you have done, are doing, or are trying to do because he told you. If you cannot, it is no wonder you have difficulty trusting him.

Not Perfection, But Trying

Of course I know that no man or woman can yet do what Christ tells him aright. But are you trying? Obedience is not perfection, but making an effort. He never gave a commandment knowing it was of no use for it could not be done. He tells us to do only things that *can* be done. He tells us a thing knowing that we must do it, or be lost. Not even his Father himself could save us but by getting us at length to do everything he commands, for there is no other way to know life, to know the holy secret of divine being.

He knows that you can try, and that in your trying and failing he will be able to help you, until at length you will do the will of God even as he does it himself. He takes the will in the imperfect deed, and makes the deed at last perfect.

The most correct notions without obedience are worthless. The doing of the will of God is the way to oneness with God, which alone is salvation. Sitting at the gate of heaven, sitting on the footstool of the throne itself, you could not be at peace, except the smallest point of consciousness, your heart, your mind, your brain, your body, your soul, were one with the living God. If you had one brooding thought that was not a joy in him, you would not be at peace. If you had one desire you could not leave absolutely to his will, you could not be at peace. God, all and in all, ours to the fulfilling of our very being, is the religion of the perfect, son-hearted Lord Christ.[3]

Did I Ever Do One Thing Because He Told Me To?

A Fictional Selection from *The Curate's Awakening*

Again his thoughts drifted into a reverie for some time, until suddenly the words rose from deep in his memory, *"Why do you call me, Lord, Lord, and do not the things which I say?"*

"Good God!" he exclaimed. "Here I am bothering over words, and questioning about this and that, as if I were examining his fitness for a job, while he has all the while been claiming my obedience! I have not once in my life done a single thing because he told me.—But then, how am I to obey him until I am sure of his right to command? I just want to know whether I am to call him Lord or not. Here I have all these years been calling myself a Christian, even ministering in the temple of Christ as if he were some heathen divinity who cared for songs and prayers and sacrifices, and yet I cannot honestly say I ever once in my life did a thing because he said so. I have *not* been an honest man! Is it any wonder that the things he said are too high and noble to be recognized as truth by such a man as me?"

With this another saying dawned upon him, *"If any man will do his will, he shall find out whether my teaching comes from God, or whether I speak on my own."*

After thinking for a few more minutes, Thomas went into his room and shut the door. He came out again not long afterward and went straight to visit a certain grieving old woman.

The next visible result showed on the following Sunday. The man who went up to the pulpit believed for the first time in his life that he now had something to say to his fellow-sinners. It was not the sacred spoil of others that he brought with him, but the message given him by a light in his own heart.

He opened no notebook, nor read words from any book except, with shaky voice, those of his text: *"Why do you call me, Lord, Lord, and do not the things which I say?"*

He looked around upon his congregation and trembling a little with a new excitement, he began, "My hearers, I come before you this morning to say the first word of truth ever given to *me* to utter. In my room, three days ago," the curate went on, "I was reading the strange story of the man who appeared in Palestine saying that he was the Son of God. And I came upon those words of his which I have just read to you. All at once my conscience awoke and asked me, 'Do you do the things he says to you?' And I thought to myself, 'Have I today done a single thing he has said to me? When was the last time I did something I heard from him? Did I *ever* in all my life do one thing because he said to me, "Do this?" ' And the answer was, 'No, never.' Yet there I was, not only calling myself a Christian, but presuming to live among you and be your helper on the road toward the heavenly kingdom. What a living lie I have been!

"Having made this confession," Wingfold proceeded, "you will understand that whatever I now say, I say to myself as much as to any among you to whom it may apply."

He than proceeded to show that faith and obedience are one and the same spirit: what in the heart we call faith, in the will we call obedience. He showed that the Lord refused the so-called faith which found its vent at the lips in worshiping words and not at the limbs in obedient action. Some of his listeners immediately pronounced his notions bad theology, while others said to themselves that at least it was common sense.[4]

Obedience

Trust him in the common light;
Trust him in the awesome night;

Trust him when the earth doth quake;
Trust him when thy heart doth ache;

Trust him when thy brain doth reel
And thy friend turns on his heel;

Trust him when the way is rough,
Cry not yet, It is enough!

But obey with true endeavour,
Else the salt hath lost his savour.

OPINION IS OF NO VALUE IN KNOWING GOD

A Fictional Selection from *The Baron's Apprenticeship*

She needed but to be told a good thing—not *told that a thing was good*—and at once she received it—that is, obeyed it, the only way of receiving a truth. She responded immediately upon every reception of light, every expansion of true knowledge. She was essentially *of* the truth; therefore when she came into relation with such a soul as Wingfold, a soul so much more developed than herself, her life was fed from his and began to grow faster. For he taught her to know the eternal Man who bore witness to her Father, and Barbara became his child, the inheritor of the universe. Fortunately, her life had not been loaded to the ground with degrading doctrines of a God whose justice is satisfied with the blood of the innocent for the punishment of the guilty. From the whole swarm of that brood of lies she was protected—by pure lack of what is generally regarded as a *re-*

ligious education. Such teaching is the mother of more tears in humble souls, and more presumption in the proud and selfish, than perhaps any other influence out of whose darkness God brings light. Neither ascetic nor mystic nor doctrinist of any sort, caring nothing for church or chapel or observance of any kind for its own sake, Barbara believed in God, and was coming to believe in Jesus Christ. And glad she was as she had never been before that there was such a person as Jesus Christ!

Wingfold never sought to influence her in any way concerning her workman-friend; he only sought to strengthen her in the truth.

One day when they were all three sitting together in the twilight, he said to his pupil:

"Now, Miss Wylder, don't try to convince the young man of anything by argument. If you succeeded, it would do no good. Opinion is all that can result from argument, and opinion concerning God—even right opinion—is of little value when it comes to *knowing* God. The god Richard denies is a being that could never exist. Talk to Richard, not of opinion, but of the God you love—the beautiful, the strong, the true, the patient, the forgiving, the loving. Let him feel God through your enthusiasm for him. You can't prove to him that there is a God. A god who could be proved would not be worth proving. Make his thoughts dwell upon a God worth having. Wake the notion of God such as will draw him to wish there were such a God. Many religious people will tell you God is different from what I say. 'God is just!' said a carping theologian to me the other day. 'Yes,' I answered, 'and he cannot be pleased that you should call that justice which is injustice, and attribute it to him!' There are many who must die in ignorance of their heavenly Father's character, because they will not of their own selves judge what is right.

"Set in Richard's eye a God worth believing in, a God like the Son of God, and he will go out and look to see if such a God may be found. He will call upon him, and the God who *is* will hear and answer him. God is God to us not that we may prove that *he is*, but *that we may know him*; and when we know him, then we are with him, at home, at the heart of the universe, the heirs of all things.

"All this is foolishness, I know, to the dull soul that cares only for things that can be proved, 'You cannot prove to me that you have a father,' says the blind sage, reasoning with the little child. 'Why should I prove it?' answers the child. 'I am sitting on his knee! If I could prove it, that would not make you see him; that would not make you happy like me! You do not care about my father, or you would not stand there disputing; you would feel about until you found him.' If a thing be true in itself, it is not capable of proof; and that man is in the higher condition who is able to believe it as it is. If there is a higher power than intellect, something that goes deeper, causing and even including our intellect, if there be a creative power of which our intellect is but a faint reflex, then the child of that power, the one who acknowledges and loves and obeys that power, will be the one to understand it.

"Men accept a thousand things without proof every day, and a thousand things may be perfectly true and have no proof. But if a man cannot be sure of a thing, does that automatically mean it is false? Neither can any man prove God's existence to be false. There is no proof of the intellect available in either direction. The very chance that a good thing *may* be true is a huge reason for an honest and continuous and unending search. But the final question is always this: have you acted, or rather, are you acting according to the conscience which is the one guide to truth?"[5]

The Asthmatic Man to the Satan That Binds Him

Satan, avaunt!
   Nay, take thine hour,
Thou canst not daunt,
   Thou hast no power;
Be welcome to thy nest,
Though it be in my breast.

Burrow amain;
   Dig like a mole;
Fill every vein
   With half-burnt coal;
Puff the keen dust about,
And all to choke me out.

Fill music's ways
   With creaking cries,
That no loud praise
   May climb the skies;
And on my labouring chest
Lay mountains of unrest.

My slumber steep
   In dreams of haste,
That only sleep,
   No rest, I taste—
With stiflings, rhymes of rote,
And fingers on my throat.

Satan, thy might
   I do defy;
Live core of night
   I patient lie:
A wind comes up the gray
Will blow thee clean away.

Christ's angel, Death,
   All radiant white,
With one cold breath
   Will scare thee quite,
And give my lungs an air
As fresh as answered prayer.

So, Satan, do
   Thy worst with me
Until the True
   Shall set me free,
And end what he began,
By making me a man.

The Truth in Christ

I press toward the mark for the prize of the high calling of God in Christ Jesus. Let us therefore, as many as be perfect, be thus minded: and if in any thing ye be otherwise minded, God shall reveal even this unto you. Nevertheless, whereto we have already attained, let us walk by the same.

Philippians 3:14–16

I t is faith that saves us.

Not faith within our*selves*, as if *we* could in our own beings mentally initiate salvation. Nor is it faith in any *work* of God.

It is faith in God *himself!*

If I did not believe God to be as good as the tenderest human heart, the fairest, the purest, the most unselfish that human heart could imagine him, yes, an infinitude better, higher than our imagined goodness as the heavens are higher than the earth—if I did not believe it, not as a mere mental proposition, but with the responsive being of my whole nature; if I did not feel every fiber of my heart and brain and body safe with him because he is the Father who made me—I would not be saved. For this faith is salvation.

It is God and the man as one. God and man together, the vital energy flowing unchecked from the Creator into his creature—that is the salvation of the created. Even the poorest faith of this kind—faith in the living God, the God revealed in Christ Jesus—if it be vital, true (that is, obedient), is the beginning of the way to know him, and to know him is eternal life.

False Faith Will Not Save

If you mean by faith anything of a different kind than an obedient faith in the *living* God, that faith will not save you.

A faith, for instance, that God does not forgive me because he loves me but because he loves Jesus Christ, cannot save me, because it is a falsehood against God. If the thing were true, such a gospel would be the preaching of a God that was not love, therefore in whom was no salvation, a God whom to know could not be eternal life. Such a faith would damn, not save a man, for it would bind him to a God whose love was not perfect and complete. Such assertions going by the name of Christianity are nothing but the poor remnants of paganism, and it is only with that part of our nature not yet Christian that we are able to believe them.

Neither will a faith in a correct system of doctrines and ideas and scriptural interpretations concerning the things of God save me. Nor a faith in this church or that church.

We must forsake such false faiths and receive the teaching of Christ heartily, not letting the interpretation of it attributed to his apostles turn us aside from the imperative of his words. I say interpretation "attributed" to his apostles, for what the New Testament writers teach is never against what Christ taught, though very often the exposition of it is, by those who would understand, and even explain, rather than obey.

We may be sure of this, that no man or woman will be condemned for any sin that is past. If he be condemned, it will be because he or she would not come to the Light when the Light came to them, because they would not learn to do as the Light instructs, because they hid their unbelief in the garment of a false faith, and would not obey. Such talk of imputed righteousness, as if this makes them worthy in the midst of their unworthiness, because they prefer such religious jargon to confessing themselves everywhere in the wrong, and repenting.

Doing the Thing We Know

We may be sure that when someone becomes a disciple of Jesus, he will not leave that one in ignorance as to what he should believe. That person will know the truth of everything it is needful for him to understand.

If we do what Jesus tells us, his light will dawn in our hearts. Till then we could not understand even if he explained everything to us. If you cannot trust Jesus to let you know what is right, but think you must hold this or that opinion before you come to him, then I justify your doubts in what you call your worst times, but which I suspect are your best times, in which you come nearest to the truth—those times, namely, in which you fear you have no faith.

So long as a man will not set himself to obey the word spoken, the word written, the word printed, the word read, of the Lord Jesus

Christ, I would not take the trouble to try to convince him concerning even the most obnoxious and false doctrines. It is those who want to believe, but who are hindered by such doctrines, whom I would help. Disputation about things only hides the living Christ, who alone can teach the truth, who is the truth, and the knowledge of whom is life.

He who believes in a God not altogether unselfish and good, a God who does not do all he can for his creatures, belongs to the same class of humankind who make sticks or stones or other idols into deities to be worshiped. His is not the God who made the heaven and the earth and the sea and the fountains of water—not the God revealed in Christ. If one sees in God any darkness at all, and especially if one defends that darkness, attempting to justify it with some low, manufactured theology, I cannot but think his blindness must have followed his ignoring of the words of the Lord. Surely, if he had been strenuously obeying Jesus, he would before now have received the truth that God is light, and in him is no darkness—a truth which cannot be acknowledged by calling the darkness attributed to him light, and the candle of the Lord in the soul of man darkness. It is one thing to believe that God can do nothing wrong; quite another to call whatever presumption one may attribute to him right.

The whole secret of progress is doing the thing we know. There is no other way of progress in the spiritual life, no other way of progress in the understanding of that life. Only as we do, can we know.

Theories—Substitutes for Faith

The duty of Christians toward their fellow men and women is to let their light shine, not to force on them their interpretations of God's designs.

If those who set themselves to explain the various theories of Christianity had set themselves instead to do the will of the Master, the one object for which the gospel was preached, how different would the world now be! Had they given themselves to understanding his Word that they might do it, and not to the quarrying from it material wherewith to buttress their systems of dogma, in many a heart by this time would the name of the Lord be loved where now it remains unknown.

Unhindered by Christians' explanations of Christianity, undeterred by having their acceptance forced on them, but attracted instead by their behavior, men would be saying to each other, as Moses said to himself when he saw the bush that burned but was not consumed, "I will now turn aside and see this great sight!" All over the world, people would be drawing near to behold how these Christians loved one another, and how just and fair they were to every one that came into contact with them! They would note that the goods Christians had to sell were the best, their weights and measures most dependable, their prices most reasonable, their word most certain, their smiles most genuine, their love most selfless! They would see that in their families there was neither jealousy nor emulation, that Mammon was not worshiped, that in their homes selfishness was neither the hidden nor the openly ruling principle, that their children were as diligently taught to share as some are to save or spend only upon themselves, that their mothers were more anxious lest a child should hoard than if he should squander, that in no Christian house was religion one thing and the daily practice of life another; that the preacher did not think first of his church nor the nobleman of his privileges. They would see, in short, a people who *lived* by their principles of belief, not merely talked and disputed about them.

I can hear some object: "But the world could not function that way! We must not take the words of the Bible too literally. We must, after all, live in the world of men."

Such an objection is but another proof of unbelief. Either you do or you do not believe the word the Lord spoke—that, if we seek first the kingdom of God and his righteousness, *all* things needful will be added to us.

Do you prefer the offers of Mammon? Perhaps you do *not* want to be saved from the snare of the too-much. Are you able to examine yourself with honesty? Do you, in fact, desire wealth—the freedom of the world? Do you *not* want to live under such restrictions as the Lord might choose to lay upon you if he saw that something precious in his sight might be made of you?

You would, if you could, inherit the earth, but not through meekness. You would have the life of this world sweet, come of the life eternal what may.

If such is your Christianity, a rude awakening will be yours. One day you will find that, unable to trust God for this world, neither can you trust him for the world to come. Refusing to obey God *in* your life now, how can you trust him *for* your life then? From this attitude comes the various substitutes you seek for true saving faith. You search the Scriptures for his promises. You appeal to the atonement. You point to the satisfaction made to God's justice, as you call it. While all the time you will take no trouble to fulfill the absolutely reasonable and necessary condition—yes, the morally and spiritually imperative condition—through which alone he can offer you deliverance from the burden of life into the strength and glory of life—that is, that you shall be true and obedient children.

You say, "Christ has satisfied the law," but you will not satisfy him by doing his words. He says, "Come unto me," and you will not rise up and go to him. You say, "Lord I believe; help mine unbelief," but when he says, "Leave everything behind you, and be as I am toward God, and you shall have peace and rest," you turn away, muttering about "figurative speech" and taking his words "too literally."

If you were faithful and had been *living* the life, had been a practicing *Christian*, as the word means—namely, one who does as Christ does—then indeed you would have drawn the world after you. In your church you would be receiving and giving out nourishment, strength to live—thinking far less of serving God on Sunday and far more of serving your neighbor throughout the week. Instead of churches filled with the wealthy, the deceitful businessman, the ambitious poor, and the self-righteous, whom you have attracted to your social community you call a church with the offer of a salvation other than deliverance from sin; the publicans and sinners would have been drawn instead, and turned into true Christian men and women. Those who stand outside looking at the proceedings inside one of these social assemblies, who are more repelled by your general worldliness than by your misrepresentation of God, would positively hasten to the company of people loving and true, eager to learn what it was that made them so good, so happy, so unselfish, so free of care, so ready to die, so willing to live, so hopeful, so helpful, so careless to possess, so undeferential to possession.

I Will Not Defend My Opinions

If you tell me my ideas are presumptuous, contrary to what is taught in the Bible and what Christian preachers and writers have always believed, I will not therefore defend my beliefs, the principles on which I try to live. And how much less will I defend my opinions!

I appeal to you instead, whether or not I have spoken the truth concerning our paramount obligation, to do the word of Christ.

If you answer that I have not, I have nothing more to say. There is no other ground on which we can meet. But if you do allow that doing the word of Christ is a prime duty, then I would only say that you should do it.

I will not attempt to change your opinions. If they are wrong, obedience alone can enable you to set them right. And where I am wrong, only my obedience will likewise set me right. I only pray for you to obey; only thus can we equip ourselves for understanding the mind of Christ.

None but he who *does* right can think right. You cannot know Christ until you do as he does, as he tells you to do. Neither can you tell others of him, until you know him as he means himself to be known, that is, as he is.

Why should I care to convince you that my doctrine is right? What does any honest person care what you think of his doctrine? To convince another by intellect alone, while the heart remains unmoved, is but to add to his condemnation.

The honest heart must see that however wrong I may or may not be in other things, at least I am right in this, that Jesus must be obeyed, and obeyed immediately, in the things he has said. For he who does not choose to see that Christ must be obeyed, must be left to the teaching of the Father, who brings all that hear and learn of him to Christ. The Father will leave no one to his own way, however much that one may prefer it. The Lord did not die to provide men with the wretched heaven they may invent for themselves, or accept what has been invented for them by others. He died to give us life, and bring us to the heaven of the Father's peace; the children must share in the essential bliss of the Father and the Son.

The Truth of Life Comes by Walking in the Truth We Know

This is and has been the Father's work from the beginning—to bring us into the home of his heart, where he shares the glories of life with the Living One, in whom was born life to light men back to the original life.

This is our destiny. And however one may refuse, he will find it hard to fight with God—useless to kick against the goads of his love. For the Father is goading him, or will goad him, if need be, into life by unrest and trouble. Even the fire of hell will have its turn if less will not do; can any need it more than such as will neither enter the kingdom of heaven themselves, nor allow them to enter it that would? The old race of the Pharisees is by no means extinct; they were St. Paul's great trouble, and are yet to be found in every religious community and every Christian church under the sun.

The one only way to truly reconcile all differences is to walk in the light. So St. Paul teaches in his epistle to the Philippians, the third chapter. After setting forth the loftiest idea of human endeavor, in declaring his own highest aspiration, he says, "let us walk by that same." The one, the only essential point with him is that we walk by that which we have seen to be true.

In such walking, and only by such walking, will love grow, will truth grow. The soul, then first in its genuine element and true relationship toward God, will see into reality which was before but a blank to it. And he who has promised to teach, will teach abundantly.

Faster and faster will the glory of the Lord dawn upon the hearts and minds of his people so walking in obedience. Then they are his people indeed! Fast and far will the knowledge of him spread, for truth of action, both preceding and following truth of word, will prepare the way before him. The man and woman walking in the truth they know will be able to think aright. Only when we begin to do the thing we know do we begin to be able to think aright. Then God comes to us in a new and higher way, and works along with the spirit he has created.

Without heaven above its head, without its life-breath around it, without its love-treasure in its heart, without its origin one with it and bound up in it, without its true self and originating life, the soul cannot think toward any real purpose—nor ever would to all eternity.

The Heritage of the Soul

When man joins with God, then is all impotence and discord cast out. Until then there can only be strife. When the man joins God, then is Satan foiled. Then for the first time is the truly natural state of the universe restored: God and man are one.

Until God and man begin to be one in reality as in the divine idea, in the flower as in the root, in the finishing as in the issuing creation, nothing can go right with the man, and God can have no rest from his labor in him. As the greatest spheres in heaven are drawn by the gravity of the least, God himself must be held in divine disquiet until every one of his family be brought home to his heart, to be one with him in a unity too absolute, profound, far-reaching, fine, and intense to be understood by any but the God from whom it comes.

For God is the heritage of the soul of origin. Man is the offspring of his making will, of his very life. God himself is man's birthplace. God is the self that makes the soul able to say, I too, *am*.

This absolute unspeakable bliss of the creature is that for which the Son died, for which the Father suffered with him—to regain the *oneness* of man and God. Then only is life right, is it as it should be and was meant to be. Then only is it as it was designed and necessitated by the eternal life-outgiving Life.

"Whereto then we have already attained, let us *walk* by that same"![1]

BEFORE EVERYTHING ELSE: OBEDIENCE!

A Fictional Selection from *Donal Grant*

N ow tell me, Davie, what is the biggest faith of all—the faith to put in the one only thoroughly good person."

"You mean God, Mr. Grant?"

"Whom else could I mean?"

"You might mean Jesus."

"They are all one there; for they mean always the same thing, do always the same thing, always agree. There is only one thing the one does that the other never does: they do not love the same person."

"What *do* you mean, Mr. Grant?" interrupted Arctura. She had been listening intently, and now first imagined the cloven foot of Mr. Grant's heresy about to appear.

"I mean this," said Donal, with a smile that seemed to Arctura such a light as she had never seen on a human face, for it arose from no fount of mere human gladness, but from the more human gladness that is only to be found in God. "I mean that God loves Jesus, not God; and Jesus loves God, not Jesus. We love one another, not ourselves—don't we, Davie?"

"You do, Mr. Grant," answered Davie modestly.

"Now tell me, Davie, what is the great big faith of all that we have to put in the Father of us, who is as good not only as thought can think, but as good as heart can wish—infinitely better than anybody but Jesus Christ can think—what is the faith to put in him?"

"Oh, it is everything!" answered Davie.

"But what first?" asked Donal.

"First it is to do what he tells us."

"Yes, Davie; it is to learn his ways by going and doing them, not trying to understand them first, or doing anything else whatever with them first than obeying them. We spread out our arms to him as a child does to his mother when he wants her to take him; then when he sets us down, saying, 'Go and do this or that,' we make all the haste in us to go and do it. And if ever we get hungry to see God, we must look at his picture."

"Where is that, sir?"

"Ah, Davie, Davie! Don't you know that besides being himself, and just because he is himself, Jesus is the living picture of God?"

"I know, sir! We have to go and read about him in the book. But may I ask you a question, Mr. Grant?" said Arctura.

"With all my heart," answered Donal. "I only hope I may be able to answer it."

"When we read about Jesus, we have to draw for ourselves the likeness of Jesus from words, and you know what kind of a likeness the best artist would make that way, who had never seen with his own eyes the person whose portrait he had to paint!"

"I understand you quite," returned Donal. "Some go to other men to draw it for them; and some go to others to tell them what they are to draw for themselves—thus acquiring all their blunders in addition to those they must make for themselves. But the nearest likeness you can see of him is the one drawn by yourself from thinking about him while you do what he tells you. No other is of any vital use to you. And right here comes in the great promise he made, in itself true, and a law of God, else it could not have been a promise of Jesus—just as no scripture is of private interpretation, but is a principle that applies to all. If God were not in us at all, we should see nothing at all of his likeness. And he has promised to come himself into our hearts, to give us his Spirit, the very presence of his soul to our souls, speaking in language that cannot be uttered because it is too great and strong and fine for any words of ours. So will he be much nearer to us than even his personal presence to us would be; and so we shall see him, and be able to draw for ourselves the likeness of God. But first of all, and before everything else, mind you, Davie, *obedience*!"

"Yes, Mr. Grant; I know," said Davie.

"Then off with you to the games God has given you."

"I'm going to fly my kite, Mr. Grant."

"Do. God likes to see you fly your kite. Don't forget it is all in his March wind it flies. It could not go up a foot but for that."[2]

Did You Go to Church?

Fictional Selection from *The Landlady's Master*

I seldom go to church," said Andrew, reddening a little, but losing no sweetness from his smile.

"I have heard that. It is wrong of you not to be regular. Why don't you go to church?"

Andrew was silent.

"I want you to tell me," persisted Alexa, with a peremptoriness she had inherited from the schoolmaster. She had known Andrew too as a pupil of her father's.

"If you insist, ma'am," replied Andrew. "I not only learn nothing from Mr. Smith, but I think that much of what he says is not true."

"Still you ought to go for the sake of example."

"Do wrong to make other people follow my example! How could that be right?"

"Wrong to go to church! What *do* you mean? Wrong to pray with your fellow Christians?"

"Perhaps the time may come when I shall be able to pray with them, even though the words they use seem addressed to a tyrant, not to the Father of Jesus Christ. But at present I cannot. I might endure to hear Mr. Smith say evil things concerning God, but the evil things he says to God make me quite unable to pray, and I would feel like a hypocrite to attempt it in such a setting."

"Whatever you may think of Mr. Smith's doctrines, it is presumptuous to set yourself up as too good to go to church."

"My difficulties with the church have nothing to do with thinking myself good, ma'am, which I do not. But I must bear the reproach. I cannot consent to be a hypocrite in order to avoid being called one."

Either Miss Fordyce had no answer to this, or did not choose to give any. She was not so much troubled that Andrew would not go to church. Like many who feel compelled to debate on matters religious, she was arguing on behalf of the traditions of men rather than from the depth of her own personal religious convictions. In truth, what offended her most was the unhesitating decision with which the unlearned young man set her counsel aside. . . .

"You seem to have some rather peculiar notions, Mr. Ingram."

"Perhaps. But for a man to have no ideas he counts as his very own is much the same as to have no ideas at all. For a person to adopt as his beliefs only and nothing more than what he has heard from others seems to me a hollow faith. A man cannot have the ideas of another man any more than he can have another man's soul, or another man's body. Ideas must be one's own or they cease to truly be *ideas* at all."

"That is dangerous doctrine."

"Perhaps we are not talking about the same thing. I mean by *ideas* what a man orders his life by."

"Your ideas may be wrong."

"The All-wise will be my judge."

"So much the worse if you are in the wrong."

"Having him as my judge is good whether I be in the right or the wrong. I want him as my judge all the more when I am wrong, for then I most keenly need his wisdom. Would I have my mistakes overlooked? Not at all! Shall he not do right? And will he not set me right? I can think of nothing so wonderful!"

"That is most dangerous confidence."

"It would be if there were any other judge. But it will be neither the church nor the world that will sit on the great white throne. He who sits there will not ask, 'Did you go to church?' or 'Did you believe this or that?' but, *Did you do what I told you?*"

"And what will you say when he asks that, Mr. Ingram?"

"I will say, 'Lord, only you know. . . .' "

"It looks as if you thought yourselves better than everybody else."

"I consider myself better than no man. Besides, if it were such that we thought, then certainly he would not be one of the gathering . . . His presence cannot be proved; it can only be known. One thing for certain, if we are not keeping his commandments, he is not among us. But if he does meet us, it is not necessary to the joy of his presence that we should be able to prove that he is there. If a man has the company of the Lord, he will care little whether someone else does or does not believe that he has it."

"Your way fosters division in the church."

"Did the Lord come to send peace on the earth? My way, as you call it, would make division, but division between those who *call* themselves his, and those who *are* his. It would bring together those that love him. Company would merge with company that they might look on the Lord together. I don't believe Jesus cares much for what is called the visible church; but he cares with his very Godhead for those that do as he tells them; they are his Father's friends; they are his elect by whom he will save the world. It is by those who obey, and by their obedience, that he will save those who do not obey, that is, will bring them to obey. It is one by one that the world will pass to his side. There is no saving of the masses. If a thousand be converted at once, it is still every single lonely man that is converted."

"You would make a slow process of it."

"It is slow, yet faster than any other. All God's processes are slow. The works of God take time and cannot be rushed."[3]

Rondel

Heart, thou must learn to do without—
　　That is the riches of the poor,
　　Their liberty is to endure;
Wrap thou thine old cloak thee about;
And carol loud and carol stout;
　　Let thy rags fly, nor wish them fewer;
Thou too must learn to do without,
　　Must earn the riches of the poor!

Why should'st thou only wear no clout?
　　Thou only walk in love-robes pure?
　　Why should thy step alone be sure?
Thou only free of fortune's flout?
Nay, nay! but learn to go without,
　　And so be humbly, richly poor.

THE HARDNESS OF THE WAY

Children, how hard is it!
Mark 10:24

Is the Lord Unfair to the Rich?

I suspect there is scarcely a young, thoughtful rich man today who does not feel our Lord's treatment of the young man in Mark 10 hard.

He is apt to ask, like many of us, "Why should it be difficult for a rich man to enter the kingdom of heaven?" We tend to look upon the natural fact as an arbitrary decree, arising perhaps from some prejudice in the divine mind, or maybe from some objection on God's part to the joys of well-being.

Why should the rich fare differently from other people with respect to the world to come?

Those who ask such a question do not perceive that the difficulty comes precisely because they *shall* fare like other people, whereas they want to fare as rich people.

I cannot conceive of a condition of things in which it would be easy for a rich man to enter into the kingdom of heaven. The reason is this: there is no kingdom of this world into which a rich man may not easily enter—in which, if he is rich enough, he may not be the first and most exalted of all men and women. The various kingdoms of this world naturally receive the rich with open arms. The rich man does not by any necessity of things belong to the kingdom of Satan, but into that kingdom he is especially welcome; whereas into the kingdom of heaven he will be just as welcome—no less but neither no more—as another man.

I suspect also that many turn from the record of this incident with the resentful feeling that there lies in it a claim upon their own having possessions. And there are many, and by no means only the rich, who cannot believe the Lord really meant to take the poor fellow's money away from him.

Both the man born to riches and the man who has made a great deal of money feel a right to have and to hold the things they possess. How hard indeed it seems to them that to enter the kingdom of heaven would require the necessity of giving up that which they feel it is their right and proper due to retain. The thing hardly seems fair!

Why should they not make the best of both worlds?

"Where is the harm in a little compromise?" I can hear such a one ask. He would serve Mammon just a little, and God much, or so he thinks. But in reality he would gain as little as may be had of heaven— but something, with the loss of as little as possible of the world. That which he desires of heaven is not its best; that which he would not yield of the world is its most worthless. He does not understand that to truly "make the best of both worlds" comes of putting the lower in utter subservience to the higher—of casting away the treasure of this world and taking the treasure of heaven instead.

How Would We Reason When His Words Hit Us?

I can well imagine an honest man or woman, educated in Christian forms, thus reasoning in contemplation of Christ's words: "Is this story to be applied to all? Is the same demand made upon me? If I make up my mind to be a Christian, will I be required to part with all I possess?

"Of course, in those times, possessions did not mean what they do today. It must have been comparatively easy to give up the kinds of things they had then. If it had been me, I am sure I should have done it at once—especially at the demand of Jesus in person.

"But things are very different now. I should be giving up so much more! And I do not love money as he was in danger of doing. He would not ask the same thing of me. I try to do good with my money. I am no Mammon-worshiper. Besides, am I not a Christian already? Why should the same thing be required of me as of this young Jew? If every person who, like me, has a conscience about money and tries to use it well, had to give everything up, the power would at once be in the hands of the irreligious. They would have no opposition, and the world would go to the devil! We read often in the Bible of rich men. How would the Lord have been buried but for the rich man Joseph? The text says, 'How hard is it for them that trust in riches to enter into the kingdom of God!' But I do not trust in my riches. I know they can do nothing to save me."

Do you find yourself raising such arguments?

If so, I care little to set forth anything called truth, except in siege for surrender to the law of liberty. If I cannot persuade, I would be silent. Nor would I labor to instruct the keenest intellect. I would rather learn for myself. To persuade the heart, the will, the action, is alone worth the full energy of a man. His strength is first for his own, then for his neighbor's manhood. He must first pluck out the beam from his own eye, then the mote out of his brother's—if indeed the mote in his brother's be more than the projection of the beam in his own. To make a man happy as a lark, *might be* to do him a grievous wrong: to make a man wake, rise, look up, and turn is worth the life and death of the Son of the Eternal.

He Does Not Say the Same to Everyone

If you find yourself reasoning against the Lord's words, I would ask you: "Have you kept—have you been keeping the commandments?"

"I will not dare to say that," you might answer. "I know, as well as the rich young ruler, how much is implied in the keeping of the commandments. I cannot make quite that bold a claim."

If that be your answer, then I would ask you further, and I ask myself as well: "Does your answer imply that, counting the Lord a hard master, you have taken the less pains to do as he would have you? Knowing him to be hard, you have not even tried to obey him completely? Or does your statement mean that you *have* bent your energies to the absolute perfection he requires, and as a result you have perceived the impossibility of fulfilling the law?"

Have you failed to note that it is the youth who has been for years observing the commandments on whom the further—and to you startling—command is laid to part with all he has? If you, like him, *have* been keeping the commandments for years, then are you one on whom the same command could be laid?

Have you, in any sense like that in which the youth answered the question, kept the commandments? Have you, unsatisfied with the result of what obedience you have given, and filled with the desire to be perfect, gone kneeling to the Master to learn more of the way to eternal life? Or are you so well satisfied with what you are that you have never hungered and thirsted after the righteousness of God, the perfection of your being, never sought eternal life?

If this latter be your condition, then be comforted—the Master does not require of you to sell what you have and give to the poor.

You follow him? *You* go with him to preach the gospel?—you who do not care for righteousness? You are not one whose company is desirable to the Master. Be comforted, I say. You are not ready to share with him in the salvation of the world. He will not ask you to open your purse for him. Your money is nothing to him. Bring him a true heart, an obedient hand; he has given his lifeblood for that. But your money—he neither needs it nor cares for it.

Once more, the sum of the matter is this: *go and keep the commandments*. It is not come to your money yet. The commandments are enough for you. You are not yet a child in the kingdom. You do not yet hunger for the arms of your Father; you value only the shelter of his roof. As to your money, let the commandments direct you how to use it. When in keeping the commandments you have found the great reward of discovering that with all the energy you can put forth you are but an unprofitable servant, when you have come to feel that you would rather die than live such a poor, miserable, selfish life as alone you can call yours, when you are aware of something beyond all that your mind can think, yet not beyond what your heart can desire, when you have therefore come to the Master with the cry, "What shall I do that I may inherit eternal life?"—it may be that then he will say to you, "Sell all you have and give to the poor, and come follow me."

If he does say this to you, then you will be of all men most honorable if you obey—of men most pitiable if you refuse. But until he says it, there is little point in pondering the question. For the young man to have sold all and followed him would have been to accept God's oneness with himself: to you it has perhaps not yet been offered. Were one of the disobedient, in the hope of honor, to part with every straw he possessed, he would only be sent back to keep the commandments in the new and easier circumstances of his poverty.

Where Is Your Trust?

Do you find comfort in the fact that perhaps the Lord does *not* require of you what he required of the rich Jewish youth? Then I am sorry for you! Your relief is to know that the Lord does not require you to part with your money and possessions, but he also does not offer you himself instead! You did not sell him for thirty pieces of silver, but you are glad not to buy him with all that you have?

How do you differ from the youth of the story? In this, that he was invited to do more, to do everything, to partake of the divine nature. You, on the other hand, have not had it in your power to refuse; you are not ready to be invited. As you are, you cannot enter the kingdom. You would not even know you were in heaven if you were in it.

"But I do not trust in my riches," you say. "I trust in the merits of my Lord and Savior. I trust in his finished work. I trust in the sacrifice he has offered."

Yes, no doubt, you will trust in anything but the Man himself who tells you it is hard to be saved! Not all the merits of God and his Christ can give you eternal life. Only God and his Christ can. But they cannot, and would not if they could, without your keeping the commandments. The knowledge of the living God *is* eternal life. What have you to do with his merits? You have to know his being—himself.

No One Really Trusts in Riches for Salvation

And as to trusting in your riches—whoever imagined he could have eternal life by his riches? No man with half a conscience, half a head, and no heart at all, could suppose that anyone could enter the kingdom by trusting in his riches to gain him entrance. The idea is too absurd. It is the last refuge of the riches-lover, the riches-worshiper, to yet say he does not trust in them. The saying of it somehow justifies to him that, though his possessions are essential for his peace, he yet trusts elsewhere for his salvation. Hundreds who think of nothing so much as their possessions, their wealth, and the state of their bank account, will yet say, "I do not trust in my riches, I trust in—." And here they enter this or that stock religious phrase.

Some will object here, thinking that I am taking exception to the Lord's own words, for did he not say: "How hard is it *for them that trust in riches* to enter into the kingdom of heaven!"

Yes, so the Authorized King James Version would have it. But I do not believe our Lord ever said those words. According to the two oldest manuscripts we have, the reading is: "Children, how hard is it to enter the kingdom of God!" The additional phrase, *for them that trust in riches*, I take to be that of some copyist, who was dissatisfied with the Lord's way of regarding money and, like many, was anxious to compromise. Adding his marginal gloss, he changed the meaning to the effect that it is not the possessing of riches, but the trusting in them, that makes it difficult to enter into the kingdom.

Difficult? Why, it is eternally impossible for the man who trusts in his riches to enter into the kingdom! For the man who *has* riches it is difficult.

You do not really suppose the Lord teaches that for a man who trusts in his riches it is possible to enter the kingdom? That, though impossible with men, this is possible with God? God take the Mammon-worshiper into his glory?

No! the Lord never said it. The annotation of Mr. Facingbothways crept into the text, and stands in the 1611 version.

Our Lord was not in the habit of explaining away his hard words. He let them stand in all the glory of the burning fire wherewith they would purge us. Where their simplicity finds corresponding simplicity of heart, they are understood. The twofold heart must mistake them. It is hard for a rich man, just because he is a rich man, to enter into the kingdom of heaven.

Some, no doubt, comfort themselves with the thought that, if it be so hard, that fact will be taken into account. In other words, some special allowance will certainly be made for them, because it is harder for them than certain other persons—namely, the poor. But this is but another shape of the fancy that the rich man must be treated differently than his fellows, that as he has had his good things here, so he must have them there too.

You may be certain they will have absolute justice, that is, fairness. But what will that avail them if they enter not into the kingdom? It is life they must have. There is no enduring of existence without life. They somehow think they can do without "eternal life," if only they might live forever.

The Simplicity of Existence Is Hard to Enter

Take the Lord's words: "Children, how hard is it to enter into the kingdom of God!" It is quite like his way of putting things. Calling on his listeners first to reflect on the original difficulty for *every* one of entering into the kingdom of God, he reasserts in yet stronger phrase the difficulty of the rich man: "It is easier for a camel to go through a needle's eye, than for a rich man to enter into the kingdom of God."

It always was, always will be, hard to enter the kingdom of heaven. It is hard even to believe that one must be born from above—must pass into a new and unknown consciousness.

The law-faithful Jew, the ceremonial Christian, shrinks from the self-annihilation, the life of grace and truth, the upper air of heavenly delight, the all-embracing love that fills the law full and sets it aside. They cannot accept a condition of being which is in itself eternal life.

Hard to believe in—this life, this kingdom of God—this simplicity of absolute existence is even harder to enter.

How hard?

As hard as the Master of salvation could find words to express the hardness: "If any man cometh unto me, and hate not . . . his own life also, he cannot be my disciple."

And the rich man must find it harder than another to hate his own life. There is so much associated with it to swell out the self of his consciousness, that the difficulty of casting it from him as the mere ugly shadow of the self God made is vastly increased.

Only Those Doing It Know How Hard

None can know how difficult it is to enter into the kingdom of heaven, except those who have tried—tried hard, are trying, and have not ceased to try.

I care not to be told that one may pass at once into all possible sweetness of assurance by murmuring a certain prayer. It is not assurance I desire, but the thing itself, not the certainty of eternal life, but eternal life.

I care not what other preachers may say about assurance and resting in the Spirit. I know that in St. Paul the spirit and the flesh were in frequent strife. Entering into the kingdom of God was, to Paul, a daily battle with his own self.

I repeat therefore, only those know how hard it is to enter into life who are in conflict every day, and are growing to have this conflict every hour—nay, who are beginning to see that no moment is life without the presence that maketh strong.

Let anyone tell me of peace and contentment and joy unspeakable as the instant result of the new birth. I will not deny them such testimony. All I care to say is that, if by salvation they mean less than absolute oneness with God, I count it no salvation at all. Neither would I be content with it if it included every joy in the heaven of their imagining. If they are not righteous even as he is righteous, they are not saved, whatever be their superficial gladness or contentment. They are only on the way to being saved.

If they do not love their neighbor—not as themselves, that is a phrase difficult to understand and not reflective of Christ's meaning, but—as Christ loves him, they are not yet entered into life, though life may have begun to enter into them.

Those whose idea of life is simply an eternal one best know how hard it is to enter into life. The Lord said, "Children, how hard is it to enter the kingdom!" and the disciples little knew what was required of them!

Demands unknown before are continually being made upon the Christian. It is the ever-fresh rousing and calling, asking and sending of the Spirit that works in the children of obedience.

When he thinks he has attained, then is he in danger. When he finds the mountain he has so long been climbing show suddenly a distant peak, radiant in eternal whiteness, and all but lost in heavenly places, a peak whose glory-crowned apex it seems as if no human foot could ever reach—then is there hope for him. Then there is proof that he has been climbing, for he beholds the yet unclimbed. He sees what he could not see before. If he knows little of what he is, he knows something of what he is not. He learns ever afresh that he is not in the world as Jesus was in the world, but the very wind that breathes courage as he climbs is the hope that one day he shall be like him, seeing him as he is.[1]

The Widow With the Two Mites

Here much and little shift and change,
    With scale of need and time;
There more and less have meanings strange,
    Which the world cannot rhyme.

Sickness may be more hale than health,
    And service kingdom high;
Yea, poverty be bounty's wealth,
    To give like God thereby.

Bring forth your riches; let them go,
    Nor mourn the lost control;
For if ye hoard them, surely so
    Their rust will reach your soul.

Cast in your coins, for God delights
    When from wide hands they fall;
But here is one who brings two mites,
    And thus gives more than all.

I think she did not hear the praise—
    Went home content with need;
Walked in her old poor generous ways,
    Nor knew her heavenly meed.

KNOWING GOD IN POVERTY

*Fictional Selections from The Marquis of Lossie
and The Marquis' Secret*

T ell me one thing before I go," said Clementina. "Are we not commanded to bear each other's burdens and so fulfill the law of Christ? I read it today."

"Then why ask me?"

"For another question: does not that involve the command to those who have burdens that they should allow others to bear them?"

"Surely, my lady. But I have no burden to let you bear."

"Why should I have so much and you so little?"

"My lady, I have millions more than you. I have been gathering the crumbs under my Master's table for thirty years."

"I believe you are just as poor as the apostle Paul when he sat down to make a tent or as our Lord himself after He gave up carpentry."

"You are wrong there, my lady. I am not so poor as they must often have been."

"But I don't know how long I may be away, and you may fall ill, or—or—see—some book you want very much."

"I have my Testament, my Plato, my Shakespeare, and one or two besides whose wisdom I have not yet quite exhausted."

"I can't bear it!" cried Clementina almost on the point of weeping. "Let me be your servant." As she spoke she rose, and walking softly up to him where he sat, knelt at his knees and held out suppliantly a little bag of white silk. "Take it—Father," she said, hesitating and with effort, "take your daughter's offering—a poor thing to show her love, but something to ease her heart."

He took it, and weighed it up and down in his hand with an amused smile, but his eyes full of tears. It was heavy. He opened it. A chair was within his reach, he emptied it on the seat of it, and laughed with merry delight as its contents came tumbling out.

"I never saw so much gold in my life, if it were all taken together," he said. "What beautiful stuff it is! But I don't want it, my dear. It would but trouble me." And as he spoke, he began to put it in the bag again. "You will want it for your journey," he said.

"I have plenty in my reticule," she answered. "That is a mere nothing to what I could have tomorrow morning for writing a cheque. I am afraid I am very rich. It is such a shame! But I can't well help it. You must teach me how to become poor. Tell me true: how much money have you?"

She said this with such an earnest look of simple love that the schoolmaster made haste to rise, that he might conceal his growing emotion.

"Rise, my dear lady," he said, as he rose himself, "and I will show you."

He gave her his hand, and she obeyed, but troubled and disappointed, and so stood looking after him, while he went to a drawer. Thence, searching in a corner of it, he brought a half-sovereign, a few shillings, and some coppers, and held them out to her on his hand, with a smile of one who has proved his point.

"There!" he said; "do you think Paul would have stopped preaching to make a tent so long as he had as much as that in his pocket? I shall have more on Saturday, and I always carry a month's rent in my good old watch, for which I never had much use, and now have less than ever."

Clementina had been struggling with herself; now she burst into tears.

"Why, what a misspending of precious sorrow!" exclaimed the schoolmaster. "Do you think because a man has not a gold mine he must die of hunger? I once heard of a sparrow that never had a worm left for the morrow, and died a happy death notwithstanding." As he spoke, he took her handkerchief from her hand and dried her tears with it. But he had enough ado to keep his own back. "Because I won't take a bagful of gold from you when I don't want it," he went on, "do you think I should let myself starve without coming to you? I promise you I will let you know—come to you if I can, the moment I get too hungry to do my work well, and have no money left. Should I think it a disgrace to take money from *you*? That would show a poverty of spirit such as I hope never to fall into. My *sole* reason for refusing it now is that I do not need it."

But for all his loving words and assurances Clementina could not stay her tears. She was not ready to weep, but now her eyes were as a fountain.

"See, then, for your tears are hard to bear, my daughter," he said, "I will take one of these golden ministers, and if it has flown from me ere you come, seeing that, like the raven, it will not return if once I let it go, I will ask you for another. It *may* be God's will that you should feed me for a time."

"Like one of Elijah's ravens," said Clementina, with an attempted laugh that was really a sob.

"Like a dove whose wings are covered with silver, and her feathers with yellow gold," said the schoolmaster.

A moment of silence followed, broken only by Clementina's failures in quieting herself.

"To me," he resumed, "the sweetest fountain of money is the hand of love, but a man has no right to take it from that fountain except he is in want of it. I am not. True, I go somewhat bare, my lady; but what is that when my Lord would have it so?"

He opened again the bag, and slowly, reverently indeed, drew from it one of the new sovereigns with which it was filled. He put it into a waistcoat pocket, and laid the bag on the table.

"But your clothes are shabby, sir," said Clementina, looking at him with a sad little shake of the head.

"Are they?" he returned, and looked down at his lower garments, reddening and anxious. "I did not think they were more than a little rubbed, but they shine somewhat," he said. "They are indeed polished by use," he went on, with a troubled little laugh, "but they have no holes yet—at least none that are visible," he corrected. "If you tell me, my lady, if you honestly tell me that my garments"—and he looked at the sleeve of his coat, drawing back his head from it to see it better—"are unsightly, I will take of your money and buy me a new suit."

Over his coat sleeve he regarded her, questioning.

"Everything about you is beautiful!" she burst out. "You want nothing but a body that lets the light through!"

She took the hand still raised in his survey of his sleeve, pressed it to her lips, and walked, with even more than her wonted state, slowly from the room. He took the bag of gold from the table, and followed her down the stair. Her chariot was awaiting her at the door. He helped her in, and laid the bag on the little seat in front.

The coachman took the queer, shabby, un-London-like man for a fortune teller his lady was in the habit of consulting, and paid homage to his power with the handle of his whip as he drove away. The schoolmaster returned to his room—not to his Plato or Shakespeare, not even to Saul of Tarsus, but to the Lord himself.[2]

To One Threatened With Blindness

I

Lawrence, what though the world be growing dark,
And twilight cool thy potent day inclose!
The sun, beneath the round earth sunk, still glows
All the night through, sleepless and young and stark.
Oh, be thy spirit faithful as the lark,
More daring: in the midnight of thy woes,
Dart through them, higher than earth's shadow goes,
Into the Light of which thou art a spark!
Be willing to be blind—that, in thy night,
The Lord may bring his Father to thy door,
And enter in, and feast thy soul with light.
Then shalt thou dream of darksome ways no more,
Forget the gloom that round thy windows lies,
And shine, God's house, all radiant in our eyes.

II

Say thou, his will be done who is the good!
His will be borne who knoweth how to bear!
Who also in the night had need of prayer,
Both when awoke divinely longing mood,
And when the power of darkness him withstood.
For what is coming take no jot of care:
Behind, before, around thee as the air,
He o'er thee like thy mother's heart will brood.
And when thou hast wearied thy wings of prayer,
Then fold them, and drop gently to thy nest,
Which is thy faith; and make thy people blest
With what thou bring'st from that ethereal height,
Which whoso looks on thee will straightway share:
He needs no eyes who is a shining light!

THE CAUSE OF SPIRITUAL IGNORANCE

How is it that ye do not understand?
Mark 8:21

The Leaven of the Pharisees

After feeding the four thousand with seven loaves and a few small fishes on the east side of the Sea of Galilee, Jesus crossed the lake, was met on the other side by certain Pharisees, whose attitude toward him was such that he got back in the boat, and recrossed the lake. On the way the disciples began talking amongst themselves that they did not have enough food for their next meal. Jesus, still occupied with the antagonism of the leaders of the people, began to warn the disciples against them, making use of a figure they had heard him use before—that of leaven as representing a hidden but potent and pervading energy. He had used it in speaking of the kingdom of heaven. Now he tells them to beware of the leaven of the Pharisees. But a leaven like that of the Pharisees was even then at work in their hearts.

It is to the man who is trying to live, to the man who is obedient to the word of the Master, that the word of the Master unfolds itself. When we understand the outside of things, we think we have them. Yet the Lord puts his things in subdefined, suggestive shapes, yielding no satisfactory meaning to the mere intellect, but unfolding themselves to the conscience and heart, to the man himself, in the process of life-effort.

Accordingly, as the new creation, in reality, advances in him, the man becomes able to understand the words, the symbols, the parables of the Lord.

For life, that is, action, is alone the human condition into which the light of the Living can penetrate. Life alone can assimilate life, can change food into growth.

See how the disciples here fooled themselves! See how the Lord calls them to their senses. He does not tell them in so many words where they are wrong; he attacks instead the cause in them which led to their mistake—a matter always of infinitely more consequence than any mistake itself. The one is a live mistake, an untruth in the soul, the other a mere dead blunder born of it. The word-connection, therefore, between their blunder and the Lord's exhortation is not to be found. The logic of what the Lord said is not on the surface.

Often he speaks not to the words but to the thought. Here he speaks not even to the thought, but to the whole mode of thinking, to the thought-matrix, the inward condition of the men.

The Lord addresses himself to rouse in them a sense of their lack of confidence in God, which was the cause of their blunder as to his meaning. He makes them go over the particulars of the miracles—hardly to refresh their memories, but to make their hearts dwell on them, for they had already forgotten or had failed to see the central revelation—the eternal fact of God's love and care and compassion.

They knew the number of the men each time, the number of the loaves each time, the number of baskets of fragments they had each time taken up. But they forgot the Love that had so broken the bread that its remnants twenty times outweighed its loaves.

Having thus questioned them like children and listened as to the answers of children, the Lord turns the light of their thoughts upon themselves, and, with an argument to the men that overleaps all the links of its own absolute logic, demands, "How is it that ye do not understand?"

Then at last they did understand. He who trusts can understand. He whose mind is set at ease can discover a reason.

Miracles Reveal the Father

The lesson Jesus would have had his disciples learn from the miracle, the natural lesson, the only lesson worthy of the miracle, was that God cared for his children, and could, did, and would provide for their necessities. This lesson they had not learned.

The ground of the Master's upbraiding is not that they did not understand him, but that they did not trust God.

Because we easily imagine ourselves in want, we imagine God ready to forsake us. The miracles of Jesus were the ordinary works of the Father, wrought small and swift that we might take them in. The lesson of them was that help is always within God's reach when his children need it. Their design was to show what God is—not that Jesus was God, but that his Father was God.

The mission undertaken by the Son was not to show himself as having all power in heaven and earth, but to reveal his Father, to show him to men such as he is, that men may know him, and knowing, may trust him. Jesus came to give men God, who is eternal life.

Those miracles of feeding gave the same lesson to their eyes, their hands, their mouths, that his words gave to their ears when he said, "Seek not ye what ye shall eat, or what ye shall drink, neither be ye of doubtful mind, for your Father knoweth that ye have need of these things. . . . Seek ye first the kingdom of God, and his righteousness, and all these things shall be added unto you." So little had they learned it yet, that they remembered the loaves but forgot the Father—as men in their theology forget the very *Word of God*. The mere mention of leaven threw them floundering afresh in the bog of their unbelief.

Trust and Obedience Have No Relation But to Now

The care of the disciples was care for the day, not for the morrow.

The word *morrow* must stand for any and every point of the future. The next hour, the next moment, is as much beyond our grasp and as much in God's care as the next hundred years. Care for the next minute is just as foolish as care for tomorrow, or for a day in the next thousand years. In neither can we do anything; in both God is doing everything.

Only those claims of the morrow that have to be prepared for today are of the duty of today. The moment that coincides with work to be done is the moment to be minded. The next is nowhere till God has made it.

The disciples' lack of bread seems to have come from no neglect, but from the hastiness of the Lord's reembarcation. Yet even if there had been a lack of foresight, that was not the kind of thing the Lord would have reproved. He did not come to set this and that fault right, but to remedy the primary evil of life without God, the root of all evils. Neither did he bother with certain minor virtues, prudence among the rest. They, too, in the end would be almost, if not altogether, superseded by his true purpose.

If a man forget a thing, God will see to that. Man is not lord of his memory or his intellect. But the man is lord of his will, his action. And he is verily to blame when, remembering a duty, he does not do it, but puts it off, and so forgets it.

If a man or woman determines to do the immediate duty of the moment, wonderfully little forethought or planning, I suspect, will be needed. Only that forethought is necessary which has to determine where obedience is called for, and then enable it to pass into action. To the foundation of yesterday's work well done, the work of tomorrow will be sure to fit. Work *done* is of more consequence for the future than all the foresight and planning of an archangel.[1]

To love the truth is a far greater thing than to know it, for it is itself truth in the inward parts—act-truth, as distinguished from fact-truth. In the highest truth the knowledge and love of it are one, or, if not identical then coincident. The very sight of the truth is the loving of it.[2] And all truth understood becomes duty. To him that obeys well, the truth comes easy. To him who does not obey, truth does not come at all, or comes in forms of fear and dismay. The true—that is, the obedient—man cannot help seeing the truth, for it is the very business of his being—the natural concern, the correlate of his soul. The religion of such men and women is obedience and prayer, and their theories but the print of their spiritual feet as they walk homeward.[3]

OBEDIENCE ALONE OPENS THE DOOR TO THE SPIRIT OF WISDOM

Fictional Selections from *Sir Gibbie*

T hus Gibbie had his first lesson in the only thing worth learning, in that which, to be learned at all, demands the united energy of heart and soul and strength and mind; and from that day he went on learning it. I cannot tell how, or what were the slow stages by which his mind budded and swelled until it burst into the flower of humanity, the knowledge of God. I cannot tell the shape of the door by which the Lord entered into that house, and took everlasting possession of it. I cannot even tell in what shape he appeared himself in Gibbie's thoughts—for the Lord can take any shape that is human. I only know it was not any unhuman shape of earthly theology that he bore to Gibbie, when he saw him with "that inward eye, which is the bliss of solitude." For happily, Janet never suspected how utter was Gibbie's ignorance. She never dreamed that he did not know what was generally said about Jesus Christ. She thought he must know as well as she the outlines of his story, and the purpose of his life and death, as commonly taught, and therefore never attempted explanations for the sake of which she would probably have found herself driven to use terms and phrases which merely substitute that which is intelligible because it appeals to what in us is low, and is itself both low and false, for that which, if unintelligible, is so because of its grandeur and truth. Gibbie's ideas of God he got all from the mouth of Theology himself, the Word of God; and to the theologian who will not be content with his teaching, the disciple of Jesus must just turn his back, that his face may be to his Master.

The mountain was a grand nursery for him, and the result, both physical and spiritual, corresponded. Janet, who, better than anyone else, knew what was in the mind of the boy, revered him as much as he revered her; the first impression he made upon her had never worn off—had only changed its color a little. More even than a knowledge of the truth, is a readiness to receive it; and Janet saw from the first that Gibbie's ignorance at its worst was but a room vacant for the truth: when it came it found bolt nor bar on door or window, but had immediate entrance. The secret of this power of reception was, that to see a truth and to do it was one and the same thing with Gibbie. To know and not do would have seemed to him an impossibility, as it is in vital idea a monstrosity.

This unity of vision and action was the main cause also of a certain daring simplicity in the exercise of the imagination, which so far from misleading him reacted only in obedience— which is the truth of the will—the truth, therefore, of the whole being. He did not do the less well for his sheep, that he fancied they knew when Jesus Christ was on the mountain, and always at such times both fed better and were more frolicsome. He thought Oscar knew it also, and interpreted a certain look of the dog by the supposition that he had caught a sign of the bodily presence of his Maker. The direction in which his imagination ran forward, was always that in which his reason printed; and so long as Gibbie's fancies were bud-blooms upon his obedience, his imagination could not be otherwise than in harmony with his reason. Imagination is a poor root, but a worthy blossom, and in a nature like Gibbie's its flowers cannot fail to be lovely. For no outcome of a man's nature is so like himself as his imaginations, except it be his fancies, indeed. Perhaps his imaginations show what he is meant to be, his fancies what he is making of himself.

It were indeed an argument against religion as strong as sad, if one of the children the kingdom specially claims could not be possessed by the life of the Son of God without losing his simplicity and joyousness. Those of my readers will be the least inclined to doubt the boy, who, by obedience, have come to know its reward. For obedience alone holds wide the door for the entrance of the spirit of wisdom. There was as little to wonder at in Gibbie as there was much to love and admire, for from the moment when, yet a mere child, he heard there was such a one claiming his obedience, he began to turn to him the hearing ear, the willing heart, the ready hand. The main thing which rendered this devotion more easy and natural to him than to others was, that, more than in most, the love of man had in him prepared the way of the Lord. He who so loved the sons of men was ready to love the Son of Man the moment he heard of him; love makes obedience a joy; and of him who obeys all heaven is the patrimony—he is fellow-heir with Christ.[4]

OBEDIENCE PRECEDES INTELLECTUAL ASSURANCE

A Fictional Selection from *The Landlady's Master*

Alexa was growing to care more about the truth. She was gradually coming to see that much of what she had taken for a more liberal creed was but the same falsehoods in weaker forms of the constricting religion from which her mind had rebelled. In Andrew she saw what was infinitely higher and more than the religion of various doctrines and prohibitions of her ancestors—namely, the denial of his very self, and the reception of God instead. She was beginning to realize that she had been, even with all her supposed progress, only a recipient of the traditions of the elders. Yet there must be a deeper something . . . somewhere—the *real* religion that would satisfy heart and soul!

Her eyes were gradually opening, but she did not yet see that the will of God lay in another direction altogether than the heartiest reception of dogma and creed and doctrine, no matter how right they may be!—that God was too great and too generous to care about anything except righteousness, and only wanted us to be good children!

She longed for something positive to believe, something in accordance with which her feelings might agree. She was still on the lookout for definite intellectual formulae to hold. Like so many seeming Christians, she could not divorce her mind from thinking of belief as a framework of viewpoints—social, political, philosophical, and theoretical; none of which the Lord had anywhere in his mind when he said, "Repent and *believe* in the Gospel." True belief consists in no cognitive convictions, no matter how pious, no matter how biblically correct, but rather in *life* as it is *lived!*

Alexa's interaction with Andrew had as yet failed to open her eyes to the fact that the faith required of us is faith in a person, not in the truest of statements concerning anything, even concerning him, for some do not discern his truth correctly. Neither was she yet alive to the fact that faith in the living One, the very essence of it, consists in obedience to him. A man can obey before he is intellectually sure; and except he obey the command he knows to be right, wherever it may come from, he will never be sure. To find the truth, a man or woman must be true.[5]

Rest

I

When round the earth the Father's hands
Have gently drawn the dark;
Sent off the sun to fresher lands,
And curtained in the lark;
'Tis sweet, all tired with glowing day,
To fade with fading light,
And lie once more, the old weary way,
Upfolded in the night.

If mothers o'er our slumbers bend,
And unripe kisses reap,
In soothing dreams with sleep they blend,
Till even in dreams we sleep.
And if we wake while night is dumb,
'Tis sweet to turn and say,
It is an hour ere dawning come,
And I will sleep till day.

II

There is a dearer, warmer bed,
Where one all day may lie,
Earth's bosom pillowing the head,
And let the world go by.
There come no watching mother's eyes,
The stars instead look down;
Upon it breaks, and silent dies,
The murmur of the town.

The great world, shouting, forward fares:
This chamber, hid from none,
Hides safe from all, for no one cares
For him whose work is done.
Cheer thee, my friend; bethink thee how
A certain unknown place,
Or here or there, is waiting now,
To rest thee from thy race.

III

Nay, nay, not there the rest from harms,
The still composed breath!
Not there the folding of the arms,
The cool, the blessed death!
That needs no curtained bed to hide
The world with all its wars,
No grassy cover to divide
From sun and moon and stars.

It is a rest that deeper grows
In midst of pain and strife;
A mighty, conscious, willed repose,
The death of deepest life.
To have and hold the precious prize
No need of jealous bars;
But windows open to the skies,
And skill to read the stars!

IV

Who dwelleth in that secret place,
Where tumult enters not,
Is never cold with terror base,
Never with anger hot.
For if an evil host should dare
His very heart invest,
God is his deeper heart, and there
He enters in to rest.

When mighty sea-winds madly blow,
And tear the scattered waves,
Peaceful as summer woods, below
Lie darkling ocean caves:
The wind of words may toss my heart,
But what is that to me!
'Tis but a surface storm—thou art
My deep, still, resting sea.

Trust God by Obeying Christ

Casting all your care upon him; for he careth for you.

1 Peter 5:7

Things Slay Trust

Both the wealthy young man who came to Jesus inquiring about eternal life and the disciples who questioned between themselves about the leaven of the Pharisees did not grasp the essential element in Jesus' responses to them. With the disciples as with the rich youth, it was *things* that prevented the Lord from being understood.

Because of possessions the young man had not a suspicion of the grandeur of the call with which Jesus honored him. He thought the Lord's dealing with him was hard, even though he was offered a right to join heaven's nobility—he was so very rich! But *things* filled his heart. Things blocked up his windows. Things barricaded his door so that the very God could not enter. His soul was not empty, swept and garnished, but crowded with idols, among which his spirit crept about upon its knees, wasting on them the gazes that belonged to his fellows and to his Master.

The disciples were a little further on than he; they had left all and followed the Lord. But neither had they yet got rid of *things*. The paltry solitariness of a loaf of bread was enough to hide the Lord from them, to make them unable to understand him. Why, having forgotten, could they not trust? Surely if he had told them that for his sake they must go all day without food, they would not have minded. But they lost sight of God, and were in a state as if he did not see, or did not care for them.

In the former case it was the *possession* of wealth, in the latter the *not having* more than a loaf, that rendered men incapable of receiving the word of the Lord. Possessing or not possessing, it matters not: the evil principle was precisely the same. If it be *things* that slay you, what does it matter whether it is the things you *have* or the things you do *not* have?

Not trusting in God, the source of his riches, the youth could not endure the word of his Son, offering him better riches, directly from the heart of the Father. The disciples, forgetting who is Lord of the harvests of the earth, could not understand his word, because they were filled with the fear of a day's hunger. The youth did not trust in God as having given; they did not trust in God as ready to give.

We are like them when we find ourselves in *any* trouble and do not trust God.

We could say it is difficult for God when his children will not let him give, when they conduct themselves in such a way that he must withhold his hand, lest he harm them. To have no concern that they acknowledge whence their help comes would be to leave them to be worshipers of idols, trusting in that which is dead and void.

Not Trusting Is Unbelief

Distrust is atheism and the barrier to all growth.

Lord, we do not understand you, because we do not trust your Father! Full of care, we foolishly think this and that escapes God's notice. While we who are evil would die to give our children bread to eat, we are not certain that the only Good in the universe will give us anything of what we desire! The things of the world so crowd our hearts that there is no room in them for the things of God's heart, which would raise ours above all fear and make us merry children in our Father's house. How many whispers of the watching Spirit do we let slip by, while we brood over a need not yet come to us! Tomorrow makes today's whole head sick, its whole heart faint. When we should be still, sleeping or dreaming, we are fretting about an hour that lies half a sun's journey away!

Not so do you do, Lord! You do the work of your Father! Were you such as we, then should we have good cause to be troubled! But you know it is difficult, *things* pressing upon every sense, to believe that the informing power of them is in the unseen, that out if it they come, that, where we can see no hand directing, a will nearer than any hand is moving them from within, causing them to fulfill his word. Help us, Lord, to obey, to resist, to trust.

The care that is filling your mind at this moment, or but waiting till you lay the book aside to consume you—that need which is no real need, is a demon sucking at the spring of your life.

Do you object, saying: "But no! you do not understand. The thing I am worrying about is a reasonable anxiety—an unavoidable care."

"Does it involve something you have to do at this very moment?" I ask.

"Well—no."

"Then you are allowing it to usurp the place of something that is required of you at this moment, the greatest thing that can ever be required of any man or woman."

"And what is that?"

"To trust in the Living God."

"What if God does not want me to have what I need at this moment?"

"If he does not want you to have something *you* value, it is to give you instead something *he* values."

"And if I do not want what he has to give me?"

"If you are not willing that God should have his way with you, then, in the name of God, be miserable—until your misery drive you to the arms of the Father."

"Oh, but this is only about some financial concern. I *do* trust him in spiritual matters."

"*Everything* is an affair of the spirit. If God has a way of dealing with you in your life, it is the only way. Every little thing in which you would have your *own* way has a mission for your redemption. And he will treat you as a willful little child until you take your Father's way for your own."

Trifles Dull the Understanding

There will be this difference between the rich that loves his riches and the poor that hates his poverty. When they die, the heart of the one will still be crowded with things and their pleasures, while the heart of the other will be relieved of their lack. The one has had his good things; the other, his sorrowful things.

But the rich man, on the other hand, who held his things lightly and who did not let them nestle in his heart, who was a channel and not a cistern, who was ever and always forsaking his money—*this* rich man starts in the new world side by side with the man who *accepted*, not hated, his poverty. Each will say, "I am free."

For the only air in which the soul can breathe and live is the present God and the spirits of the just. That is our heaven, our home, our all right place. Cleansed of greed, jealousy, vanity, pride, possession, all the thousand forms of the evil self, we shall see God's children on the hills and in the fields of heaven, not one desiring to be ahead of any other, any more than to cast that other out. For ambition and hatred will then be seen to come from one and the same spirit. Then we will say, "What you have, I have. What you desire, I pray for. I give to myself ten times in giving once to you. My desire for *you* to have is my richest possession."

But let me be practical. If you are ready to be miserable over trifles and do not believe God good enough to care for your care, then I would reason with you to help you get rid of your troubles, for they hide from you the thoughts of your God.

The things most urgent to be done, those which lie not at the door but on the very table of a person's mind, are the things most often neglected, let alone, and postponed.

If the Lord of life demands high virtue of us, can it be that he does not care for the first principles of justice? May a person become strong in righteousness without learning to speak the truth to his neighbor? Shall one climb the last flight of the stairs who has never set foot on the first?

Truth is one. He who is faithful in the small thing at hand is of the truth. He who will only do the great thing, who postpones the small thing at hand for the sake of the great thing farther from him, is not of the truth.

Let me suggest some possible parallels between ourselves and the disciples murmuring over their one loaf—with the Bread of Life at their side in the boat.

We, too, dull our understanding with trifles, fill heavenly spaces with phantoms, waste heavenly time with hurry. To those who possess their souls in patience come the heavenly visions. When I trouble myself over a trifle, even a trifle confessed—the loss of some little article, say—spurring my memory, and searching the house, not from immediate need, but from dislike of loss, am I not like the disciples? When one of my books has been borrowed, and I have forgotten the borrower, and I fret over the missing volume while there are hundreds on my shelves from which the moments thus lost might gather treasure, holding relation with neither moth nor rust nor thief, am I not then being like the disciples? When I am absorbed with the bug in the dirt and see not the glories of the sunset filling the sky, am I not then pondering a loaf while missing life? Am I not a fool whenever loss troubles me more than recovery would gladden?

God would have me wise and smile at the trifle. Is it not time I lost a few things when I care for them so unreasonably? The losing of things is of the mercy of God; it comes to teach us to let them go.

Or have I forgotten a thought that came to me, which seemed of the truth, and a revelation to my heart? I wanted to keep it, to have it, to use it by and by, and it is gone! I keep trying and trying to call it back. I feel like a poor man till I can recover that nugget of truth—to be far more lost, perhaps, in a notebook or written in the margin of my Bible, where I shall never look again to find it!

Do I, in some special book I love, whose author I revere, read a pearl of great wisdom, and underline it and make reference to it alongside, as if the notation of the truth will enliven its reality in my heart? Do I make notes of a moving sermon, thinking the writing of truth will awaken truth in my inward parts?

No, I say, a thousand times no to these trifles, these mere externals, these entombed monuments to dead analysis! Arise, awake, my soul, to obedient and *living* truth!

Many who from Sunday to Sunday read the poems of a certain king brought up a shepherd lad never stop to bring the truths of those poems into their daily lives. They read, "I will both lay me down in peace and sleep, for thou, Lord, only makest me to dwell in safety." Yet these readers never think that such a feeling ought to rule in their own hearts in consequence. . . . Such men and women build stone houses, but never a spiritual nest. They cannot believe . . . a *practical* faith possible. And they may never believe it before they begin to do it.

I can hardly wonder that so many reject Christianity when they see so many would-be champions of it holding their beliefs at arm's length—in their Bibles, in their theories, in their churches, in their clergymen, in their prayerbooks, in the last devotional page they have read—all things separate from their real selves—rather than in their hearts on their beds in the stillness. God is nearer to me than the air I breath, nearer to me than the heart of wife or child, nearer to me than my own consciousness of myself, nearer to me than the words in which I speak to him, nearer than the thought roused in me by the story of his perfect Son. The unbelievers might well rejoice in the loss of such a God as many Christians would make of him. But if he be indeed the Father of our Lord Jesus Christ, then to all eternity let me say only, "Amen, Lord, your will be done!"[1]

It is *live* things God cares about—live truths, not things set down in a book, or in a memory, or embalmed in the joy of knowledge, but things lifting up the heart, things active in an active will.

True, my lost thought might have so worked. But had I faith in

God, the maker of thought and memory, I should know that, if the thought was a truth and so alone worth anything, it must come again. For it is in God—so, like the dead, not beyond my reach; kept for me, I shall have it again.

Cast Out Anxiety to Make Room for Truth

With every haunting trouble, great or small—the loss of thousands of pounds or the lack of a shilling—go to God and appeal to him, the God of your life, to deliver you, his child, from that which is unlike him and which is therefore antagonistic to your nature. If your trouble is such that you think you cannot appeal to him, then you need to appeal to him all the more!

Where one cannot go to God, there is something especially wrong. If you let thought for the morrow, or the next year, or the next month, distress you, if you let the chatter of what is called the public, peering blindly into the sanctuary of motive, annoy you, if you seek or even greatly heed the judgment of men, capable or incapable, you set open your windows to the mosquitoes of care, to drown with their buzzing the voice of the Eternal! It is true that by letting go of all your cares and your strivings you are not likely to get rich, but neither will you block up the gate of the kingdom of heaven against yourself.

Ambition in every form has to do with *things*, with outward advantages for the satisfaction of self-worship. It is that form of pride, foul shadow of Satan, that usurps the place of aspiration.

The sole ambition that is of God is the ambition to rise above oneself; all other is of the devil. Yet ambition is nursed and cherished in many a soul that thinks itself devout, filling it with petty cares and disappointments, that swarm like bats in its air, and shut out the glory of God.

The love of the praise of men, the desire for fame, the pride that takes offense, the puffing-up of knowledge, these and every other form of ever-changing self-worship—we must get rid of them all.

We must be free!

The man whom *another* enslaves may still be free in God. But he who is a slave in himself, in him God will not enter. God will not sup with him, for God cannot be his friend. Jesus will sit by the humblest hearth where the daily food is prepared. But he will not eat in the fanciest room, be it filled with thrones and crowns, with one who does not invite him.

Will not, did I say? *Cannot* is closer to the truth. Men full of *things* would not once partake with God even if he were beside them all the day.

God will force no door in order to enter. He may send a tempest about the house. The wind of his admonishment may burst doors and windows and shake the house to its foundations, but he will not enter.

The door must be opened by the willing hand before the foot of Love will cross the threshold.

God watches to see the slightest move of the door from within. Every tempest is but an assault in the siege of love. The terror of God is but the other side of his love; it is love outside the house that would be inside—love that knows the house is no house, only a place, until love enters—no home, but a tent, until the Eternal dwells there.

Things must be cast out to make room for their souls—the eternal truths which in things find shape and show.[3]

Would Proof of Eternity Make Men Believe?

A Fictional Selection from *The Curate's Awakening*

There are a thousand individual events in the course of every man's life by which God takes a hold of him—a thousand little doors by which he enters, however little the man may realize it. But in addition, there is one universal and unchanging grasp that God keeps on the race, no matter how men may ignore him all their lives long and ignore these thousand ways he would enter and give them his life. And that grasp is death and its shroud of mystery. Imagine a man who is about to die in absolute loneliness and cannot tell where he will go—to whom, I say, can such a man go for refuge? Where can he take the doubts and fears that assail him, but to the Father of his being?"

"But," objected Drew, "I cannot see what harm would come of letting us know a little—enough at least to assure us that there is *something* on the other side."

"Just this," returned Polwarth. "Their fears relieved, their hopes encouraged from any lower quarter—men would, as usual, turn away from the fountain to the cistern of life. They would not turn to the ever-fresh, original, creative Love to sustain them, but would rely on their knowledge instead. Satisfy people's desire to know this and what have they gained? A little comfort perhaps—but not a comfort from the highest source, and possibly gained too soon for their well-being. Does it bring them any nearer to God than they were before? Is he filling one more cranny of their hearts in consequence? Their assurance of immortality has not come from knowing him in their hearts, and without that it is worthless knowledge. Little would be gained, and possibly much would be lost—and that is the need to trust him beyond what our minds can see. Trust is born in love, and our need is to *love* God, not apprehend facts concerning him. Remember Jesus' words: 'If they do not listen to Moses and the prophets, neither would they listen or would they be persuaded though one rose from the dead.' He does not say they would not believe in a future state though one rose from the dead— though most likely they would soon persuade themselves it had been nothing more than an illusion—but they would not be persuaded to repent, to turn to God, to love and trust and believe in him with their whole hearts. And without love for God, what does it matter whether someone believes in a future state or not? It would only be worse for him if he did. No, Mr. Drew! I repeat, it is not a belief in immortality that will deliver a man from the woes and pains and sins of humanity, but faith in the God of life, the Father of lights, the God of all consolation and comfort."

Polwarth paused, then said, "Witness our friend Lingard. His knowledge of God's love and forgiveness *in his heart*—not in his intellect—brought peace to his troubled soul. He knows of the afterlife now, because he is in it, with his Lord who loved him in the midst of his guilt. But what good would that mere *knowledge* have done him before, without the cleansing power of the Savior's love to wash the bloodstains from his hands and make his heart once again white as snow? Believing in the Father of Jesus, a man can leave his friends, his family, and his guilt-ridden past, with utter confidence in his hands. It is in *trusting* him that we move into higher regions of life, not in knowing *about* him. Until we have his life in us, we shall never be at peace. The living God dwelling in the heart he has made, and glorifying it by inner communion with himself—that is life, assurance, and safety. Nothing less can ever give true life."[4]

A Vision Without Result

A Fictional Selection from *The Highlander's Last Song*

There was once a woman whose husband was well-to-do, but he died and she sank into poverty. She did her best, but she had a large family and work was hard to find. But she trusted in God, and said whatever he pleased must be right, whether he sent it with his own hand or not.

Now, whether it was that she could not find her children enough to eat, or that she could not keep them warm enough, I do not know. But whatever the cause, they began to die. One after the other became sick and lay down, and did not rise again, and for a long time her life was nothing but waiting upon death. She would have wanted to die herself, but there was always another to die first and she had to see them all safe home before she dared wish to go herself. At length when the last of them was gone, and she then had no more to provide for, the heart of work went out of her: what was the good of working for herself alone? But she knew it was the will of God she should work and eat until he chose to take her back to himself, so she worked on for her living and comforted herself that every day brought death a day nearer. Then she fell ill herself and could work no more and thought God was going to let her die.

But just as she was going to her bed for the last time, she thought to herself that she was bound to give her neighbor the chance of doing a good deed; any creature dying at *her* door without letting her know he was in want would do her a great wrong. She saw it was the will of God that she should beg. So she put on her clothes again and went out to beg. And beg she did—enough to keep her alive, and no more.

As she went her way begging, one night she came to a farmhouse where a rich miserly farmer lived. She knew about him, and had not meant to stop there, but she was weary and the sun went down as she reached his gate and she felt as if she could go no further. So she went up to the door and knocked and asked if she could have a night's lodging. The woman who opened the door to her went and asked the farmer. Now the old man did not like hospitality, and in particular did not like it toward those that stood most in need of it. At the same time, however, he was very fond of hearing all the country rumors, and he thought to himself that he would invite her in and buy her news with a scrap of something to eat. So he told his servant to bring her in.

He received her kindly enough, for he wanted her to talk, and he let her have a share of the supper, such as it was. But not until he had asked every question about everybody he could think of, and drawn her own history from her as well, would he allow her to have the rest her tired body was so in need of.

Now it was a poor house, like most in the country, and nearly without interior walls, and the man had done little to better his surroundings despite his wealth. He had his warm box-bed and slept on feathers where no wind could reach him, and the poor woman had her bed of short rumpled straw on the earthen floor at the foot of the wall in the coldest corner. Yet the heart of the man had been somewhat moved by her story, for, without dwelling on her sufferings, she had been honest in telling it. He had indeed, before he went to sleep, thanked God that he was so much better off than she. For if he did not think it the duty of the rich man to share with his neighbors, he at least thought it his duty to thank God for being richer than they.

Now it may seem strange that such a man should be privileged to see a vision, especially when the woman saw nothing of it. But she did not require to see any vision, for she had truth in the inward parts, which is better than all visions. His vision was this: In the middle of the night the man came wide awake, and looking out of his bed saw the door open and a light come in, burning like a star. It was a faint rosy color, unlike any light he had ever seen before. Another and another came in, and more still, until he counted six of them. They moved near the floor, but he could not see clearly what sort of little creatures they were that were carrying them. They went up to the woman's bed, walked around it slowly in a hovering kind of way, stopped, moved up and down, and then went on again. And when they had done this three times they went slowly out of the door again, stopping for a moment several times as they went.

The man fell asleep again, and when he woke late the next

morning, he was surprised to see his guest still on her hard couch—as quiet as any rich woman on her feather bed. He woke her, told her he wondered how she could sleep so far into the morning, and narrated the curious vision he had had. "Does that not explain it to you," she said, "how I have slept so long? Those were my dead children you saw. They died young and God lets them come and comfort their poor mother. I often see them in my dreams. If, when I am gone, you will look at my bed, you will find every straw laid straight and smooth. That is what they were doing last night." Then she gave him thanks for the good fare and fine rest, and continued on her way, leaving the farmer better pleased with himself than he had been for a long time, partly because there had been granted him a vision from heaven.

At last the woman died also and was carried by angels into Abraham's bosom. She was now with her own people at last, with God and all the good. The old farmer did not know of her death till a long time later, but it was upon the night she died, as near as he could make out, that he dreamed another strange dream. He never told it to anyone but the priest from whom he sought comfort when he lay dying some time later, and the priest told it to no one until everybody belonging to the old man was gone.

The old man was lying awake in his own bed, as he thought, in the dark night, when the poor woman came in at the door. She had in her hand a wax candle, but it was not lit. He said to her, "You extravagant woman! Where did you get that candle?" She answered, "It was put into my hand when I died, with the word that I was to wander till I found a fire at which to light it." "There!" he said, "there's the fire. Blow and get a light; poor thing! It shall never be said I refused a body a light!"

She went to the hearth and began to blow at the smoldering peat; but for all she kept trying she could not light her candle. The old man thought it was because she was dead, not because he was dead in sin, and losing his patience, he cried, "You foolish woman! Haven't you wit enough to light a candle? It's small wonder you came to beggary!"

Still she went on trying, but the more she tried, the blacker grew the peat she was blowing at. It would indeed blaze up at her breath, but the moment she brought the candle near it to catch the flame, it grew black, and each time blacker than before. "Give me the candle!" cried the farmer, springing out of bed; "I will light it for you!" But as he stretched out his hand to take it, the woman disappeared and he saw that the fire was dead and cold.

"This is a fine thing!" he said. "How am I to get a light?" For they were miles from the next house. And with that he turned to go back to his bed. When he came near it he saw somebody lying in it. "What! Has the old hag got into my very bed?" he cried, and went to drive her out of the bed and out of the house. But when he came close, he saw that it was he himself lying there, and at least he knew that he was out of the body, if not downright dead. The next moment he found himself on the moor, following the woman, some distance ahead of him, with her unlighted candle still in her hand. He walked as fast as he could to get up with her, but could not. He called after her but she did not seem to hear.

When he first set out he knew every step of the ground, but by and by he ceased to know it. The moor stretched endlessly before him, and the woman walked on and on. Without a thought of turning back he followed. At length he saw a gate, seemingly in the side of a hill. The woman knocked and by the time it opened he was near enough to hear what passed. It was a grave, and he knew at once that the stately but very happy-looking man that opened it was St. Peter. When he saw the woman he stooped and kissed her. The same moment a light shone from her, and the old man thought her candle was lighted at last. But presently he saw it was her head that gave out the shining. And he heard her say, "I pray you, St. Peter, remember the rich tenant of Balmacoy. He gave me shelter one whole night, and would have let me light my candle but I could not." St. Peter answered, "His fire was not fire enough to light your candle, and the bed he gave you was of short straw." "True, St. Peter," said the woman, "but he gave me some supper, and it is hard for a rich man to be generous. You may say that the supper was not very good, but at least it was more than a cup of cold water." "Yes," answered the saint, "but he did not give it to you because you loved God, or because you were in need of it, but because he wanted to hear your news." Then the woman was sad, for she could not think of anything more to say for the poor old rich man. And St. Peter saw that she was sad and said, "But if he dies tonight, he shall have a place inside the gate, because you prayed for him. He shall lie there." And he pointed to just such a bed of short crumpled straw as she had lain upon in his house.

But she said, "St. Peter, you ought to be ashamed of yourself. Is that the kind of welcome to give a poor man? Where would he have lain if I had not prayed for him?" "In the dog kennel outside there," answered St. Peter. "Oh, then please let me go back and warn him what comes of loving money!" she pleaded. "That is not necessary," he replied. "The man is hearing every word you and I are this moment saying to each other." "I am so glad," rejoined the woman, "it will make him repent." "He will not be a straw better for it," answered the saint. "He thinks now that he will behave differently, and perhaps when he wakes up he will think so still. But in a day or two he will mock it all as a foolish dream. To gather money will seem again to him a good thing to do, and to lay up treasure in heaven will appear as nonsense. A bird in the hand will be to him worth ten in the heavenly bush. And the end of that will be he will not get the straw inside the gate, and there will be many worse places than the dog kennel which will be too good for him!"

And with that the man awoke. "What an odd dream!" he said to himself. "I had better mind what I am about!" So he was better that day, eating and drinking more freely, and giving more to his people. But the rest of the week he was worse than ever, trying to save what he had that day spent, and so he went on growing worse. When he found himself dying, the terror of his dream came upon him, and he told it all to the priest. But the priest could not comfort him.[5]

Come To Me

Come to me, come to me, O my God;
    Come to me everywhere!
Let the trees mean thee, and the grassy sod,
    And the water and the air!

For thou art so far that I often doubt,
    As on every side I stare,
Searching within, and looking without,
    If thou canst be anywhere.

How did men find thee in days of old?
    How did they grow so sure?
They fought in thy name, they were glad and bold,
    They suffered, and kept themselves pure!

But now they say—neither above the sphere
    Nor down in the heart of man,
But solely in fancy, ambition, and fear
    The thought of thee began.

If only that perfect tale were true
    Which ages have not made old,
Which of endless many makes one anew,
    And simplicity manifold!

TRUTH IS OF THE SPIRIT NOT THE LETTER

I have yet many things to say unto you, but ye cannot bear them now. Howbeit when he, the Spirit of truth, is come, he will guide you into all truth.

John 16:12–13

Are the Gospel Words to Be Revered?

How near we come in the New Testament to the exact words of the Lord we cannot know of a certainty. I cannot doubt that they are different than he actually spoke them. For one thing, I do not believe he spoke in Greek. I cannot imagine that the thoughts of God would come out of the heart of Jesus in anything but the mother tongue of the simple people to whom he spoke. No doubt he knew Greek, and spoke it upon occasion, but not the majority of the time.

Then in addition, are we bound to believe that John Boanerges, who perhaps understood Jesus better than any other man, after such a lapse of years was able to give us in his Gospel, even supposing the Lord did speak to his disciples in Greek, the *very* words he uttered? I do not say he was *not* able, but are we *bound* to believe such is the case?

When the disciples, by the divine presence in their hearts, became capable of understanding the Lord, they remembered things he had said that they had forgotten. Possibly the very words in which he said them returned to their memories. But must we believe the evangelists always precisely recorded his words? The little differences between their records is answer enough to the contrary.

The Gospel of John is the outcome of years and years of remembering, recalling, and pondering the words of the Master, one thing understood recalling something new to mind. Certainly the memory, in its best condition—that is, with God in the man activating his brain—is capable of more than we can imagine. But I do not believe that John would have always given us the *very* words of the Lord, even if, as I do not think he did, he had spoken them in Greek.

God has not cared that we should anywhere have assurance of his very words—not merely because of the tendency in his children to word-worship, false logic, and corruption of the truth, but also because he would not have his people oppressed by words. For words, being human, therefore but partially capable, could not absolutely contain or express what the Lord meant. No matter how precise the words used, to be understood the Lord must depend on the spirit of his disciple.

Seeing it could not give life, the letter should not be throned with power to kill. It should be only the handmaid to open the door of the truth to the mind that was *of* the truth.

God Speaks to All

"Then you believe in an individual inspiration to anyone who chooses to lay claim to it?" you may ask.

Yes, to everyone who claims it from God. And not to everyone who claims from men the recognition of his possessing it.

He who has a thing does not need to have it recognized. If I did not believe in a special inspiration to every man or woman who asks for the Holy Spirit, the good thing of God, I should have to throw the whole thing aside as an imposture. For the Lord has promised such inspiration to those who ask for it. If an objector does not have this Spirit, is not inspired with the truth, he can know nothing of the words that are spirit and life, and his objections are not worth heeding. His agreement with you also is but the blowing of an idle horn.

"But how is one to tell whether it is the spirit of God that is speaking in a man, or the spirit of himself?"

You are not called upon to tell. The question for you is whether *you* have the Spirit of Christ yourself. The question is for you to put to *yourself*, and the question is for you to answer yourself: Am *I* alive with the life of Christ? Is his Spirit dwelling in me?

Everyone who desires to follow the Master has the Spirit of the Master, and will receive more, that he may follow closer, nearer, in his very footsteps. He is not called upon to prove to this or that or any man that he has the light of Jesus. He has but to let his light shine. It does not follow that his work is to teach others, or that he is able to speak large truths in true forms. When the strength or the joy or the pity of the truth urges him, let him speak it out and not be afraid—content to be condemned for it, comforted that if he makes a mistake, the Lord himself will condemn him, and save him too. The condemnation of his fellow men will not hurt him. If he speak the truth, the Lord will say, "I sent him." For all truth is of the Lord. No man can see a thing to be true but by the Lord, the Spirit.

Doing the Truth Reveals the Truth

How are you to know if a thing is true? By *doing* what you know to be true, and calling nothing true until you see it to be true. By shutting your mouth until the truth opens it. Are you meant to be silent? Then woe to you if you speak.

"But if, as you suggest, we do not take the words attributed to him in the Gospels for the certain, absolute, exact words of the Master, how are we to know that they represent his truth? What if the whole thing be folly?"

By seeing in them what corresponds to the plainest truths he speaks and commends itself to the power that is working in you to make of you a true man or a true woman. By their appeal to your power of judging what is true. By their rousing of your conscience.

If they do not seem to you true, either they are not the words of the Master, or you are not true enough to yet understand them. Be certain of this, that, if any words that are his do not show their truth to you, you have not received his message in them; they are not yet to you the word of God, for they are not in you spirit and life. They may be the nearest to the truth that words can come. They may have served to bring many into contact with the heart of God. But for you they remain as yet covered by scales.

If yours be a true heart, it will revere these words because of the probability that they are words with the meaning of the Master behind them. To you they are the rock in the desert before Moses spoke to it. If you wait, your ignorance will not hurt you. If you presume to reason from them, you are a blind man disputing of that which you never saw. To reason from a thing not understood is to walk straight into the mire. To dare to reason of truth from words that do not show to us that they are true is the presumption of pharisaical hypocrisy. Only they who are not true are capable of such blind reasoning.

Humble mistakes will not hurt us. The truth is there, and the Lord will see that we come to know it. We may think we know it when we have scarce a glimpse of it. But the error of a true heart will not be allowed to ruin it. Certainly that heart would not have mistaken the truth except for the untruth yet remaining in it. But he who casts out devils will cast out that devil.

Spiritual Logic—Revelation Through Creation

In the words of Jesus as recorded by the Gospel writers, I see enough to enable me to believe that the words embody the mind of Christ. If I could not say this about some certain passage, I should say, "Here is a record of a saying of Christ, yet in it I have not yet been able to recognize the mind of Christ. Therefore I conclude that I cannot have understood it, for to understand what is true is to know it is true."

I have yet seen no words credibly reported as the words of Jesus, concerning which I would dare to say, "His mind is not therein; therefore the words are not his."

The mind of man can receive any word only in proportion as it is the word of Christ, and in proportion as the man is one with Christ. To him who does verily receive Christ's word, it is a power, not of argument, but of life. The words of the Lord are not for the logic that deals with words as if they were things, but for the spiritual logic that reasons from divine thought to divine thought, dealing with spiritual facts.

No thought, human or divine, can be conveyed from man to man except through the symbolism of the creation. The heavens and the earth are around us that it may be possible for us to speak of the unseen by the seen, for the outermost husk of creation has correspondence with the deepest things of the Creator.

He is not a God that hides himself, but a God who made all that he might reveal himself. He is consistent and one throughout. There are things with which an enemy has meddled. But there are more things with which no enemy could meddle, and by which we may speak of God. They may not have revealed him to us, but at least when he is revealed, they show themselves so much of his nature that we at once use them as spiritual tokens in the commerce of the spirit to help convey to other minds what we may have seen of the unseen.[1]

Waiting

I waited for the Master
  In the darkness dumb;
Light came fast and faster—
  My light did not come!

I waited all the daylight,
  All through noon's hot flame:
In the evening's gray light,
  Lo, the Master came!

Nature Teaches Us to Know God

A Fictional Selection from *The Highlander's Last Song*

Macruadh, Mr. Ian and you often say things about *nature* that I cannot understand. I wish you would tell me what you mean by it."

"By what?" asked Alister.

"By *nature*," answered Mercy. "I heard Mr. Ian say, for instance, the other night, that he did not like *nature* to take liberties with him; you said she might take what liberties with you she pleased; and then you went on talking so that I could not understand a word either of you said. . . ."

Silence fell for a moment, then Ian said, "We mean by *nature* every visitation of the outside world through our senses."

"More plainly please, Mr. Ian. You cannot imagine how stupid I am."

"I mean by *nature*, then, all that you see and hear and smell and taste and feel of the things round about you."

"If that is all you mean, why should you make it seem so difficult?"

"But that is not all. The things themselves hold value for the sake of what they say to us. As our sense of smell brings us news of fields far off, so those fields, or even the smell that comes from them, tell us of things, meaning, thoughts, intentions beyond them, and embodied in them."

"And that is why you speak of nature as a person?" asked Mercy.

"Whatever influences us must be personal. But God is the only real person, being in himself and without help from anybody. And so we talk even of the world, which is his living garment, as if that were a person; we call it *she* as if it were a woman, because so many of God's loveliest influences come to us through her. She always seems to me a beautiful old grandmother."

"But there now! When you talk of her influences, I do not know what you mean. She seems to do and be something to you which certainly she does not and is not to me."

"I think I can let you see into it, Miss Mercy," said Ian. "Imagine for a moment how it would be if, instead of having the sky over us as it is, we only had a roof we could see, with clouds hanging down, as in a theater, only a yard or two from our heads!"

Mercy was silent for a moment, then said, "It would be horribly wearisome."

"It would indeed be wearisome. But how do you think it would affect your nature, your being?"

Mercy held her peace, which is the ignorant man's wisdom.

"We should have known nothing of astronomy," said Christina.

"True; and the worst of it would have been that the soul would have had no notion of heavenly things."

"There you leave me again," said Mercy.

"I mean," said Ian, "that it would have had no sense of outstretching, endless space, no feeling of heights above and depths below. When the soul wakes up, it needs all space for room!"

"Then my soul is not waked up yet!" rejoined Christina with a laugh.

Ian did not reply, and Christina felt that he accepted the proposition, as absurd as it seemed to herself.

"But there is more than that," he resumed. "What notion

could we have had of majesty if the heavens seemed scarcely higher than the earth? What feeling of the grandeur of God, of the vastness of his being, of the limitlessness of his goodness? For space is the body to our idea of God. Over and around us we have the one perfect geometrical shape—a dome, or sphere. I do not say it is put there for the purpose of representing God. I say it is there of necessity, because of its nature in relation to God's nature and character. It is of God's thinking, and that half sphere above our heads is the beginning of all revelation of him to men. We must begin with that. It is the simplest as well as most external likeness of him, while its relation to him goes so deep that it represents things in his very nature that nothing else could."

"You bewilder me," said Mercy.

"If it were not for the outside world," resumed Ian, "we should have no inside world to understand things by. Least of all could we understand God without these millions of sights and sounds and scents and motions, weaving their endless harmonies. They come out of his heart to let us know a little of what is in it."

Alister had been listening intently.

"I have never heard you put a thing better, Ian!" he said.

"You gentlemen," said Mercy, "seem to have a place to think in that I don't know how to get into. . . ."

"My brother has always been opening doors for me to think in," said Alister. "But here no door needs to be opened. All you have to do is step straight into the temple of nature and let her speak to you."

"Why should we trouble about religion more than is required of us?" interposed Christina.

"Why indeed?" returned Ian. "But then how much is required?"

"You require far more than my father, and he is good enough for me."

"The Master says we are to love God with all our hearts and souls and strength and mind."

"How then can you worship in the temple of nature?" said Mercy.

"Just as he did. It is nature's temple, remember, for the worship of *God*, not of herself!"

"But how am I to get into it? That's what I want to know."

"You *are* in it! True, the innermost places of the temple are open only to such as already worship in a greater temple; but it has courts into which any honest soul may enter. Yet some of nature's lessons you must learn before you can understand them."[2]

Shadows

All things are shadows of thee, Lord;
*   The sun himself is but thy shade;*
My spirit is the shadow of thy work,
*   A thing that thou hast said.*

Diamonds are shadows of the sun,
*   They gleam as after him they hark:*
My soul some arrows of thy light hath won,
*   And feebly fights the dark!*

All knowledges are broken shades,
*   In gulfs of dark a scattered horde:*
Together rush the parted glory-grades—
*   Then, lo, thy garment, Lord!*

My soul, the shadow, still is light
*   Because the shadow falls from thee;*
I turn, dull candle, to the center bright,
*   And home flit shadowy.*

Shine, Lord; shine me thy shadow still;
*   The brighter I, the more thy shade!*
My motion be thy lovely moveless will!
*   My darkness, light delayed!*

RECOGNIZING THE SON

Ye have neither heard his voice at any time, nor seen his shape. And ye have not his word abiding in you; for whom he hath sent, him ye believe not.

John 5:37–38

Two Kinds of Seeing

There seems almost a contradiction in this passage at first glance, as if Jesus is reproaching his listeners for something they cannot help. John himself says, "No man hath seen God," and Paul says no man can see him. Is Jesus here speaking as a paradoxical sophist? "No man hath seen God, but ye are condemned that ye have not seen God!"

But there cannot be contradiction. The reason is this: the word *see* is used in one sense in the one statement, and in another sense in the other. In the one it means *see with the eyes*; in the other, *with the soul*. The one statement is made of all people, the other is made to certain of the Jews of Jerusalem concerning themselves. It is true that no man hath seen God, and true that some men ought to have seen him. No man hath seen him with his bodily eyes, but those Jews ought to have seen him with their spiritual eyes.

No man has ever seen God in any outward, visible, close-fitting form of his own. He is revealed in no shape except that of his Son. But multitudes of men have with their mind's, or rather their heart's eye, seen more or less of God. And perhaps every man might have and ought to have seen something of him.

We cannot follow God into his infinitesimal intensities of spiritual operation, any more than into the atomic life-potencies that lie deep beyond the eye of the microscope: God may be working in the heart of a heathen savage, in a way that no wisdom of his wisest, humblest child can see, or imagine that it sees. Many who have never beheld the face of God may yet have caught a glimpse of the hem of his garment. Many who have never seen his form may yet have seen the vastness of his shadow. Thousands who have never felt the warmth of its folds have yet been startled by the sight of the passing of his white robe. Some have dreamed his hand laid upon them, who never knew themselves gathered to his bosom.

The reproach in the words of the Lord is the reproach of those who ought to have had an experience they had not had.

We Ought to See and Hear

"Ye have not heard his voice at any time," might mean, "*You have never listened to his voice,*" or "*You have never obeyed his voice.*"

But the following phrase, "nor seen his shape," keeps us rather to the primary sense of the word *hear:—"The sound of his voice is unknown to you. You have never heard his voice so as to know it for his."*

"You have not seen his shape," means, "*You do not know what he is like.*" Plainly Jesus implies, "*You ought to know his voice. You ought to know what he is like.*"

"You have not his word abiding in you," means, "*The word that is in you from the beginning, the word of God in your conscience, you have not kept with you; it is not dwelling in you. By yourselves accepted as the witness of Moses, the scripture in which you think you have eternal life does not abide with you, is not at home in you. It comes to you and goes from you. You hear, heed not, and forget. You do not dwell with it, and brood upon it, and obey it. It finds no acquaintance in you. You are not of its kind. You are not of those to whom the word of God comes. Their ears are ready to hear. They hunger after the word of the Father."*

On what does the Lord base his accusation of them? "For whom he hath sent, him ye believe not."

"How so?" the Jews might answer. "We are ready to believe you. Have we not asked you for a sign from heaven, and have you not point-blank refused to give it? How is it that you blame us?"

The argument of the Lord was indeed of small weight, and of little use, to those to whom it most applied. For the more it applied, the more incapable they were of seeing that his words *did* apply to them. Yet his words had, no doubt, a great effect upon some that stood nearby listening, for their minds were more or less open to the truth, and their hearts drawn to the man before them.

His argument was this: "If you had ever heard the Father's voice, if you had ever known his call, if you had ever imagined him, or a God anything like him, if you had cared for his will so that his Word was at home in your hearts, you would have known me when you saw me—known that I must come from him, that I must be his messenger, and you would have listened to me. The least acquaintance with God, such as any true heart must have, would have made you recognize that I came from the God of whom you knew something.

"If you were intimate with the Father's voice, you would have been capable of knowing me by the light of his Word abiding in you, by the shapes you had beheld however vaguely, by the likeness of my face and my voice to those of my Father. You would have seen my Father in me. You would have known me by the little you knew of him. The family feeling would have been awake in you, the holy instinct of the same spirit, making you know your elder brother.

"That you do not know me now, as I stand here speaking to you, is evidence that you do not know your own Father, even my Father, evidence that throughout your lives you have refused to do his will, and so have not heard his voice, evidence that you have shut your eyes from seeing him, and have thought of him only as a partisan of your ambitions. If you had loved my Father, you would have known his Son."

And I think Jesus might have said, "If even you had loved your neighbor, you would have known me, neighbor to the deepest and best in you."[1]

The Obediently Childlike Would Be the First to Recognize Him

If our Lord were to come again visibly, now, which do you think would come crowding around him in greater numbers—the respectable churchgoers or the people from the slums? I do not know. I dare not judge. But the fact that the church draws so few of those that are despised, of those whom Jesus drew and to whom most expressly he came, gives ground for question as to how far the church is like her Lord. Certainly many a one would find the way to the feet of the Master from whom the respectable churchgoer, the Pharisee of our time, would draw back with disgust. And doubtless it would be in the religious world that a man like Jesus would meet with the chief opponents of his doctrine and life.[2]

If the Lord were to appear today in England or America, as he did once in Palestine, he would not come in the halo of the painters, or with that wintry shine of effeminate beauty, of sweet weakness, in which it is their helpless custom to represent him.

Neither would he probably come as a carpenter, or mason, or gardener. He would come in such form and condition as might bear to the present England, Scotland, Canada, or the United States, a relation like that which the form and condition he then came in, bore to the motley Judea, Samaria, and Galilee.

If he came thus, in a form altogether unlooked for, who would they be that recognized and received him?

The idea is not an absurd one to consider. He is not far from us at any moment. He might at any moment appear. And who, I ask, would be the first to receive him?

Now, as then, it would of course be the childlike in heart, the truest, the least selfish. They would not be the highest in the estimation of any church, for the childlike are not yet the many, nor considered among the important, even in so-called religious or spiritual circles. It might not even be those that knew most about the former visit of the Master who would now recognize him, nor those that had pondered or expounded upon every word of the Greek New Testament. The first to cry, "It is the Lord!" would be neither "good churchman" nor "good Protestant" nor "good Catholic" nor "good Evangelical." It would be no one with so little of the mind of Christ as to imagine him caring about the stupid outside matters that divide us into sects. It would not be the man that holds by the mooring-ring of the letter, fast in the quay of what he calls theology, and from his rotting deck abuses the presumption of those that go down to the sea in ships—lets the wind of the Spirit blow where it listeth, but never blow him out among its wonders in the deep. It would not be he who, obeying a command, does not care to see reason in the command, and who thinks faith to be somehow opposed to reason and common sense; not he who, from very barrenness of soul, cannot receive the meaning and will of the Master, and so fails to fulfill the letter of his Word, making it of no effect.

It would rather be those who were most like the Master—those, namely, that did the will of their Father and his Father, that built their house on the rock by hearing and doing Christ's sayings.

But are there any enough like Christ to know him at once by the sound of his voice, by the look of his face? There are multitudes who would at once be taken by a false Christ fashioned after their fancy and would at once reject the Lord as a poor imposter.

One thing is certain: they who first recognized him would be those that most loved righteousness and hated iniquity and falsehood.

Foolish Forms Cannot Hide the Truth Forever

There are many in whom foolish forms cover a live heart, warm toward everything human and divine. For the worst fitting and ugliest robe may hide the loveliest form.

Every covering is not a clothing. The grass clothes the fields. The glory surpassing Solomon's clothes the grass. But the traditions of the worthiest elders will not clothe any soul—how much less the traditions of the unworthy! Its true clothing must grow out of the live soul itself.

Some naked souls need but the sight of truth to rush to it, as Dante says, like a wild beast to his den. Others, heavily clad in the garments the scribes have left behind them, and fearful of tearing those burdensome robes which are fit only to be trodden underfoot, cautiously approach the truth, going round and round it like a shy horse that fears a hidden enemy.

But let each be true after the fashion possible to him, and he shall have the Master's praise.

If the Lord were to appear, the many who take the commonest presentation of thing or person for the thing or person itself could never recognize the new vision of him as another form of the old. The Master has been so misrepresented by such as have claimed to present him—especially in the relation between him and his Father—that it is impossible they should see any likeness.

For my part, I would believe in no god rather than in such a god as is generally offered for believing in. How far those may be to blame who, righteously disgusted, cast the idea from them, I cannot say. It is true, if such loved the truth, they would make inquiry whether something in the old tale may not be true, and would feel some claim toward investigation on the chance that some that call themselves his prophets may have taken spiritual bribes:

> To mingle beauty with infirmities,
> And pure perfection with impure defeature.

Yet how far such may be to blame, I say, it is not my work to inquire.

Some would grasp with gladness the hope that such a chance might be proved a fact. Those with true hearts are ever willing to leave behind old dogmas and preconceptions for new revelations of deeper truth.

Others, however, would not care to discern upon the palimpsest*

---

*Palimpsest—an ancient parchment or tablet that has been written on or inscribed two or three times, the previous text or texts having been imperfectly rubbed off or erased, and therefore remaining visible under the new inscriptions.

covered but not obliterated, a credible tale of a perfect man revealing a perfect God. Like the false prophets whose cumbersome theology led such, not unbelievers but *mis*believers, astray in the first place, they are not true enough to desire that discovery to be a fact. No doubt they have some inkling that an acknowledgement of its truth would immediately demand the modeling of their lives upon its claims.

For all who *truly* see the Son, that is, know him as he *is* not as men say he is, do not—indeed, *cannot*—remain any more as they were. But we all, beholding the glory of the Lord, are changed into his image.[3]

OBEDIENCE AWAKENS US TO THE SPIRIT

A Fictional Selection from *The Baron's Apprenticeship*

The God Barbara believed in was like Jesus Christ, not at all like the God his mother believed in. Jesus was someone who could be loved. He was gentle and cared for individuals. And he said he loved the Father! And how could such a one as he be the Son of any but an equally kind, equally gentle, equally loving Father? Yet Richard's eyes saw such disharmony in the world around him. Nature herself could be mild one moment, cruel the next. And how could he reconcile the seemingly indiscriminate suffering which existed everywhere? How could, he asked again, as he had been asking for years, a good and loving and kind God have created a world where so much was wrong?

The thought, halfway to an answer, did not come to Richard then: What if we are not yet able to understand nature's secret, therefore not able to see it although it lies open to us? What if the difficulty lies in us? What if nature is doing her best to reveal? What if God is working to make us know—if we could but let him—as fast as he can?

One idea will not be pictured, cannot be made present to the mind by any effort of the imagination—one idea requires the purest faith: a man's own ignorance and incapacity. When a man knows, then first he gets a glimpse of his ignorance as it vanishes. Ignorance cannot be the object of knowledge. We must *believe* ourselves ignorant. And for that we must be humble of heart. For God is infinite, and we are his little ones, and his truth is eternally better than the best shape in which we see it.

Jesus is perfect, but our idea of him cannot be perfect. Only obedient faith in him and in his Father is changeless truth in us. Even that has to grow, but its growth is not change. We glimpse a greater life than we can feel; but no man will arrive at the peace of it by struggling with the roots of his nature to understand them, for those roots go down and out, out and down infinitely into the infinite. By acting upon what he sees and knows, hearkening to every whisper, obeying every hint of the good, following whatever seems light, man will at length arrive. Thus obedient, instead of burying himself in the darkness about its roots, he climbs to the treetop of his being; there, looking out on the eternal world, he understands at least enough to give him a rest.

In his climbing, the man will somewhere in his upward progress of obedience awake to know that the same Spirit is in him that is in the things he beholds. God is in the world, the atmosphere, the element, the substance, the essence of his life. In him he lives and moves and has his being. Now he lives indeed; for his Origin is his, and this rounds his being to eternity. God himself is his, as nothing else *could* be his.[4]

Much and More

When thy heart, love-filled, grows graver,
  And eternal bliss looks nearer,
Ask thy heart, nor show it favor,
  Is the gift or giver dearer?

Love, love on; love higher, deeper;
  Let love's ocean close above her;
Only, love thou more love's keeper,
  More, the love-creating lover.

How Old Must One Be to Obey the Lord's Words?

A Fictional Selection from *The Landlady's Master*

He said, 'Lo, I am with you always!' " continued Andrew. "And even suppose he weren't, we wouldn't dare do behind his back what we shouldn't do before his face."

"Do you really think it *was* him, Andrew?"

"Well," replied Andrew, "if the devil goes about like a roaring lion seeking who he can devour, as Father says, it's not likely *He* wouldn't be going about as well, seeking to hold him off us."

"Aye," said Sandy.

They were silent a minute. Then at last the elder spoke again. "And so now," he proposed, "what do you suppose we are to do?"

For Andrew, whom both father and mother judged the dreamiest of mortals, was in reality one of the most practical beings in the whole parish: to him, every truth must be accompanied by some corresponding act. If any of my readers say he was too young to take spiritual things so seriously, I reply by asking if the fact that so few children do take the Lord's words to heart be justification for discounting what he himself prayed when he said, "I thank thee, Father, because thou hast hid these things from the wise and learned, and revealed them to little children." Truly Andrew and Sandy were unusual children in what followed, but unusual because they were *more* what children were intended to be, not *less*; more childlike, therefore nearer the heart of God. As Andrew grew through the years, by and by people began to mock him, calling him nothing but a poet and a heretic, because he constantly sought to *do* the things that they said they believed. Most unpractical must every man appear who genuinely believes in the things that are unseen. The man called practical by the men of this world is he who busies himself building his house on the sand, while he does not even acknowledge a lodging in the inevitable beyond for which he needs to prepare.

"What are we going to do?" repeated Andrew. "If the Lord is going about like that, looking after us, we've surely got something to do looking after him!"

Sandy did not have a ready answer. And it was a good thing, with the reticence of children, that neither thought of bringing up the affair and laying the case of the question before their parents; the traditions of the elders would have ill agreed with the doctrine of obedience the sons were now under.

Suddenly one day it came into Andrew's mind that the Bible they read at church, to which he had never paid much attention, told all about Jesus. *There* must be the answer to his question!

He began at the beginning and grew so interested in the stories that he forgot why he had begun to read them. But at length it dawned on him that nothing he had read told anything about the man who was going up and down the world, gathering up their sins and carrying them away in his pack. He turned to the New Testament to see if there might be something in that book about Jesus Christ. Here also it was well they asked no advice, for they would probably have been directed to the Epistle to the Romans, with explanations yet more foreign to the heart of Paul than false to his Greek. They began to read the story of Jesus as told by his friend Matthew, and when they had ended it, went on to the gospel according to Mark. But they had not read far when Sandy cried out, "Eh, Andrew, it's all just the same thing over again!"

"Not altogether," answered Andrew. "Let's go on and see."

Finally Andrew came to the conclusion that it was close enough to the same thing that he would rather go back and read the other again, for the sake of some particular things he remembered he wanted to make sure about. So they went back and read St. Matthew a second time, and came eventually to these words:

If two of you shall agree on earth as touching anything that they shall ask, it shall be done for them of my Father which is in heaven.

"There's two of us here!" cried Andrew, laying down the book. "Let's try it!"

"Try what?" asked Sandy. His brother read the passage again.

"Let the two of us ask him for something!" concluded Andrew. "What will it be?. . ."

"Happy children," I say, "who could blunder into the very heart of the will of God concerning them, and *do* the thing immediately that the Lord taught them, using the common sense which God had given and the fairy tale had nourished!" The Lord of the promise is the Lord of all true parables and all good fairy tales.

Andrew prayed:

"O, Lord, tell Sandy and me what to ask for."

They got up from their knees. They had said what they had to say: why say more?

They felt rather dull. Nothing came to them. The prayer was prayed, and they could make out no answer. They put the Bible away in a rough box where they kept it among rose-leaves—ignorant priests of the lovely mystery of him who was with them always—and without a word went each his own way. Andrew was disconsolate the rest of the day. They had prayed and nothing had come of it, and he did not know what to do.

In the evening, while it was yet light, Andrew went alone to the elder tree, where it was their custom to meet, took the Bible from its humble shrine, and began turning over its leaves.

And why call ye me, Lord, Lord, and do not the things which I say?

He read the words over a second time, then a third, and sank deep in thought.

This is something like the way his thoughts went:

"What is he talking about? What had he been saying before? Let me look and see what he says, that I may begin to *do* it!"

He read all the chapter again and found it full of *tellings*. When he read it before, he had not thought of actually doing a single one of the things Jesus said. He had not seen himself as involved in any of the matters at hand.

"I see!" he exclaimed. "We must begin at once to *do* what he tells us, not just read about it!"

He ran to find his brother.

"I've got it!" he cried. "I've got it!"

"What?"

"What we're to do."

"What is it?"

"Just what he tells us."

"We were doing that," said Sandy, "when we prayed for him to tell us what to pray for."

"So we were! That's good."

"So are we supposed to pray for anything more?"

"We'll soon find out. But first we must look for something to do."

They began at once to search through the whole book of Matthew for things the Lord told them to do. And of all they found the plainest and simplest for their young minds to grasp was: "Whosoever shall smite thee on thy right cheek, turn to him the other also."

This needed no explanation! It was as clear as the day to both of them. The very next morning the schoolmaster, who, though of a gentle disposition, was irritable, took Andrew for the offender in a certain breach of discipline, and gave him a smart box on the ear. As readily as if it had been instinctive, Andrew turned to him his other cheek.

An angry man is an evil interpreter of holy things, and Mr. Fordyce took the action for one of rudest mockery, and did not think of the higher master therein mocked, if indeed it had been a mockery: he struck the offender a yet harder blow. Andrew stood for a minute like one dazed, but the red on his face was not that of anger; rather, he was perplexed as to whether he ought now to turn the former cheek again to the striker. Uncertain, he turned away and went back to his work.

Does one of my readers stop here to say, "Do you really mean to tell us we ought to take the words of the Bible literally as Andrew did?"

I answer, "When you have earned the right to understand, you will not need to ask me. To explain what the Lord means to one who is not obedient is the work of no man who truly knows his work."[5]

Death

Mourn not, my friends, that we are growing old:
A fresher birth brings every new year in.
Years are Christ's napkins to wipe off the sin.
See now, I'll be to you an angel bold!
My plumes are ruffled, and they shake with cold,
Yet with a trumpet-blast I will begin.
—Ah no; your listening ears not thus I win!
Yet hear, sweet sisters; brothers, be consoled:—
Behind me comes a shining one indeed;
Christ's friend, who from life's cross did take him down,
And set upon his day night's starry crown!
Death, say'st thou? Nay—thine be no caitiff creed!—
A woman-angel! see—in long white gown!
The mother of our youth!—she maketh speed.

SELF-DENIAL

And he said unto all, If any man would come after me, let him deny himself. . . .

Luke 9:23 (RV)

The World

Jesus Christ is the way out, *and* the way in.

He is the way out of slavery, whether conscious or unconscious, into liberty. He is the way from the unhomeliness of things to the home we desire but do not know. He is the way from the stormy skirts of the Father's outer garments to the peace of his bosom.

To picture Jesus, we need not only endless figures and descriptions, but sometimes quite opposing figures.

He is not only the door of the sheepfold, but the shepherd of the sheep. He is not only the way, but the leader in the way, the rock that followed, and the captain of our salvation. We must become as little children, and Christ must be born in us. We must learn of him, and the one lesson he has to give is himself: he *does* first all he wants us to do; he *is* first all he wants us to be.

We must not merely do as he did, we must see things as he saw them, regard them as he regarded them. We must take the will of God as the very life of our being. We must neither try to get our own way, nor trouble ourselves as to what may be thought or said of us.

The world must be to us as nothing.

I would not be misunderstood if I may avoid it. When I say *the world*, I do not mean the world God makes and means. Even less do I mean the human hearts that live in that world. Rather I mean the world man makes by choosing the perversion of his own nature—a world apart from and opposed to God's world.

By *the world* I mean all ways of judging, regarding, and thinking, whether political, economical, ecclesiastical, social, or individual, which are not divine, which are not God's ways of thinking, regarding, or judging. These are ways which do not take God into account, do not set his will supreme, as the one only law of life, which do not care for the truth of things, but the customs of society, or the practice of the trade, which heed not what is right, but what is acceptable by the times.

From everything that is against the teaching and thinking of Jesus, from the world in the heart of the best man in it, especially from the world in his *own* heart, the disciple must turn to follow Jesus.

The first thing in all progress is to leave something behind. To follow Jesus is to leave one's self behind. "If any man would come after me, let him deny himself."

Subjugating the Self

Some seem to take this denial of self to mean that the disciple must go against his likings *because* they are his likings, must be unresponsive to the tendencies and directions and inclinations that are his, just because they are *his*. They seem to think something is gained by abstinence from what is pleasant, or by the doing of what is disagreeable— that to thwart the lower nature is in itself a good, independent of God's work within the man's soul.

Now I will not dare say what a man may not get good from, if the thing be done in simplicity and honesty. I believe that even when a man makes a mistake and does something that is not right, if he is motivated by *trying* to do the thing that is right, God will take care that he be shown the better way—will perhaps use the very thing which is his mistake to reveal to him the mistake it is. Thus I will allow that the mere effort of will, arbitrary and not motivated by attempted obedience to Christ's commands, *may* add to a man's power over his lower nature. But such is not the best means to subjugate the self. For in that very nature it is God who must rule and not the man, however well the man may mean in the attempts of his own.

From a man's rule of himself, in smallest opposition, however devout, to the law of his being, arises the huge danger of nourishing, by the pride of self-conquest, a far worse than even the unchained animal self—the demoniac self.

True victory over self is the victory of God in the man, not of the man alone. It is not subjugation that is enough, but subjugation *by God*. In whatever man does without God, he must fail miserably—or succeed more miserably.

No portion of a man can rule another portion, for God, not the man, created it, and the part is greater than the whole. In trying to do what God does not mean, a man but falls into fresh unhealthy conditions. In crossing his natural—therefore, in themselves, right—inclinations, a man may develop a self-satisfaction, which in its very nature is a root of all sin. Doing a thing God does not require of him, the man puts himself in the place of God, becoming not a law, but a lawgiver to himself, one who commands, not one who obeys.

The diseased satisfaction which some minds feel in laying burdens on themselves is a pampering, little as they may suspect it, of the most dangerous appetite of the very self which they think they are punishing and subduing.

All the creatures of God are good, received with thanksgiving. They can become evil only when used in relations which a higher law forbids, or when refused for the sake of self-discipline, in relations which God *does* allow. For a man to be his own schoolmaster is a dangerous position. The pupil cannot be expected to make progress—except, indeed, in the wrong direction. To enjoy heartily and thankfully, and do cheerfully without, *when* God wills we should, is the way to live in regard to things of the lower nature.

These must not be confused with the things of *the world*. If anyone says this is dangerous doctrine, I answer, "The law of God is enough for me, and as for laws invented by man, I will have none of them. They are false, and all come of rebellion. God and not man is our judge."

Abandonment of Self

Verily we are not to thwart or tease the poor self, Jesus tells us. That was not the purpose for which God gave the self to us!

Jesus tells us we must leave the self altogether—yield it, deny it, refuse it, lose it. Thus *only* shall we save it. Thus only shall we have a share in our own being. The self is given us that we may sacrifice it. It is ours in order that we, like Christ, may have something to offer—not that we should torment it, but that we should deny it; not that we should cross it, but that we should abandon it utterly.

"What can this mean—we are not to thwart, but to abandon? How do we abandon without thwarting?"

It means this: we must refuse, abandon, deny self altogether as a ruling, or determining, or originating element in us. It is to be no longer the regent of our action. We are no more to think, "What would I like to do?" but "What would the Living One have me do?"

It is not selfish to take that which God has made us to desire. Neither are we particularly to be praised for giving it up—we should only be wrong not to do so—when he would deny it of us. But to yield it up heartily, willingly, without a struggle or regret, is not merely to deny the self a thing it would like, but to deny the self itself, to refuse and abandon it and leave it altogether. The self is God's making—only it must be the "slave of Christ," that the Son may make it also the free son of the same Father. It must receive all from him—not as from nowhere. Just like the deeper soul, it must follow him, not its own desires. It must not be its own law; Christ must be its law.

The time will come when the self shall be so possessed, so enlarged, so idealized by the indwelling God, who is its deeper, its deepest Self, that there will no longer be any enforced denial of it needful. It will finally have been denied and refused and sent into its own obedient place. It will have learned to receive with thankfulness, to demand nothing, to turn no more upon its own center, or think any more to minister to its own good. God's eternal denial of himself, revealed in Christ who for our sakes in the flesh took up his cross daily, will have been developed in the man. His eternal rejoicing will be in God—and in his fellows, before whom he will cast his glad self to be a carpet for their walk, a footstool for their rest, a stair for their climbing.

The Life of Self-Denial

To deny oneself, then, is to act no more from the standing-ground of self, to allow no private communication, no passing influence between the self and the will, not to let the right hand know what the left hand does. No grasping or seeking, no hungering of the individual, shall give motion to the will. No desire to be conscious of worthiness shall order the life. No ambition whatever shall be a motive of action. No wish to surpass another be allowed a moment's respite from death. No longing after the praise of men influence a single throb of the heart.

To deny the self is to shrink from no disapproval, condemnation or contempt of the community, circle, or country that is against the mind of the Living One. To deny the self is to forsake all loves and entreaties of father or mother, wife or child, friend or lover as ruling or ordering powers in our lives. We must do nothing to please them that would not first be pleasing to him. Right deeds, and not the judgment thereupon; true words, and not what reception they may have, shall be our concern.

Not merely shall we not love money, or trust in it, or seek it as the business of life, but, whether we have it or not, we must never think of it as a windfall from the tree of event or the cloud of circumstance, but as the gift of God. We must draw our life by the uplooking, acknowledging will, every moment fresh from the Living One, the causing Life, not glory in the mere consciousness of health and being.

It is God who feeds us, warms us, quenches our thirst. The will of God must be to us all in all. To our whole nature the life of the Father must be the joy of the child. We must know our very understanding his—that we live and feed on him every hour in the closest, most certain way. To know these things in the depth of our knowing is to deny ourselves and take God instead.

To leave all is to begin the denial, to follow him who never sought his own. So we must deny all anxieties and fears. When young, we must not mind what the world calls failure. As we grow old, we must not be frustrated that we cannot remember, must not regret that we cannot do what we once could, must not be miserable because we grow weak or ill. We must not mind anything. We have to do with God who *can*; we do not have to do with ourselves where we *cannot*. We have to do with the will, the eternal life of the Father of our spirits, and not with the being, which we could not make, and which is his sole concern.

He is our concern. We are his. Our care is to will his will; his care, to give us all things. This is to deny ourselves.

"Self, I do not have to consult you, but him whose idea is the soul of you, and of which as yet you are completely unworthy. I have to do, not with you, but with the source of you, by whom it is that any moment you exist. You may be my consciousness, but you are not my being. If you were, what a poor, miserable, dingy, weak wretch I should be! But my *life* is hid with Christ in God, whence it came, and whither it is returning—with you certainly, but as an obedient servant, not a master. Submit, or I will cast you from me and pray to have another consciousness given me. For God is more to me than my consciousness of myself. He is my life; you are only so much of it as I can now know at once. Because I have fooled and spoiled you, treated you as if you were indeed my own self, you have dwindled yourself and lessened me, till I am ashamed of myself. If I were to pay attention to what you say, I should soon be sick of you. Even now I am disgusted with your paltry, mean face, which I meet at every turn. No! let me have the company of the Perfect One, not of you! of my elder brother, the Living One! I will not make a friend of the mere shadow of my own being! Good-bye, self! I deny you, and will do my best every day to leave you behind me!"[1]

THE DEMAND UPON CHRISTIANS—TO BE LIKE JESUS

A Fictional Selection from *The Highlander's Last Song*

There are very few who can be said to really believe in any hereafter worth believing in. The life beyond is no factor in the life of such people. I think they fancy the life beyond will be of an utterly different kind than life here. But I look to that life to give me *more* life, *more* strength, *more* love. God is not shut up in heaven, neither is there one law of life there and another here. I desire more life here, and shall have it, for what is needed for this world is to be had in this world. In proportion as I become one with God, I shall have it. This world never did seem my home; I have never felt quite comfortable in it. I have yet to find the perfect home. And does not the Bible itself tell us that we are pilgrims and strangers in the world? This is but a place we come to be made ready for another. Yet it seems that those who *do* regard it as their home are not half so well pleased with it as I. They are always grumbling at it. They complain that their plans are thwarted, and when they succeed, that they do not give them the satisfaction they expected. Yet they mock him who says he seeks a better country! But I am keeping you awake, Alister! I will talk no more. You must go to sleep."

"It is better than any sleep to hear you talk, Ian," returned Alister. "How far you are ahead of me! I do love this world! . . . I love every foot of the earth that remains to us—every foot that has been taken from us. When I stand on the top of this rock and breathe the air of this mountain, I bless God we still have a spot to call our own. . . ."

"That is all very true, Alister. I understand your feelings perfectly. I have it myself. But we must be weaned from that kind of thing; we must not love the outside as if it were the inside! Everything comes that we may know the sender, of whom it is a symbol, a far-off likeness of something in him. And to him it must lead us—the self-existent, true, original love, the making love."

———

Early in the morning they fell asleep, and it was daylight, late in the winter, when Alister rose. He roused the fire, asleep all through the night, and prepared their breakfast of porridge and butter, tea, oatcake, and mutton-ham. When it was nearly ready, he woke Ian, and when they had eaten, they read together a portion of the Bible, that they might not forget, and start the life of the day without trust in the life-causing God.

"All that is not rooted in him," Ian would say, "all hope or joy that does not turn its face upward, is an idolatry. Our prayers must rise that our thoughts may follow them."

The portion they read contained the saying of the Lord that we must forsake all and follow him if we would be his disciples.

"It is sometimes almost terrifying," said Ian, "to stop and think of the scope of the demands made upon us as Christians, at the perfection required, at the totality of self-abandonment expected of us. Yet outside of such absoluteness can be no salvation. In God we live every mundane as well as every exalted moment of our lives. To trust in him when no great need is pressing, when things all seem to be going right, may be even harder than when things seem to be going wrong. At no time is there any danger, except in *ourselves* forgetting that it is God who breathes life into everything, that we are nothing—without wisdom or insight—in and of ourselves. O, Alister, take care you do not love the land more than the will of God. Take care you do not love even your people more than the will of God. . . .

"Be sure we shall not have to part with them. We shall yet walk, I think, with our father as we did when we were young. The wind of the twilight will again breathe about us like a thought of the living God haunting our goings and watching to help us. 'Be independent!' cries the world. But the Lord says, 'Seek ye first the kingdom of God and his righteousness, and all these things shall be added unto you.' Our dependence is our eternity. We cannot live on bread alone; we need every word of God. We cannot live on air alone; we need an atmosphere of living souls."[2]

———121———

Smoke

Lord, I have laid my heart upon thy altar
  But cannot get the wood to burn;
It hardly flares ere it begins to falter
  And to the dark return.

Old sap, or night-fallen dew, makes damp the fuel;
  In vain my breath would flame provoke;
Yet see—at every poor attempt's renewal
  To thee ascends the smoke!

'Tis all I have—smoke, failure, foiled endeavour,
  Coldness and doubt and palsied lack:
Such as I have I send thee!—perfect Giver,
  Send thou thy lightning back.

We Believe in Jesus Christ—We Take Orders From Him

A Fictional Selection from *The Highlander's Last Song*

You're a brace of woodcocks!" cried Sercombe. "It's a good thing you're not out in the world. You would be in hot water from morning to night. I can't imagine how the deuce you get on at all!"

"Get on! To where?" asked Ian with a curious smile.

"Come now! You're not such fools as you want me to think. A man must make a place for himself somehow in the world."

He rose, and they walked in the direction of the cottage.

"There is something better than getting on in the world," said Ian.

"What?"

"To get out of it."

"What! Cut your throats?"

"I mean that to get out of the world altogether is better than merely to get on in it."

"I don't understand you. I begin to think the man who thrashed me is a downright idiot!" growled Sercombe.

"What you call success," said Ian, "we count not worth a thought. Look at our clan. It is but a type of the world itself. Everything is passing away. We believe in the kingdom of heaven."

"Come, come! Fellows like you must know that's bosh! Nobody nowadays—nobody with any brains—believes such rot."

"We believe in Jesus Christ," said Ian, "and are determined to do what he wants us to do and to take our orders from nobody else."

"I don't understand you."

"I know you don't. You could not until you set about to change your whole way of life."

"What an idea! An impossible idea!"

"As to its being an impossible idea, we hold it and live by it. I know it must seem perfectly absurd to you. But we do not live in your world, and you do not see the light of ours."

"Well, there may be a world beyond the stars. I know nothing about it. I only know there is one on this side of it, a very decent sort of world, too. And I mean to make the best of it!"

"And have not even begun yet."

"Indeed I have! I deny myself nothing. I live as I was made to live."

"If you were not made to obey your conscience, you are differently made from us."

"That's all moonshine! Things are as they appear, nothing more."

The brothers exchanged a look and a smile.[3]

Song of a Poor Pilgrim

Roses all the rosy way!
*   Roses to the rosier west*
Where the roses of the day
*   Cling to night's unrosy breast!*

Thou who mak'st the roses, why
*   Give to every leaf a thorn?*
On thy rosy highway I
*   Still am by thy roses torn!*

Pardon! I will not mistake
*   These good thorns that make me*
fret!
Goads to urge me, stings to wake,
*   For my freedom they are set.*

Yea, on one steep mountainside,
*   Climbing to a fancied fold,*
Roses grasped had let me slide
*   But the thorns did keep their hold.*

Out of darkness light is born,
*   Out of weakness make me strong:*
One glad day will every thorn
*   Break into a rose of song.*

Though like sparrow sit thy bird
*   Lonely on the housetop dark,*
By the rosy dawning stirred
*   Up will soar thy praising lark;*

Roses, roses all his song!
*   Roses in a gorgeous feast!*
Roses in a royal throng,
*   Surging, rosing from the east!*

Following Christ

*And he said unto all, If any man would come after me, let him
. . . take up his cross daily, and follow me.*

Luke 9:23 (RV)

To Follow Jesus

When Jesus tells us we must come to him, believe in him, and
follow him, he speaks first and always as *the Son* of the Father.
And I mean this in the active sense—as an obedient Son—not
merely as one who claims sonship because he is a son, and so an heir.
He is the Son of the Father as the Son who obeys the Father, as the
Son who came expressly and only to do the will of the Father, as the
messenger whose delight is to do the will of him that sent him.

At the same moment Jesus says, "Follow me," he is following the
Father. His face is set homeward. He will have us follow him because
he is bent on the will of his Father.

It is nothing to think of him merely as the Son, except as we *believe*
in him—and that implies action. To believe in him is to do as he does,
to follow him where he goes. We must believe in him *practically*—
altogether practically, as he believed in his Father. Our belief must not
be in an impersonal "deity" concerning whom we have to hold certain
views, but in one whom we have to follow out of the body of this death
into life eternal. To follow him is not to take him in any way theoreti-
cally, to hold this or that theory or opinion about why he died, or
wherein lay his atonement. Such things can be revealed only to those
who follow him in his active being and the principle of his life—those
who *do as he did, live as he lived*. There is no other way to follow him.

He is all for the Father. We must be all for the Father, too, otherwise
we are not following him. To follow him is to be learning of him, to
think his thoughts, to use his judgments, to see things as he sees them,

to feel things as he feels them, to be of the same heart, soul, and mind, as he is—that we also may be of the same mind with his Father.

This is what it is to deny self and follow after him. Nothing less is to be his disciple—even if it be working miracles and casting out devils. Busy from morning to night doing great things for him on any other grounds, we will only earn the reception, "I never knew you."

When Jesus says, "Take my yoke upon you," he does not mean a yoke that he would lay upon our shoulders. It is his *own* yoke he tells us to take and to learn of him. It is the yoke he is himself carrying, the yoke his perfect Father gave him to carry. The will of the Father is the yoke he would have us take and bear also with him. It is of this yoke that he says, "It is easy," of this burden, "It is light." He is not saying, "The yoke I lay upon you is easy, the burden light." What he says is, "The yoke *I* carry is easy, the burden on *my* shoulders is light." With the Garden of Gethsemane before him, with the hour and the power of darkness waiting for him, he declares his yoke easy, his burden light.

There is no magnifying of himself. *He first* denies himself, and takes up his cross—then tells us to do the same. The Father magnifies the Son, not the Son himself. The Son magnifies the Father.

The Cunning Self Will Deceive Us If It Can

We must be jealous for God against ourselves and look keenly to the cunning and deceitful self—ever cunning and deceitful until it is informed of God—until it is thoroughly and utterly denied. The self will attempt to have its way with us until God is to it also All-in-all—until we have left it quite empty of our will and our regard, and God has come into it, and made it—not a shrine, but a gateway for himself.

Until then, the self's very denials, its very turnings from things dear to it for the sake of Christ, will tend to foster self-regard, and generate in it a yet deeper self-worship. While self is not denied, only thwarted, we may, through satisfaction with conquered difficulty and supposed victory, minister yet more to its self-gratulation.

The self, when it finds it cannot have honor because of its gifts, because of the love lavished upon it, because of its conquests, and the "golden opinions bought from all sorts of people," will please itself with the thought of its abnegations, of its unselfishness, of its devotion to God, of its forsakings for his sake.

It may not *call* itself a saint, but it will soon *feel* itself one, a superior Christian, looking down upon the foolish world and its ways, walking on "high above" the crowded byways of "average" Christians—all the time dreaming a dream of utter folly, worshiping itself with all the more concentration that it thinks it has yielded the praises of the world and dismissed the regard of others; even they are no longer necessary to its assurance of its own worth and merits!

In a thousand ways self will delude itself, in a thousand ways befool its own slavish being. Christ sought not his own, sought not anything but the will of his Father. We have to grow diamond-clear, true as the white light of the morning.

Hopeless task!—were it not that he offers to come himself and dwell in us.

Take Up Your Cross

I have wondered whether the admonition, "take up his cross," was a phrase in use at the time. When the Lord first used it he had not yet told his disciples that he would himself be crucified. I can hardly believe this form of execution such a common thing that the figure of bearing the cross had come into ordinary speech.

As the Lord's idea was new to people, so too I think was the image in which he embodied it. I grant that it *might*, being such a hateful thing in the eyes of the Jews, have come to represent the worst misery of a human being. But would they be ready to use as a figure a fact which so sorely manifested their slavery under Rome? I hardly think so. Certainly it had not come to represent the thing he was now teaching, that self-abnegation which he had only recently brought to light in his teaching—no, hardly to the light yet—only the twilight. And nothing less, it seems to me, can have suggested the terrible symbol.

But we must note that, although the idea of the denial of self is an entire and absolute one, yet the thing has to be done *daily*. We must keep on denying self.

It is a deeper and harder thing than any one-time effort of the most herculean will may finally bring about. For indeed the will itself is not pure, is not free, until the self is absolutely denied. It takes long for the water of life that flows from the well within us to permeate every outlying portion of our spiritual frame, subduing everything to itself, making it all of the one kind, until at last, reaching the outermost folds of our personality, it casts out disease, our bodies by indwelling righteousness are redeemed, and the creation delivered from the bondage of corruption into the liberty of the glory of the children of God. Every day until then we have to take up our cross; every hour we must see that we are carrying it. A birthright may be lost for a mess of pottage, and what Satan calls a trifle must be a thing of eternal significance.

Trying to Find Some Comfortable Middle Ground

Is there not many a Christian who, having *begun* to deny himself, yet spends much strength in the vain, foolish, and evil endeavor to accommodate matters between Christ and the dear self? He seeks to save that which by such a tactic he must certainly lose! But in how different a way from that in which the Master would have him lose it.

It is one thing to have the loved self devoured of hell in hate and horror and disappointment, but another to yield it to conscious possession by the loving God himself, who will raise it then first and only to its true individuality, freedom, and life. With its cause within it, then, indeed, it shall be saved! How then should it but live!

Here is the promise to those who will leave all and follow him: "Whosoever shall lose his life, for my sake, the same shall save and find it."

What speech of men or angels will serve to shadow the dimly glorious hope! To lose ourselves in the salvation of God's heart! To be no longer any care to ourselves, but to know that God is taking the most divine care of us, his own! To feel and to be just a resting place for the divine love—a branch of the tree of life for the dove to alight upon and fold its wings! To be an open air of love, a thoroughfare for the thoughts of God and all holy creatures! To know one's self by the reflex action of endless brotherly presence—yearning after nothing from any other, but ever pouring out love by the natural motion of the Spirit! To revel in the hundredfold of everything good we may have had to leave for his sake—above all, in the unsought love of those who love us as we love them—circling us round, bathing us in bliss—never reached after, ever received, ever welcomed, altogether and divinely precious! To know that God and we mean the same thing, that we are in on the secret, the child's secret of existence, that we are pleasing in the eyes and to the heart of the Father! To live nestling at his knee, climbing to his bosom, blessed in the mere and simple being which is one with God, and is the outgoing of his will, justifying the being by the very facts of the being, by its awareness of itself as bliss! What a self is this to receive again from him for that which we left, forsook, refused!

We left it paltry, low, mean. He took up the poor cinder of a consciousness, carried it back to the workshop of his Spirit, made it a true thing, radiant, clear, fit for eternal dwelling and indwelling, and restored it to our having and holding for ever!

The Imperfection of Symbols

All high things can be spoken only in figures. Yet these figures, having to do with matters too high for them, cannot *fit* intellectually.

They can be interpreted truly, understood aright, only by such as have the spiritual fact they are trying to convey *already* dwelling in themselves.

When we speak of a man and his soul, we imply a self and another self interacting with each other. But we cannot divide ourselves so; the figure suits but imperfectly.

It was never the design of the Lord to explain things to our understanding nor would that in the least have helped our necessity. What we require is a means, a word, whereby to think with ourselves of high things. That is what a true figure will always be to us, for a figure may be true while still far from perfect.

But the imperfections of the Lord's figures cannot lie in excess. Be sure that, in dealing with any truth, its symbol, however high, must come short of the glorious meaning it is intended to hold.

It is the low ignorance of an unspiritual nature that would interpret the Lord's meaning as less than his symbols. The true soul sees, or will come to see, that his words, his figures always represent more than they are able to present. For, as the heavens are higher than the earth, so are the heavenly things higher than the earthly signs of them, though they may be as good as signs ever may be.[1]

A Christmas Prayer

Loving looks the large-eyed cow,
Loving stares the long-eared ass
At Heaven's glory in the grass!
Child, with added human birth
Come to bring the child of earth
Glad repentance, tearful mirth,
And a seat beside the hearth
At the Father's knee—
Make us peaceful as thy cow;
Make us patient as thine ass;
Make us quiet as thou art now;
Make us strong as thou wilt be.
Make us always know and see
We are his as well as thou.

The End of Wingfold's Search

A Fictional Selection from *The Curate's Awakening*

I t is time, my hearers," he began, "to bring to a close this period of uncertainty about the continuation of our relationship together. As you are well aware, in the springtime of this year I felt compelled to think through whether I could in good faith go on as a servant of the church. For very dread of the honesty of an all-knowing God, I forced myself to break through the established conventions of the church and speak to you of my most private thoughts. I told you I was unsure of many things which are taken for granted concerning clergymen. Since then, as I have wrestled with these issues, I have tried to show you the best I saw, yet I dared not say I was sure of anything. And I have kept those of you who cared to follow my path acquainted with the progress of my mental history. And now I come to tell you the practical result at which I have arrived.

"First, I tell you that I will not forsake my curacy, still less my right and duty to teach whatever I seem to know. But I must not convey the impression that all my doubts are suddenly gone. All I now can say is that in the story of Jesus I have seen grandeur—to me altogether beyond the reach of the human invention, and real hope for man. At the same time, from the attempt to obey the word recorded as his, I have experienced a great enlargement of my mind and a deepening of my moral strength and a wonderful increase of faith, hope, and love toward all men. Therefore, I now declare with the consent of my whole man—I cast my lot with the servants of the Crucified. If they be deluded, then I am content to share in their delusion, for to me it is the truth of the God of men. I will stand or fall with the story of my Lord. I speak not in irreverence, but in honesty. I will take my chance of failure or success in this life or the life to come on the words and the will of the Lord Jesus Christ. Impressed as I am with the truth of his nature, the absolute devotion of his life, and the essential might of his being, if I yet obey him not, I shall not only deserve to perish, but in that very refusal I would draw ruin upon my own head. Before God I say it—I would rather be crucified with that man than reign with an earthly king over a kingdom of millions. On such grounds as these I hope I am justified in declaring myself a disciple of the Son of Man, and in devoting my life and the renewed energy of my being to his brothers and sisters of my race. Henceforth, I am not *in* holy orders as a professional clergyman, but *under* holy orders as the servant of Christ Jesus.

"And if any man would still say that because of my lack of absolute assurance I have no right to the sacred post, I answer, let him cast the first stone who has never been assailed by such doubts as mine. And if such doubts have never been yours, if perhaps your belief is but the shallow absence of doubt, then you must ask yourself a question. Do you love your faith so little that you have never battled a single fear lest your faith should not be true? For what are doubts but the strengthening building blocks toward summits of yet higher faith in him who always leads us into the high places? Where there are no doubts, no questions, no perplexities, there can be no growth into the regions where he would have us walk. Doubts are the only means through which he can enlarge our spiritual selves.

"You have borne with me in my trials, and I thank you. One word more to those who call themselves Christians among you but who, as I so recently did myself, present such a withered idea of Christianity that they cause the truth to hang its head rather than ride forth on a white horse to conquer the world for Jesus. You dull the luster of the truth in the eyes of men. You do not represent that which it is, but yet you call yourselves by its name. You are not the salt of the earth, but a salt that has lost its savor. I say these things not to judge you, for I was one of you such a short time ago. But I say to you simply, it is time to awake! Until you repent and believe afresh, believe in a nobler Christ, namely the Christ of history and the Christ of the Bible rather than the vague form which false interpretations of men have substituted for him—until you believe in him rightly you will continue to be the main reason why faith is so scanty on the earth. And whether you do in some sense believe or not, one fact remains—while you are not a Christian who obeys the word of the master, *doing* the things he says rather than merely listening to them, talking about them, and hiding certain opinions about them, then you will be one of those to whom he will say, 'I never knew you: go forth into the outer darkness.'

"But what unspeakable joy and contentment awaits you when you, like St. Paul, can be crucified with Christ, to live no more from your own self but to be thereafter possessed with the same faith toward the Father in which Jesus lived and did the will of the Father. Truly our destiny is a glorious one—because we have a God supremely grand, all-perfect. Unity with him alone can be the absolute bliss for which we were created. Therefore, I say to you, as I say to myself: awaken your spirits, and give your hearts and souls to him! For this you were created by him, and to this we are called—every one."[2]

Love Is Home

Love is the part, and love is the whole;
*   Love is the robe, and love is the pall;*
Ruler of heart and brain and soul,
*   Love is the lord and the slave of all!*
I thank thee, Love, that thou lov'st me;
I thank thee more that I love thee.

Love is the rain, and love is the air,
*   Love is the earth that holdeth fast*
Love is the root that is buried there,
*   Love is the open flower at last!*
I thank thee, Love all round about,
That the eyes of my love are looking out.

Love is the sun, and love is the sea;
*   Love is the tide that comes and goes;*
Flowing and flowing it comes to me;
*   Ebbing and ebbing to thee it flows!*
Oh my sun, and my wind, and tide!
My sea, and my shore, and all beside!

Light, oh light that art by showing;
*   Wind, oh wind that liv'st by motion;*
Thought, oh thought that art by knowing;
*   Will, that art born in self-devotion!*
Love is you, though not all of you know it;
Ye are not love, yet ye always show it!

Faithful Creator, heart-longed-for father,
*   Home of our heart-infolded brother,*
How to thee all thy glories gather—
*   All are thy love, and there is no other!*
O Love-at-rest, we loves that roam—
Home unto thee, we are coming home!

THE RESULTS OF FOLLOWING CHRIST

For whoever would save his life shall lose it; but whosoever shall lose his life for my sake, the same shall save it.

Luke 9:24 (RV)

God's Gifts to His Children

There is no joy belonging to human nature, as God made it, that shall not be increased a hundredfold to the man who gives up himself. In so doing, however, he may *seem* to be yielding the very essence of life.

To yield self is to give up grasping at things in their second causes, as men call them, but which are merely God's means. In the yielding of self is a new way of receiving things direct from their source—to take them knowing where they come from, and not as if they came from nowhere or by accident.

The careless soul receives the Father's gifts as if they had by chance dropped into his hand. He thus makes himself a slave, dependent on chance and his own blundering efforts—yet he is always complaining, as if someone were accountable for the checks and difficulties that meet him at every turn. For the good that comes to him he gives no thanks—who is there to thank? At the disappointments that befall him he grumbles—there must be someone to blame!

It is the children who shall inherit the earth. Such as will not be children cannot truly possess at all. They cannot possess themselves, they cannot possess what they call their possessions, nor can they possess the earth.

The hour is coming when all that art, science, nature, and even

animal nature can afford, shall be the possession—in ennobling subjugation to the higher, even as man is subject to the Father—of the
sons and daughters of God. To him to whom he is all in all, God is
able to give these things. To another God cannot give them, for that
one is unable to receive them; he stands outside the truth of them.

Assuredly we are not to love God for the sake of what he can give
us. Indeed, it is impossible to love him except because he is our God
and altogether good and faithful and beautiful. But neither may we
forget what the Lord does not forget, that, in the end, when the truth
is victorious, God will answer his creature in the joy of his heart.[1] It is
the narrow ways trodden of men that are miserable—those ways that
have high walls on each side, with but an occasional glimpse of the
sky above. But the true narrow way is not unlovely! It may be full of
toil, but cannot be full of misery. In the world itself are many more
lovely footpaths than high roads. The true path has not walls, but fields
and forests and gardens around it, and limitless sky overhead. It has
its sorrows, but they lie on its sides, and many leave the path to pick
them up.[2]

The Joy of the Father

What is joy but the harmony of the Spirit! The good Father made
his children to be joyful. Only before they can enter into his joy, they
must be like himself, ready to sacrifice joy to truth.

No promise of such joy is an appeal to selfishness. Every reward
held out by Christ is a pure thing. Nor can it enter the soul except as
a death to selfishness. The heaven of Christ is a loving of all, a forgetting
of self, a dwelling of each in all, and all in each. Even in our nurseries,
a joyful child is rarely selfish, generally giving and righteous.

It is not selfish to be joyful. What power could prevent him who
sees the face of God from being joyful? That bliss is his which lies
beyond all other bliss, without which no other bliss could ripen or last.
The one bliss of the universe is the presence of God—which is simply
God being to the man, and felt by the man as being, that which in his
own nature God is—the indwelling power of the man's life.

God must be to his creature what God is in himself, for it is by his
essential being alone, that by which he *is*, that he can create. His presence is the continual call and response of the creative to the created,
of the Father to the child. Where can be the selfishness in being thus
made happy?

It may be deep selfishness to refuse to be happy. Is there selfishness
in the Lord's seeing of the travail of his soul and being satisfied? Self-

ishness consists in taking the bliss from another. But to find one's bliss in the bliss of another is not selfishness. Joy is not selfishness; and the greater the joy thus reaped, the farther is that joy removed from selfishness.

The one bliss, next to the love of God, is the love of our neighbor. If anyone says, "You love because it makes you happy," I deny it. "We are blessed and happy," I say, "because we love." No one could attain to the bliss of loving his neighbor who was selfish and sought that bliss from love of himself.

Love is unselfish. We love because we cannot help it. There is no merit in it—how should there be any in love?—but neither is it selfish. There are many who confuse righteousness with merit, and think there is nothing righteous where there is nothing meritorious.

"If it makes you happy to love," they say, "where is your merit? It is only selfishness!"

There is no merit, I reply, yet the love that is born in us is our salvation from selfishness. Because a thing is joyful, it does not follow that I do it for joy of it; yet when the joy is in others, the joy is pure. That *certain* joys should be joys is the very denial of selfishness. The man would be a demoniacally selfish man whom love itself did not make joyful. It is selfish to contentedly enjoy seeing others in lack. Even in the highest spiritual bliss, to sit unconcerned of others would be selfishness, and the higher the bliss, the worse the selfishness. But surely that bliss is fullest when a great part of it consists in an effort that others may share it.

I speculate, yet I will not doubt it: the effort to bring others to share with us will make up a great part of our heavenly gladness and contentment. There would be no bliss in merely existing in joy while others still did not share it. The creating, redeeming Father will find plenty of like work for his children to do.

Dull are those—at least they can have little of Christian imagination—who think that where all are good, things must be dull. It is because there is so little good yet in them that they know so little of the power or beauty of the merest life divine. Let such make haste to be true. Interest will there be, and variety enough, not without pain, in the ministration of help to those yet wearily toiling up the heights of truth—perhaps yet unwilling to part with miserable self, which cherishing they are not yet worth being, or capable of having.

Forsaking the Good to Follow Christ

Some of the things a man or woman may have to forsake in following Christ, he does not have to leave because the things are bad in themselves.

Neither nature, art, science, nor good society are the kinds of things a man will lose in forsaking himself: they are God's, and have no part in the world of evil, false judgments, low desires, and the general unrealities that make up the conscious life of the self, which has to be denied. These latter will never be restored to the man.

But in forsaking himself to do what God requires of him—his true work in the world—a man may find he has to leave some of God's things for a season—not to repudiate them, but for the time to forsake them, because they draw his mind from the absolute necessities of the true life in himself or in others. He may have to deny himself in leaving them—not as bad things, but as things for which there is not room until those of paramount claim have been so heeded, that these will no longer impede but further them.

Then he who knows God will find that knowledge which opens the door of his understanding of all other things. He will become able to behold all things from within, instead of having to search wearily into them from the outside. This knowledge of God gave to King David more understanding than had all his teachers.

Then, when God is truly known, will the things a man has had to leave be restored to him a hundredfold.

So will it be in the forsaking of friends. To forsake them for Christ is not to forsake them as evil. It is not to cease to love them; "for he that loveth not his brother whom he hath seen, how can he love God whom he hath not seen?" Perhaps we will have to forsake them for a season, in order that their love casts not even a shadow between us and our Master. Perhaps we must forsake the need for their approval, their interaction with us, even their affection, where the Master says one thing and they another. To forsake them may be the Lord's means to teach us to learn to love them in a far higher, deeper, more tender, truer way than before—a way which keeps all that was genuine in the former way, and loses all that was false. We shall love them for their selves, and disregard our own.

I do not forget the word of the Lord about "hating father and mother." I have a glimpse of the meaning of it, but dare not attempt explaining it now. It is all against the self—not against the father and mother.

Forsaking Even False Notions About God

There is another kind of forsaking that may fall to the lot of some, and which they may find very difficult.

I speak of forsaking such notions of God and his Christ as they were taught in their youth—which they held, and could not keep from holding, when they first began to believe. And now that deep inside their heart of hearts they have begun to doubt the truth of some of these, it seems that to cast them away is to part with every assurance of safety.

There are so-called doctrines long accepted by good people, of which I find it hard to understand how any man or woman can love God and hold, except indeed by a tight closing of the spiritual eyes. If a man care more for opinion than for life, it is not worth any other man's while to persuade him to renounce the opinions he happens to entertain. Were he to be convinced to let them go, he would only proceed to place new opinions in the same place of honor—a place which can belong to no opinion whatever. It matters nothing what such a man may or may not believe, for he is not a true man. By holding with a school of thought he supposes to be right, he but bolsters himself up with the worst of all unbelief—opinion calling itself faith—unbelief calling itself religion.

But for him who is in earnest about the will of God, not opinions about him, it is of endless importance that he should think rightly of God. Theory matters nothing. Opinion matters nothing. Theology matters nothing. But true knowledge of God matters everything! No man or woman can come close to God, cannot truly know his will, as long as his notion of him is in any point that of a false god.

Such a man or woman, in yielding such ideas of God as are unworthy of God, may even seem to himself to be giving up his former assurance of salvation. To turn one's back on his spiritual upbringing can be fearsome indeed, before the liberation is felt. Yet if he would be true, if he would enter into life, if he would know God as he truly is, he must take up that cross also.

He will come to see that he must follow *no* doctrine, be it true as word of man could state it, but the living Truth, the Master himself. Many good souls will one day be horrified at the things they now believe.

Denying Sacred Prejudices to Follow Jesus

Many good souls will one day be horrified at the things they now believe of God.

If they have not thought about them, but have given themselves to obedience, their false ideas may not have done them much harm as yet. But they can make little progress in the knowledge of God, while, even if only passively, holding evil things to be true of him.

On the other hand, if they *do* think about them, and find in their concepts no obstruction, they must indeed be far from anything that could be called a true knowledge of God.

But there are others who find them a terrible obstruction, and yet imagine, or at least fear them true. Such must take courage to forsake *any* form of the false. They must take courage to deny their old selves in the most seemingly sacred of prejudices, and follow Jesus—not as he is presented in the tradition of the elders, but as he is presented by himself, his apostles, and the Spirit of truth.

There are "traditions of men" which have been erected after Christ as well as before him. And far worse, for they make "of none effect" the highest and best things about him.[3]

Hymn for a Sick Girl

Father, in the dark I lay,
*   Thirsting for the light,*
Helpless, but for hope alway
*   In thy father-might.*

Out of darkness came the morn,
*   Out of death came life,*
I, and faith, and hope, new-born,
*   Out of moaning strife!*

So, one morning yet more fair,
*   I shall, joyous-brave,*
Sudden breathing loftier air,
*   Triumph o'er the grave.*

Though this feeble body lie
*   Underneath the ground,*
Wide awake, not sleeping, I
*   Shall in him be found.*

But a morn yet fairer must
*   Quell this inner gloom—*
Resurrection from the dust
*   Of a deeper tomb!*

Father, wake thy little child;
*   Give me bread and wine*
Till my spirit undefiled
*   Rise and live in thine.*

THE FALSE FAITH OF MERE THEORY AND DOCTRINE

A Fictional Selection from *The Highlander's Last Song*

S he did not believe that God was unceasingly doing and would do his best for every man; therefore, she was unable to claim the assurance that he was doing his best for Ian. But her longing to hear what her son had proposed telling her was becoming possible between them through her learning more clearly what his views were. Therefore, the night after that spent by her sons on the hill, after Alister had retired, she said to him, "You never told me, Ian, the story you began about something that made you pray."

"Are you sure you will not take cold, Mother?" he said.

"I am warmly clad, my son; and my heart is longing to hear all about it."

"I am afraid you will not find my story so interesting as you expect, Mother."

"What concerns you is more interesting to me than anything else in the whole world, Ian."

"Not more than God, Mother?" said Ian.

The mother was silent. She was as honest as her sons. The question showed her, however dimly and in shadow, something of the truth concerning herself—even though she could not fully grasp it—namely, that she cared more about salvation than about God. If she could but keep her boy out of hell, she would be content to live on without growing close to the Lord. God was to her an awe, not yet a ceaseless growing delight!

There are centuries of paganism yet in many lovely Christian souls—paganism so deep, therefore so little recognized, that their earnest endeavor is to plant that paganism ineradicably in the hearts of those dearest to them.

She did not yet understand that salvation lies in being one with Christ, even as the branch is one with the vine—that any salvation short of knowing God is no salvation at all. The moment a man feels that he belongs to God utterly, the atonement is there and the Son of God is reaping his harvest.

The good mother was, however, not one of those conceited, stiff-necked souls who have been the curse of the church in all ages; she was but one of those in whom reverence for its passing form dulls the perception of unchangeable truth. Fortunately she was not of the kind who shut up God's precious light in the horn lantern of human theory, whose shadows cast on the path to the kingdom seem to dim eyes like insurmountable obstructions. For the sake of what they count revealed, they refuse all further revelation, and what satisfies them is merest famine to the next generation of believers. Instead of God's truth, they offer man's theory, and accuse of rebelling against God those who cannot live on the husks they call food. But ah, home-hungry soul! God is not the elder brother of the parable, but the father with the best robe and the ring—a God high above all your longing, even as the heavens are high above the earth.[4]

BELIEF IN JESUS—BEGINNING AT ONCE TO DO WHAT HE SAID

A Fictional Selection from *Donal Grant*

From very childhood her mind had been filled with traditional utterances concerning the divine character and the divine plans—the merest inventions of men far more desirous of understanding what they were not required to understand, than of doing what they were required to do, of obeying what they were commanded to obey—whence their crude and false utterances concerning a God of their own fancy—in whom it was a good man's duty, in the name of any possible God, to disbelieve. And just because she was in a measure true, authority had an immense power over her. The very sweetness of their nature forbids such to doubt the fitness of the claims of others.

She had a governess of the so-called orthodox type, a large proportion of whose teaching was of the worst kind of heresy, for it was lies against him who is Light, and in whom is no darkness at all; her doctrines were so many smoked glasses held up between the mind of her pupil and the glory of the living God—such as she would have seen for herself in time, had she gone to the only knowable truth concerning God, the face of Jesus Christ. Had she set herself to understand him the knowledge of whom is eternal life, she would have neither believed these things nor taught them to her little cousin. Nor had she yet met with anyone to help her to cast aside the doctrines of men and lead her face to face with the Son of Man, the visible God.

The first lie of all she had been taught was that she must believe so and so before God would let her come near him or listen to her. The old cobbler could have taught her differently; but she would have thought it altogether improper for her to hold conversation with such a man, even if she had known him for the best man in Auchars. She was in sore and sad earnest notwithstanding to do the thing that was required of her and to believe as she was told she must believe. Instead of believing in Jesus Christ, that is beginning at once to do what he said—what he told people they must do if they would be his disciples—she tried hard to imagine herself one of the chosen, tried hard to believe herself the chief of sinners.

No one told her that it is the man who sees something of the glory of God, the height and depth and breadth and length of his love and unselfishness, not a child dabbling with mindless doctrines, who can ever be able to feel that position and that condition. She tried to feel that she deserved to be burned in hell for ever and ever, and that it was boundlessly good of God who made her so that she could not help being a sinner, to give her the least chance of escaping it. She tried to feel that, though she could not be saved without something she did not have, if she was not saved it would be all her own fault; while at the same time the God of perfect love could save her by giving her that something if he pleased, but he might not so please—and so on through a whole miserable treadmill of contradictions.

The misery is that the professional teacher of religion has for centuries practically so disbelieved in the oneness of the God-head as to separate Father and Son so that innumerable hearts have loved the Son yet hated the idea of the Father: hated the Father they have not, for he that hath the Son hath the Father also. But I have undertaken a narrative, and not an attack on the serpents of hell; but the same lies under the name of doctrines are still creeping about everywhere, though they do not now hiss so loudly in the more educated circles, and I must set my foot on one when I can. The rattlesnake may bite after he is unable any more to rattle: and the weakness of every human heart breeds its own stinging things.[5]

THE BIGNESS OF GOD'S DESIGN

A Fictional Selection from *Donal Grant*

M aist fowk see but like the blin' man when he was half cured, and could tell fowk frae trees only by their gangin'. Man, did it ever strick ye 'at maybe deith micht be the first waukin' to come fowk?"

"It has occurrt to me," answered Donal; "but mony things come intil a body's heid 'at there's nae time, for the time, to think oot! They lie and bide their time though."

"Ye're richt there. Dinna ye lat the clergy, or the lovers o' the law an' the letter, perswaud ye 'at the Lord wadna hae ye think. Him 'at obeys, though nane ither, can think wi' safety. We maun do first the thing 'at we ken, an' syne we may think aboot the thing at we dinna ken. I think 'at whiles he wadna say a thing jist no to stop fowk thinkin' aboot it. He was aye at gettin' them to make use o' the can'le o' the Lord. It's my belief 'at ae main obstacle to the growth o' the kingdom is first the oonbelief o' believers, an' neist the w'y 'at they lay doon the law. Afore they hae learnt the rudimen's o' the trowth themsel's they begin to lay the grievous burden o' their dullness an' their ill-conceived notions o' holy things upo' the min's and consciences o' their neebours, fain to haud them frae growin' ony mair nor themsel's. Eh, man, but the Lord's won'erfu'! Ye may daur an' daur, an' no come i' sicht o' 'im!"

"Mr. Grant," she said, coming toward him, "St. Paul said that should an angel from heaven preach any other gospel than his, he was accursed. 'Let him be accursed,' he said. Even an angel from heaven, you see, Mr. Grant! It's terrible!"

"It is terrible, and I say amen to it with all my heart," replied Donal. "But the gospel you have received is not the Gospel of Paul, but one substituted for it—by no angel from heaven, neither with any design of substitution, but by men with hide-bound souls, who in order to get them into their own intellectual pockets, melted down the gold of the kingdom and recast it in the molds of wretched legal thought, learned of the Romans, who crucified their Master. Grand childlike heavenly things they would explain by vulgar worldly notions of law and right! But they meant well, seeking to justify the ways of God to men, therefore the curse of the apostle does not fall I think upon them. They sought a way out of their difficulties, and thought they had found one, when in reality it was their faith that carried them over the top of their enclosing walls. But gladly would I see discomfited such as taking their inventions at the hundredth hand, and moved by none of the fervor to those who first promulgated the doctrines, lay them as the word and will of God—lumps of iron and heaps of dust—upon the live, beating, longing hearts that cry out after their God—vanished afresh in the clouds these have raised around the Master, the express image of the Father's person."

"Oh, I do hope what you say is true!" panted Arctura. "I think I shall die if I find it is not!"

"You can find nothing but what the Lord teaches you. If you find what I tell you untrue, it will be in not being enough—in not being grand and free and bounteous enough. To think anything too good to be true is to deny God—to say the untrue is better than the true—to commit the sin against the Holy Ghost. It will be something better and better, lovelier and lovelier that Christ will teach you. Only you must leave human teachers altogether, and give yourself to him to be taught. If there is any truth in these things, then Christ is in the world now as then, and within our call."

"Anyone who is willing to be taught of God will be taught, and thoroughly taught by him. People tell such terrible lies about God, judging him by their own foolish selves."

"I am afraid I am doing wrong in listening to you Mr. Grant! I do wish that what you say might be true, but are you not in danger—you will pardon me for saying it—of presumption: how could all the good people be wrong?"

"Because the greater part of the teachers among them have always set themselves more to explain God than to obey him. The gospel is given not to redeem our understandings, but our hearts; that done, and only then, our understandings will be free. Our Lord said he had many things to tell his disciples, but they were not able to hear them. If the things be true which I have heard from Sunday to Sunday in church since I came here, then I say, the Lord brought us no salvation at all, but only a change of shape to our miseries. It has not redeemed you, Lady Arctura, and never will. Nothing but Christ himself for your very own teacher and friend and brother, not all the doctrines about him, even if every one of them were true, can save you. When we poor orphan children cannot find our God, they would have us take instead something that is not God at all—but a very bad caricature of him!"

"But how should wicked men know that such is not the true God?"

"If a man desires God, he cannot help knowing enough of him to be capable of learning more. His idea of him cannot be all wrong. But that does not make him fit to teach others all about him—only to go on to learn for himself. But Jesus Christ is the very God I want. I want a father like him, like the Father of him who came as our big brother to take us home. No other than the God exactly like Christ can be the true God. Cast away from you that doctrine of devils, that Jesus died to save us from our Father. There is no safety, no good of any kind but with the Father, his Father and our Father, his God and our God."

"But you must allow that God hates and punishes sin—and that is a terrible thing."

"It would be ten times more terrible if he did not hate and punish it. Do you think Jesus came to deliver us from the punishment of our sins? He should not have moved a step for that. The terrible thing is to be sinful, and all punishment is to help to deliver us from it, nor will it cease until we have given up being sinful. God will have us good; and Jesus works out the will of his Father."

I do not myself believe that *mere* punishment exists anywhere in the economy of the highest. I think *mere* punishment is a human idea, not a divine one. But the consuming fire is more terrible to the evildoer than any idea of punishment invented by the most riotous of human imaginations. Punishment it is, though not *mere* punishment, which is a thing not of creation but of destruction: it is a power of God and for his creature. As love is God's being and a creative energy in one, so the pains of God are to the recreating of the things his love has made, and sin has unmade.[6]

After an Old Legend

The monk was praying in his cell,
  With bowed head praying sore;
He had been praying on his knees
  For two long hours and more.

As of themselves, all suddenly,
  His eyelids opened wide;
Before him on the ground he saw
  A man's feet close beside;

And almost to the feet came down
  A garment wove throughout;
Such garment he had never seen
  In countries round about!

His eyes he lifted tremblingly
  Until a hand they spied:
A chisel-scar on it he saw,
  And a deep, torn scar beside.

His eyes they leaped up to the face,
  His heart gave one wild bound,
Then stood as if its work were done—
  The Master he had found!

With sudden clang the convent bell
  Told him the poor did wait
His hand to give the daily bread
  Doled at the convent-gate.

Then Love rose in him passionate,
  And with Duty wrestled strong;
And the bell kept calling all the time
  With merciless iron tongue.

The Master stood and looked at him
  He rose up with a sigh:
"He will be gone when I come back
  I go to him by and by!"

He chid his heart, he fed the poor
  All at the convent-gate;
Then with slow, dragging feet went back
  To his cell so desolate:

His heart bereaved by duty done,
  He had sore need of prayer!
Oh, sad he lifted the latch!—and, lo,
  The Master standing there!

He said, "My poor had not to stand
  Wearily at thy gate:
For him who feeds the shepherd's sheep
  The shepherd will stand and wait."

Yet, Lord—for thou wouldst have us judge,
  And I will humbly dare—
If he had stayed, I do not think
  Thou wouldst have left him there.

Thy voice in far-off time I hear,
  With sweet defending, say:
"The poor ye always have with you,
  Me ye have not alway!"

Thou wouldst have said: "Go feed my poor,
  The deed thou shalt not rue;
Wherever ye do my father's will
  I always am with you."

$\mathcal{S}$EEING GOD

> *Blessed are the pure in heart, for they shall see God.*
>
> Matthew 5:8

The Deepest Cry of Man

The cry of the deepest in man has always been to see God. It was the cry of Moses and the cry of Job, the cry of psalmist and of prophet. And to the cry, there has ever been faintly heard a far approach of the coming answer.

In the fullness of time the Son appears with the proclamation that certain people shall behold the Father: "Blessed are the pure in heart," he cries, "for they shall *see* God." He who saw God, who sees him now, who always did and always will see him, says, "Be pure, and you also shall see him."

To see God was the Lord's own, eternal, one happiness. Therefore, he knew that the essential bliss of the creature is to behold the face of the Creator. In that face lies the mystery of a man's own nature, the history of a man's own being. He who can read no line of it, can know neither himself nor his fellow. Only he who knows God a little can understand man at all. The blessed in Dante's *Paradise* ever and always read each other's thoughts in God. Looking to him, they find their neighbor. All that the creature needs to see or know, all that the creature can see or know, is the face of God from whom he came. Not seeing and not knowing it, the creature will never be at rest. Seeing and knowing it, his existence will yet indeed be a mystery to him and an awe, but no more a dismay. To know that it is, and that it has power neither to continue nor cease, must, to any soul alive enough to appreciate the fact, be merest terror, unless also it knows one with the Power by which it exists.[1]

A man may look another in the face for a hundred years and not know him. Men *have* looked Jesus Christ in the face, and not known either him or his father. It was necessary that he should appear, to begin the knowing of him, but his visible presence was quickly taken away so that it would not become a veil to hide men from the Father of their spirits. Many long for some sensible sign or intellectual proof. But such would only delay and impair that better, that best, vision— a contact with the heart of God himself, a perception of his being imparted by his spirit. For the sake of the vision God longs to give you, you are denied the vision you want. The Father of our spirits is not content that we should know him as we now know each other. There is a better, closer, and nearer way than any human way of knowing, and he is guiding us to that across all the swamps of our unteachableness, the seas of our faithlessness, the deserts of our ignorance.

Is it so very hard to wait for that which we cannot yet receive? Shall we complain of the shadows cast upon the mirrors of our souls by the hand and the polishing cloth, to receive more excellent glory? Have patience, children of the Father. Pray always, and do not faint. The mists and the storms and the cold will pass; the sun and the sky are forever. The most loving of you cannot imagine how one day the love of the Father will make you love.

From the man who comes to know and feel that Power in him and one with him, loneliness, anxiety, and fear vanish. He is no more an orphan without a home, a little one astray on the cold waste of a helpless consciousness.

"Father," he cries, "hold me fast to thy creating will, that I may know myself one with it, know myself its outcome, its willed embodiment, and rejoice without trembling. Be this the delight of my being, that thou hast willed, hast loved me forth. Let me know that I am thy child, born to obey thee. Dost thou not justify thy deed to thyself by thy tenderness toward me? Dost thou not justify it to thy child by revealing to him his claim on thee because of thy separation from him, because of his utter dependence on thee? Father, thou art in me, otherwise I could not be in thee, could have no house for my soul to dwell in, or any world in which to walk abroad."

Knowing Our Relation to Our Origin

These truths are, I believe, the very necessities of fact. But a man does not therefore, at a given moment, necessarily know them.

Nonetheless, it is absolutely necessary to his real being that he should know these spiritual relations in which he stands to his Origin.

Even more, it is necessary that they should be always present and potent with him, and become the heart and sphere and all-pervading substance of his consciousness, of which they are the ground and foundation.

Once to have seen them is not always to see them.

There are many times when the cares of this world—with no right to any part in our thought, seeing either they are unreasonable or God imperfect—so blind the eyes of the soul to the radiance of the eternally true, that they see it only as if it ought to be true, not as if it must be true; as if it *might* be true in the region of *thought*, but could not be true in the region of fact. Our very senses, filled with the things of our passing sojourn on this earth, combine to cast discredit upon the existence of any world for the sake of which we are furnished with an inner eye, an eternal ear.

But had we once seen God face to face, should we not always and forever be sure of him? Yet what if we *had* seen God face to face, but had again become impure of heart (if such a fearful thought be a possible idea)? I have no doubt that we should then no more believe that we had ever beheld him.

None but the pure in heart see God, and continue to see him. Only the growing-pure hope to see him. Even those who saw the Lord in the flesh did not see God. They only saw Jesus—and then but the outward Jesus, or a little more.

They were not pure in heart. They saw him and did not see him. They saw him with their eyes, but not with those eyes which alone can see God. That vision was not yet born in them. Neither the eyes of the resurrection-body, nor the eyes of unembodied spirits can see God. Only the eyes of that eternal quality that is of the very essence of God, the thought-eyes, the truth-eyes, the love-eyes, can see him.

It is not because we are created and he uncreated, it is not because of any difference involved in that difference of all differences that we cannot see him. If he were pleased to take a shape, and that shape were presented to us, and we saw that shape, we should not therefore be seeing God. Even if we knew it was a shape of God—call it even God himself our eyes rested upon. If we had been told the fact and believed the report, yet if we did not see the *Godness*, were not capable of recognizing him, so as without the report to know the vision him, we should not be seeing God. We should be seeing only the tabernacle in which for the moment he dwelt.

In other words, not seeing what in the form made it a form fit for him to take, we should not be seeing a presence which could only be God.[3]

CHAPTER 12

The Pinnacle of Created Being

When we rise into the mountain air, we require no other testimony than that of our lungs that we are in a healthful atmosphere. We do not find it necessary to submit it to a quantitative analysis; we are content that we breathe with joy, that we grow in strength, become lighter-hearted and better-tempered. Truth is a very different thing from fact; it is the loving contact of the soul with spiritual fact, vital and potent. It does its work in the soul independently of all faculty or qualification there for setting it forth or defending it. Truth in the inward parts is a power, not an opinion. It were as poor a matter as any held by those who deny it, if it had not its vitality in itself, if it depended upon any buttressing of other and lower material.

How should it be otherwise? If God be so near as the very idea of him necessitates, what other availing proof of His existence can there be, than such *awareness* as must come of the developing relation between him and us? The most satisfying of intellectual proofs, if such were to be had, would be of no value. God would be no nearer to us for them all. They would bring about no blossoming of the mighty fact. While he was in our very souls, there would yet lie between him and us a gulf of misery, of no knowledge.[4]

Peace is for those who *do* the truth, not those who believe it intellectually. The true man troubled by doubts is so troubled into further health and growth. Let him be alive and hopeful, above all obedient, and he will be able to wait for the deeper contentedness which must follow with more complete insight. It is said by some that men who walk in this truth deceive themselves. But this is at least worth reflecting on—that while the man who aspires to higher regions of life sometimes does fear he deceives himself, it is the man who aspires for nothing more whose eyes are not looking for truth from whatever quarter it pleases to come. The former has his eyes open, the latter his eyes closed. And so, as more and more truth is revealed, one day the former may be sure, and the latter begin to doubt in earnest![5]

To see God is to stand on the highest point of created being.

Not until we see God—no partial and passing embodiment of him, but the abiding presence—do we stand upon our own mountain-top, the height of the existence God has given us, and up to which he is leading us.

That there we should stand is the end of our creation.

This truth is at the heart of everything, means all kinds of completions, may be uttered in many ways. But language will never compass it, for form will never contain it. Nor shall we ever see, that is know

God perfectly. We shall indeed never absolutely know man or woman or child. But we may know God as we never can know a human being— as we never can know ourselves.

We not only may, but we *must* so know God, and it can never be until we are pure in heart. Then shall we known him with the infinitude of an ever-growing knowledge.

Do Not Define Purity; Be Pure

"What is it, then, to be pure in heart?"

I answer: It is not necessary to define this purity, or to have in the mind any clear form of it. For even to know perfectly what purity of heart is, were that possible, would not be the same as to *be* pure in heart.

"How then am I to try to seek such purity? How can I do so without even knowing what it is?"

Though you do not know any definition of purity, you know enough to begin to be pure. You do not know what a man is, but you know how to make his acquaintance—perhaps even how to gain his friendship. Your brain may not know what purity is, but your heart has some acquaintance with purity itself. Your brain, in seeking to analyze its components, may even obstruct your heart in bettering its friendship with it.

To know what purity is, a man must already be pure. But he who can ask the question already knows enough of purity, I repeat, to begin to become pure. If this moment you determine to start moving toward purity, your conscience will at once tell you where to begin. If you reply, "My conscience says nothing definite," I answer, "You are but playing with your conscience. Determine to be pure, and your conscience will speak."

If you care to see God, be pure.

If you will not determine to be pure, you will grow more and more impure, and instead of seeing God, will at length find yourself face to face with a vast void of empty space—a vast void, yet filled full of one inhabitant, that devouring monster, your own false self. If you do not care that you are bound to face such, I tell you there is a Power that will not have it so; a Love that will make you care through the consequences of not caring.

You who seek purity, and would have your fellowmen also seek it, spend not your thoughts and labor on the stony ground of their intellect, endeavoring to explain what purity is. Give to their imagination a picture of the one pure man. Call up their conscience to witness against their own deeds. Urge upon them the grand resolve to be pure.

With the first endeavor of a soul toward it, purity will begin to draw nigh, calling for admittance. And never will a man have to pause in the divine toil, asking what next is required of him. The demands of indwelling purity will ever be ahead of his slow-laboring obedience.[6]

REPENTANCE

A Fictional Selection from *The Minister's Restoration*

Thus wrought in young James Blatherwick—pastor, sinner, and soon to be child of God—that mighty power, mysterious in its origin as marvelous in its result, which had been at work in him all the time he lay sick and overwhelmed with feverish phantasms. But the result was certainly no phantasm. His repentance was true. He had been dead, and was alive again! God and the man met at last! As to *how* God turned the man's heart, that shall remain the eternal mystery. We can only say, "Thou, God, knowest." To understand that, we should have to go down below the foundation of the universe itself, underneath creation, and there see God send out from himself man, the spirit, forever dependent upon and growing in him, never complete outside of him because his origin, his very life is founded in the Infinite; never outside of God, because in him only he lives and moves and breathes and grows, and *has* his being.

Brothers and sisters, let us not linger to ask how these things can be. Let us turn at once to this Being in whom the *I* and *me* are created and have meaning, and let us make haste to obey him. Only in obeying shall we become all we are capable of being; thus only shall we learn and understand all we are capable of learning and understanding. The pure in heart shall see God; and to see him is to know all things.[7]

GOD IS LIGHT

A Fictional Selection from *The Lady's Confession*

I s it not strange," asked the curate, "that we are so prone to hide behind the veil of what is not? To seek refuge in lies? To run from the daylight for safety deeper into the cave? In the cave live the creatures of night, while in the light are the true men and women and clear-eyed angels. But the reason is clear. They are more comfortable with the beasts of darkness than with the angels of light. They dread the peering of eyes into their hearts. They feel themselves ashamed and therefore put the garment of hypocrisy around themselves, hiding their true selves and trying to appear other than they really are.

"But God hides nothing. His work from the very beginning has been *revelation*—a throwing aside of veil after veil, a showing to men of truth after deeper truth. On and on, from fact to fact, he advances, until at length in his Son Jesus he unveils his very face and character. When the Son is fully known, we shall know the Father also. The whole of creation, its growth, its history, the gathering of all human existence, is an unveiling of the Father.

"He loves light and not darkness. Therefore he shines, reveals. There are infinite gulfs in him into which our small vision cannot see. But they are gulfs of light, and the truths there are only invisible through excess of their own clarity.

"But see how different we are—until we learn of him! See the tendency of man to conceal his treasures, to claim even *truth* as his own by discovery, to hide it and be proud of it, gloating over that which he thinks he has in himself. We would be forever heaping together possessions, dragging things into the cave of our finitude, our individual *self*, not perceiving that the things which pass that dreariest of doors come to nothing inside. When a man tries to bring a truth in there, as if it were of private interpretation, he drags in only the bag which the truth, remaining outside, has burst and left."

With this the curate's voice softened, as he drew the undivided attention of each one there. "If then, brother or sister, you have that which would hide, make haste and drag the thing from its hiding place into the presence of your God, your light, your Savior. If it be good, he can cleanse it. If evil, it can be stung through and through with the burning arrows of truth and perish in glad relief. For the one bliss of an evil thing is to perish and pass out of existence. If we have such things within ourselves, we must confess them to ourselves and to God. And if there be anyone else who has need to know it, to that one also we must confess, casting out the vile thing that we may be clean. Let us hurry to open the doors of our lips and the windows of our humility, to let out the demon of darkness and let in the angels of light.

"If we do not thus open our house, the day will come when a roaring blast of his wind, or the flame of his keen lightning will destroy every defense of darkness and set us shivering before the universe in our nakedness. For there is nothing covered that shall not be revealed, neither hid that shall not be known! It is good that we cannot hide! Some of our souls would grow great vaults of uncleanness. But for every one of them, just as for the universe, the day of cleansing is coming. Happy are they who hasten it, who open wide the doors, take the broom in hand, and begin to sweep! It may be painful, but the result will be a clean house, with the light and wind of heaven shining and blowing clear and fresh through all its chambers. Better to choose such cleansing than to have a hurricane from God burst in door and window and sweep clean with his broom of destruction every lie."[8]

The Thorn in the Flesh

Within my heart a worm had long been hid.
I knew it not when I went down and chid
Because some servants of my inner house
Had not, I found, of late been doing well,
But then I spied the horror hideous—
Dwelling defiant in the inmost cell—
No, not the inmost, for there God did dwell!
But the small monster, softly burrowing,
Nearby God's chamber had made itself a den,
And lay in it and grew, the noisome thing!
Aghast I prayed—'twas time I did pray then!
But as I prayed it seemed the loathsome shape
Grew livelier, and did so gnaw and scrape
That I grew faint. Whereon to me he said—
Someone, that is, who held my swimming head,
"Lo, I am with thee: let him do his worst;
The creature is, but not his work, accurst;
Thou hating him, he is as a thing dead."
Then I lay still, nor thought, only endured.
At last I said, "Lo, now I am inured
A burgess of Pain's town!" The pain grew worse.
Then I cried out as if my heart would break.
But he, whom, in the fretting, sickening ache,
I had forgotten, spoke: "The law of the universe
Is this," he said: "Weakness shall be the nurse
Of strength. The help I had will serve thee too."
So I took courage and did bear anew.
At last, through bones and flesh and shrinking skin,
Lo, the thing ate his way, and light came in,
And the thing died. I knew then what it meant,
And, turning, saw the Lord on whom I leant.

Hungering After Righteousness

Blessed are they which do hunger and thirst after righteousness, for they shall be filled.

Matthew 5:6

W e are called to be pure. Yet the more we know ourselves, the keener are we aware how distant that purity is from us.

"Alas, I am shut out from this blessing!" we say. "I am not pure in heart. I shall never see God, for how shall I ever be pure!"

To such a heart, here is another word from the same eternal heart to comfort him, making his grief its own consolation. For this man also there is blessing from the messenger of the Father. Unhappy would be we, if God were the God of the perfected only, and not of the growing, the becoming!

"Blessed are they," says the Lord to the not yet pure, "which do hunger and thirst after righteousness, for they shall be filled." Filled with righteousness, they are pure. Pure, they shall see God.

Long before the Lord appeared, ever since man was on the earth, no, surely, from the very beginning, was his Spirit at work in it for righteousness. In the fullness of time he came in his own human person to fulfill all righteousness. He came to his own of the same mind with himself, who hungered and thirsted after righteousness. They should be fulfilled of righteousness!

The Passion to Be Good

To hunger and thirst after anything implies a sore personal need, a strong desire, a passion for that thing.

Those who hunger and thirst after righteousness seek with their whole nature the design of that nature. Nothing less will give them satisfaction. That alone will set them at ease. They long to be delivered from their sins, to send them away, to be clean and blessed by their absence—in a word, to become true men.

It was not in such a righteousness-hungry heart that the revolting legal fiction of imputed righteousness first arose. Righteousness, God's righteousness, righteousness in their own being, in heart and brains and hands, is what such righteousness-hungry men and women want, not some make-believe *pretend* form of what is not righteousness but is called righteousness.

Of such men was Nathanael, in whom was no guile. Such, perhaps, was Nicodemus, too, although he did come to Jesus by night. Such was Zacchaeus. The temple could do nothing to deliver these men. But, its observances, by their very futility, had done their work, developing the desires mere observance could not meet; making the men hunger and thirst the more after genuine righteousness—for this, the Lord must bring them bread from heaven.

With him, the live, original *rightness*, in their hearts, they will quickly become righteous. With that Love as their friend, who is at once both the root and the flower of things, they would strive vigorously as well as hunger eagerly after righteousness. Love is the father of righteousness, which could not be, and could not be hungered after, but for love. The lord of righteousness himself could not live without Love, without the Father in him. Every heart was created for, and cannot live otherwise than in and upon love eternal, perfect, pure, unchanging. And love necessitates righteousness.

In how many souls has not the very thought of a real God awakened a longing to be different, to be pure, to be good!

The fact that this feeling is possible, that a soul can become dissatisfied with itself, reveals that God is an essential part of its being. For in itself the soul is aware that it cannot be what it would, what it ought—that it cannot set itself right. A need has been generated in the soul for which the soul can generate no supply. A presence higher than itself must have caused that need. A power greater than itself must supply it, for the soul knows its very need, its very lack, is of something greater than itself.

The Primal Need of the Human Soul

The primal need of the human soul is even greater than this hunger. The longing after righteousness is only one of the manifestations of it.

The need itself is that of an existence which is not merely self-existent, for the consciousness of the Presence which has caused the existence of self. It is the man's need of God.

A moral, that is, a human spiritual being, must either *be* God, or be one *with* God. This truth begins to reveal itself when man begins to feel that he cannot cast out the thing he hates, cannot be the thing he loves. The fact that he hates thus, and that he loves thus, is because God is in him, but he finds he has not enough of God. His awaking strength manifests itself in his sense of weakness, for only strength can know itself weak. The negative cannot know itself at all; weakness cannot know itself weak. It is a little strength that longs for more; it is infant righteousness that hungers after full righteousness.

To every soul dissatisfied with itself, this rousing and consoling word comes from the Power that lives and makes him live—that in his hungering and thirsting he is blessed, for he shall be filled. His hungering and thirsting is the divine pledge of the divine meal. The more he hungers and thirsts the more blessed is he; the more room there is in him to receive that which God is yet more eager to give than he is to have.

It is the miserable emptiness that makes a man hunger and thirst. And, as the body hungers and thirsts for food and drink, so the soul hungers and thirsts after righteousness because the man's nature needs it—needs righteousness because he was made for it; and the soul desires its own. Man's nature is good, and desires more good. Therefore, no one need be discouraged because he is empty of good, for what is emptiness but room to be filled? Emptiness is need of good. And the emptiness that desires good is itself good.

Even if the hunger after righteousness should in part spring from a desire after self-respect, it is not therefore *all* false. A man could not even be ashamed of himself without feeling some sense of the beauty of rightness. By divine degrees the man will at length grow sick of himself and desire righteousness with a pure hunger—just as a man longs to eat that which is good, without thinking of the strength it will restore.

God Awakes and Will Fill the Hunger

God made man, and awoke in him the hunger for righteousness. The Lord Jesus came to enlarge and rouse this hunger.

The first and lasting effect of Jesus' words must be to make the hungering and thirsting yet more. If their passion grow to a despairing sense of the unattainable, a hopelessness of ever gaining that without which life would be worthless, let them remember that the Lord congratulates the hungry and thirsty, so surely does he know that they will one day be completely satisfied.

Their hunger is a precious thing to have, nonetheless a bad thing if retained unappeased. It springs from the lack but also from the love of good, and its presence makes it possible to supply the lack.

Happy, then, you pining souls! The food you would have is the one thing the Lord wants to give you, the very thing he came to bring you!

Fear not, ye hungering and thirsting! You shall have righteousness enough, though none to spare—none to spare, yet enough to overflow upon every man.

See how the Lord goes on filling his disciples—John and Peter and James and Paul—with righteousness from within! What honest soul, interpreting the servant by the master, and unbiased by the tradition of them that would shut the kingdom of heaven against men, can doubt what Paul means by "the righteousness which is of God by faith?" Paul was taught of Jesus Christ through the words Jesus had spoken, and the man who does not understand Jesus Christ will never understand his apostles. What righteousness could Paul have meant but the same the Lord would have men hunger and thirst after—the very righteousness with which God is righteous!

They that hunger and thirst after such righteousness shall become pure in heart, and shall see God.

Be Patient in Your Hungering

If your hunger seems long in being filled, it is well it should seem long.

But what if your righteousness tarry because your hunger after it is not eager? There are those who sit long at the table because their appetite is slow; they eat like those who would say, "We need no food."

In spiritual things, increasing appetite is the sign that satisfaction is drawing near. But it would be better to hunger after righteousness forever than to dull the sense of lack with the husks of the Christian scribes and theologians—some of whom trust in some theory of the atonement instead of in the Father of Jesus Christ, filling their fancy with the vestments of a vulgar legalism, and not the heart with the righteousness of God.

Hear another word of the Lord: He assures us that the Father hears the cries of his elect—those whom he seeks to worship him because they worship in spirit and in truth.

"Shall not God avenge his own elect," Jesus says, "which cry day and night unto him?"

Now what can God's elect have to keep on crying for, night and day, but righteousness? Jesus allows that God seems to put off answering them, but assures us that he will answer them speedily. Even now God must be busy answering their prayers; increasing hunger is the best possible indication that he is doing so.

For some divine reason it is good they should not yet know in themselves that he is answering their prayers. But the day must come when we shall be righteous even as he is righteous, when no word of his will miss being understood because of our lack of righteousness, when no unrighteousness will hide from our eyes the face of the Father.[1]

A Prayer from
CASTLE WARLOCK

Breathe o' God, eh! come an' blaw
Frae my hert ilk fog awa;
Wauk me up, an' mak' me strang,
Fill my hert wi' mony a sang.

GOD WILL KEEP MAKING US BIGGER TO ALL ETERNITY

A Fictional Selection from *Donal Grant*

N ow, Davie," said Donal, "what have you done since our last lesson?"

Davie stared.

"You didn't tell me to do anything, Mr. Grant!"

"No, but did it come into your mind what I could have given you the lesson for? Where is the good of such a lesson if it makes no difference to you! What was it I told you?"

Davie, who had never thought about it since, for the lesson had been broken off before Donal could bring it to its natural fruit, thought back, and said—

"That Jesus Christ rose from the dead."

"I did tell you that! Now where is the good of knowing that?"

Davie was silent; he knew no good of knowing it. He would probably have made up something had he known how, but he did not. The Shorter Catechism, of which he had learned about half, suggested nothing. He held his peace.

"Come, Davie, I will try to help you: Is Jesus dead, or is he alive?"

Davie considered.

"Alive," he answered.

"What does he do?"

Davie did not answer.

"What did he die for? Do you know?"

Here Davie had a good answer, though a cut and dried one: "To take away our sins," he said.

"Then what does he live for?"

Davie was again silent.

"Do you think if a man died for a thing, he would be likely to forget it the minute he rose again?"

"No, sir."

"I should say he would just go on doing the same thing as before; therefore he also lives to take away our sins. What are sins, Davie?"

"Bad things, sir."

"Yes; the bad things we think, and the bad things we feel, and the bad things we do. Have you any sins, Davie?"

"Yes; I am very wicked."

"Oh! How do you know that?"

"Arkie told me."

"What is being wicked?"

"Doing bad things."

"What bad things do you do?"

"I don't know, sir."

"Then you don't know that you are wicked; you only know that Arkie told you so!"

Lady Arctura drew herself up, indignant at his familiar use of her name; but Donal was too intent to perceive the offense he had given.

"I will tell you," Donal went on, "something you did wicked today." Davie grew rosy red. "When we find out one wicked thing we do, it is a beginning, that is, if we put it right, to finding out all the wicked things we do. Some people would rather not find them out, but have them hidden from themselves and from God too. But let us find them out, every one of them, that we may ask Jesus to take them away, and help Jesus to take them away by fighting them with all our strength. There are bad things in you, Davie, worse than you can know yet; but I will tell you one thing: I saw you pull the little pup's ears till he screamed out." Davie hung his head. "And you stopped a while, and then did it again! So I knew it wasn't because you didn't know that it hurt the pup. Was that a thing that Jesus would have done when he was a little boy?"

"No, sir."

"Why?"

"Because it would have been wrong."

"I suspect, rather, it was because he would have loved the little pup. He didn't have to think about its being wrong. He loves every kind of living thing; and he wants to take away your sin because he loves you—not merely to make you not cruel to the little pup, but to take away the wrong *thing* that doesn't love the little pup, and make you, too, love every living creature. Ah, Davie, you cannot do without Jesus!"

The silent tears were flowing down Davie's cheeks.

"The lesson's done, Davie," said Donal, and rose and went, leaving the boy with his cousin.

But just as he reached the door, he turned with a sudden impulse, and said, "Davie, I love Jesus Christ and his Father more than I can tell you—more than I can put into words—more than I can think; and if you love me, you will mind what Jesus tells you."

"What a good man you must be, Mr. Grant! Isn't he, Arkie?" sobbed Davie.

Donal laughed aloud.

"What, Davie!" he exclaimed; "you think me very good for loving the only good person in the whole world? That is very odd! Why, Davie, I should be the most contemptible creature, knowing him as I do, not to love him with all my heart—yes, with all the heart I shall have one day when he is done making me!"

"Is God making you yet, Mr. Grant? I thought you were a grown-up man!"

"Well, I don't think he will make me any taller," answered Donal; "but what is inside me, the thing I love you with, and the thing I think about God with, and the thing I love poetry with, the thing I read the Bible with—that thing God keeps on making bigger and bigger. I do not know where it will stop, but I know where it will not stop. That thing is *me*, and God will keep on making it bigger to all eternity, though he has not even got me into right shape yet."

"Why is he so long about it?"

"I don't think he is long about it; but I know he could do it quicker, if I was as good as by this time I ought to have been, with the father and mother I have had, and all my long hours on the hillsides with my New Testament, and the sheep. I prayed to God on the hill and in the fields, and he heard me, Davie, and made me see the foolishness of a great many things, and the grandeur and beauty of the true things. Davie, God wants to give you the whole world and everything in it, and when you have begun to do the things Jesus tells you, then you will be my brother, and we shall both be his little brothers."

With that he turned again and went.

The tears were rolling down Arctura's face without her being aware of it; for she was saying to herself, "He is a well-meaning man, but dreadfully mistaken; the Bible says believe, not obey!"

The poor girl, though she read her Bible through and through regularly, was so blinded by the dust and ashes of her teaching that she knew very little indeed of what was actually in it. The most significant things slipped from her as if they were merest words without a shadow of meaning or intent; they did not support the doctrines she had been taught, and therefore said nothing to her. She did not know that the story of Christ and the appeals of those who had handled the Word of life had a very different end in view than that of making people understand how it was that God arranged matters for their salvation by a terror of their imagining. God would have us live, and if we live we cannot but know; while all the knowledge in the universe could not make us live. Obedience is the road to all things. It is the only way to grow able to trust him. Love and faith and obedience are sides of the same prism.[2]

To My Sister
On her twenty-first birthday

I

Old fables are not all a lie
    That tell of wondrous birth,
Of Titan children, father Sky,
    And mighty mother Earth.

Yea, now are walking on the ground
    Sons of the mingled brood;
Yea, now upon the earth are found
    Such daughters of the Good.

Earth-born, my sister, thou art still
    A daughter of the sky;
Oh climb forever up the hill
    Of thy divinity!

To thee thy mother Earth is sweet,
    Her face to thee is fair;
But thou, a goddess incomplete,
    Must climb the starry stair.

II

Wouldst thou the holy hill ascend,
    Wouldst see the Father's face?
To all his other children bend,
    And take the lowest place.

Be like a cottage on a moor,
    A covert from the wind,
With burning fire and open door,
    And welcome free and kind.

Thus humbly doing on the earth
    The things the earthly scorn,
Thou shalt declare the lofty birth
    Of all the lowly born.

III

Be then thy sacred womanhood
    A sign upon thee set,
A second baptism—understood—
    For what thou must be yet.

For, cause and end of all thy strife,
    And unrest as thou art,
Still stings thee to a higher life
    The Father at thy heart.

A FAMILY OF PEACEMAKERS

Blessed are the peacemakers, for they shall be called the children of God.

Matthew 5:9

T he two promises Jesus gives in what are called the Beatitudes—seeing God and being filled with righteousness—have their place between the individual and his Father in heaven. The promise I would now address has its place between a man and his God, as the God of other men also, but primarily between man and man. Its relation to God is as the Father of the whole family in heaven and earth. "Blessed are the peacemakers," Jesus says, "for they shall be called the children of God."

The True Idea of the Universe Is Family

Those that are on their way to see God, those who are growing pure in heart through hunger and thirst after righteousness, are indeed the children of God. But especially the Lord calls those his children who, on their way home, are peacemakers in the traveling company. For, surely, those in any family are especially the children who make peace with and among the rest.

The true idea of the universe is the whole family in heaven and earth. All the children in this part of it, the earth, are not good children yet. But however far, therefore, the earth is from being a true portion of a real family, the life-germ at the root of the world, that by and for which it exists, is its relation to God the Father of men.

The church—whose idea is the purer family within the mixed family, ever growing as leaven within the meal, but which is, unfortunately, not easily distinguishable from the world it would change—is one of the passing means for the development of this germ in the consciousness of God's whole family of children. For the same purpose, the whole divine family is made up of countless human families, that in these, men and women may learn and begin to love one another.

God's purpose, then, is to make of the world a true, divine family.

Peacemakers Work Unity Within the Family

Now the primary necessity to the very existence of a family is peace. Many a human family is no *family*, and the world is no true family yet, because of the lack of peace. Wherever peace is growing, there of course is the live peace, counteracting disruption and disintegration and division, and helping the development of the true essential family.

The one question, therefore, as to any family is, whether peace or strife be on the increase in it. For peace alone makes it possible for the binding grassroots of life—namely, love and justice—to spread throughout what would otherwise be but a wind-blown heap of still drifting sand.

The peacemakers quiet the winds of the world which are always ready to be up and blowing disharmony, disunity, and strife among the people of it. The peacemakers tend and cherish the interlacing roots of the ministering grass. They spin and twist many uniting cords, and they weave many supporting bands. They are the servants, for the truth's sake, of the individual, of the family, of the world, and of the great universal family of heaven and earth.

The peacemakers are the true children of that family, the allies and ministers of every clasping and consolidating force in it. They are fellow-workers with God in the creation of the family. They help him to get across his mind, to perfect his father-idea. Ever radiating peace, they welcome love, but do not seek it. They provoke no jealousy. They are the children of God, for they, like him, would be one with his creatures.

His eldest Son, his very likeness, was the first of the family-peacemakers. Preaching peace to them that were afar off and to them that were nigh, he stood undefended in the turbulent crowd of his fellows, and it was only over his dead body that his brothers began to come together in the peace that will not be broken. He rose again from the dead, and his peacemaking brothers, like himself, are dying unto sin, and not yet have the evil children made their Father hate or their elder Brother flinch.

Dividers and Separators

On the other hand, those whose influence is to divide and separate, causing the hearts of men to lean away from each other, make themselves the children of the evil one. Born of God and not of the devil, they turn from God, and adopt the devil as their father instead. They set their God-born life against God, against the whole creative, redemptive purpose of his ever-unifying will. They thus continually obstruct the one prayer of the First-born—that the children may be one with him in the Father.

Against the heart-end of creation, against that for which the Son yielded himself utterly, these sowers of strife, these fomenters of discord, ceaselessly contend. They do their part with all the other powers of evil to make the world which the love of God holds together—a world at least, though not yet a family—one heaving mass of dissolution. But they labor in vain.

Through this disharmonious mass, that it may cohere, this way and that as a shuttle in and around unconnected threads of a loom, guided in dance inexplicable of prophetic harmony, move the children of God—the lights of the world, the lovers of men, the fellow-workers with God, the peacemakers—ever weaving, after a pattern devised by and only known to him who orders their ways, the web of the world's history.

If it were not for them, the world would have no history. It would vanish, a cloud of windborne dust. As in God's labor, so shall these share in God's joy, in the divine fruition of victorious endeavor.

Blessed are the peacemakers, for they shall be called the children of God—*the* children because they set the Father on the throne of the family.

Perhaps the most potent of strife-encouragers are not those powers of the visible church who care more for rules and dogma than for truth, and for the church, or their little corner of it, more than for Christ. To be sure, these do sufficient damage, they who take uniformity for unity, who strain at a gnat and swallow a camel, not knowing what spirit they are of. Such men, I say, are perhaps neither the most active nor the most potent force working for the disintegration of the body of Christ.

I imagine also that neither are the party liars of religious politics the worst foes to divine unity, ungenerous and often knowingly false as they are to their opponents, to whom they seem to have no desire to be honest and fair. I think, rather, that the worst of the lot must be the babbling liars and gossips of the social circle, and the faithless brothers and unloving sisters of disunited human families.

But why inquire which is most devastating? *Every* self-assertion, *every* form of self-seeking, however small or poor, world-noble or repugnant, is a separating and scattering force. And these forces are multitudinous, these points of radial repulsion are innumerable, because of the prevailing passion of mean and self-seeking souls to seem great and feel important. If such cannot hope to attract the attention of their own little world, if they cannot make themselves seem important enough to neighboring eyes, they will—in what sphere they may call their own, however small it be—try to make a party for themselves, each revolving on his or her own axis, attempting to self-center a private whirlpool of human monads. To draw such a surrounding to its own being, the partisan of self will sometimes gnaw asunder the most precious of bonds, poison whole broods of infant loves.

Such real schismatics go about, not always inventing evil, yet rejoicing in iniquity—mishearing, misrepresenting, paralyzing affection, separating hearts. Their chosen calling is that of the strife-maker, the child of the dividing devil. They belong to the class of *the perfidious*, whom Dante places in the lowest infernal gulf as their proper home. Many a one who now imagines himself or herself standing well in morals and religion, will find at last that they are just such a child of the devil, and the misery of such will be the hope of their redemption.

What, Therefore, Must the Peacemakers Do?

The main practical difficulty, at least with some peacemakers, is how to conduct themselves toward the undoers of the peace, the disuniters of souls. I do not write the above for the sake of those who are most concerned. Were I to put it down as close as words could draw it, would such a one recognize his or her own likeness? It is doubtful. Rather I am as one groping after some light on what should be the true behavior of the peacemaker toward ones of this kind.

Are we to treat persons known to be liars and strife-makers as the children of the devil, or not? Are we to turn away from them, and refuse to acknowledge them, rousing an ignorant strife of tongues concerning our conduct? Are we guilty of connivance, when silent as to the ambush, when we know where the silent and secretive arrow is shot from? Are we to call the traitor in the cause of Christ to account?

Are we to give warning of any sort that their behavior is from the evil one, though they may not know it?

I have no answer. Each must carry the question that perplexes him to the Light of the World. To what purpose is the Spirit of God promised to them that ask it, if not to help them order the behavior of their way aright?

One thing is plain—that we must love the strife-maker. Another is nearly as plain—that, if we do not love him, we must leave him alone. For without love there can be no peacemaking, and words will but occasion more strife. Until we genuinely love, we must say nothing, for fear our words may be somehow an attempt to elevate our own self. And while awaiting words—though the time for them may never come—we can always, indeed, we *must* always be kind. To be kind neither hurts nor compromises. Kindness has many phases, and the fitting form of it may avoid offense and must avoid untruth.

We must not fear what man can do to us, but commit our way to the Father of the family. We must in no way be anxious to defend ourselves. And if God is our defense, is he not our friend's as much as ours? Therefore, commit your friend's cause also to him who judges righteously. Be ready to bear testimony for your friend, as you would to receive a blow aimed at him. But do not plunge into a nest of scorpions to rescue his handkerchief. Be true to him yourself, and do not spare any opportunity to show that you love and honor him. But defense may dishonor: men may say, "What! is your friend's esteem then so small?" He is unwise who drags a rich veil from a cactus bush.

Whatever our relation, then, with any peace-breaker, our mercy must ever be within call. And it may help us against an indignation too strong to be pure to remember that when any man is reviled for righteousness' sake, then is he blessed.[1]

THE SHOPS IN HEAVEN

A Fictional Selection from *The Curate's Awakening*

"Tell them your vision of the shops in heaven, Uncle," said Rachel after a long silence.

"Oh, no, Rachel," said Polwarth.

"I know the gentlemen would like to hear it."

"That we should," insisted both men at once.

"I venture my objections are not likely to stand in this company," returned Polwarth with a smile. "Agreed, then. This was no dream, Mr. Wingfold. It is something I have thought out many times. But the only form I could find for it was that of a vision."

He stopped, took a deep breath while the others waited expectantly. Then he began.

" 'And now,' said my guide to me, 'I will take you to the city of the righteous, and show you how they buy and sell in the kingdom of heaven.' So we journeyed on and on and I was weary before we arrived. After I had refreshed my soul, my conductor led me into a large place that we would call a shop here, although the arrangements were different and an air of stateliness dwelt in and around the place. It was filled with the loveliest silk and woolens—all types and colors, a thousand delights.

"I stood in the midst of the place in silence and watched those that bought and sold. On the faces of those that sold I saw only expressions of a calm and concentrated ministration. As soon as one buyer was contented, they turned graciously to another and listened until they perfectly understood what he had come seeking. And once they had provided what the customer had desired, such a look of satisfaction lingered on their faces, as of having just had a great success.

"When I turned to watch the faces of those who bought, in like manner I saw complete humility—yet it was not humility because thy sought a favor, for with their humility was mingled the total confidence of receiving all that they sought. It was truly a pleasure to see how everyone knew what his desire was, and then made his choice readily and with decision. I perceived also that everyone spoke not merely respectfully, but gratefully, to him who served him. And the kindly greetings and partings made me wonder how every inhabitant of such a huge city would know every other. But I soon saw that it came not of individual knowledge, but of universal love.

"And as I stood watching, suddenly it came to me that I had yet to see a single coin passed. So I began to keep my eyes on those who were buying. A certain woman was picking out a large quantity of silk, but when she had make her purchase, she simply took it in her arms and carried it out of the shop and did not pay. So I turned to watch another, but when he carried away his goods, he paid no money either. I said to myself, 'These must be well-known persons who trade here often. The shop-keeper knows them and will bill them at a later time.' So I turned to watch another, but he did not pay either! Then I began to observe that those who were selling were writing nothing down concerning each sale. They were making no record of each purchase or keeping track of what was owed them.

"So I turned to my guide and said, 'How lovely is this honesty. I see that every man and woman keeps track of his own debts in his mind so that time is not wasted in paying small sums or in keeping accounts. But those that buy count up their purchases and undoubtedly when the day of reckoning comes, they each come and pay the merchant what is owed, and both are satisfied.'

"Then my conductor smiled and said, 'Watch a little longer.'

"And I did as he said and stood and watched. And the same thing went on everywhere. Suddenly at my side a man dropped on his knees and bowed his head. And there arose a sound as of soft thunder, and everyone in the place dropped upon his knees and spread out his hands before him. Every voice and every noise was hushed and every movement had ceased.

"Then I whispered in his ear, 'It is the hour of prayer; shouldn't we kneel also?' And my guide answered, 'No man in the city kneels because another does, and no man is judged if he does not kneel.'

"For a few moments all was utter stillness—every man and woman was kneeling with hands outstretched, except him who had first kneeled, and his hands hung by his sides and his head was still bowed to the earth. At length he rose up, and his face was wet with tears, and all the others rose also. The man gave a bow to those around him, which they returned with reverence, and then, with downcast eyes, he walked slowly from the shop. The moment he was gone the business of the place began again as before.

"I went out at last with my guide and we seated ourselves under a tree on the bank of a quiet stream and I began to question him. 'Tell me, sir,' I said, 'the meaning of what I have seen. I do not yet understand how these happy people do their business without passing a single coin.'

"And he answered, 'Where greed and ambition and self-love rule, there must be money; where there is neither greed nor ambition nor self-love, money is useless.'

"And I asked, 'Is it by barter that they go about their affairs? For I saw no exchange of any sort.'

" 'No,' answered my guide, 'if you had gone into any shop in the city, you would have seen the same thing. Where no greed, ambition, or selfishness exists, need and desire can have free rein, for they can work no evil. Here men can give freely to whoever asks of him without thought of return, because all his own needs will be likewise supplied by others. By giving, each also receives. There are no advantages to be gained or sought. The sole desire is to more greatly serve. This world is contrary to your world. Everything here is upside down. The man here that does the greatest service, that helps others the most in the obtaining of their honest desires, is the man who stands in the highest regard with the Lord of the place, and his great reward and honor is to be enabled to spend himself yet more for the good of his fellows.

" 'There is even now a rumor among us that before long one shall be ripe to be enabled to carry a message from the King to the spirits that are in prison. That is indeed a strong incentive to stir up thought and energy to find things that will serve and minister to others, that will please their eyes and cheer their brains and gladden their hearts. So when one man asks, 'Give me, friend, of your loaves of bread,' the baker or shopkeeper may answer, 'Take of them, friend, as many as you need.' That is indeed a potent motive toward diligence. It is much stronger than the desire to hoard or excel or accumulate passing wealth. What a greater incentive it is to share the bliss of God who hoards nothing but always gives liberally.

" 'The joy of a man here is to give away what he has made,

to make glad the heart of another and in so doing, grow. This doctrine appears strange and unbelievable to the man in whom the will of life is yet sealed. There have never been many at a time in the old world who could thus enter into the joy of their Lord. Surely you know of a few in your world who are thus in their hearts, who would willingly consent to be as nothing, so to give life to their fellows. In this city so it is with everyone.'

"And I said, 'Tell me one thing: how much may a man have for the asking?'

" 'What he wants. What he can well use.'

" 'But what if he should turn to greed and begin to hoard?'

" 'Did you not see today the man because of whom all business ceased for a time? To that man had come the thought of accumulation instead of growth, and he dropped on his knees in shame and terror. And you saw how immediately that shop was made what below they call a church. For everyone hastened to the poor man's help. The air was filled with praying and the atmosphere of God-loving souls surrounded him, and the foul thought fled and the man went forth glad and humble, and tomorrow he will return for that which he needed. If you should be present then, you will see him all the more tenderly ministered unto.'

" 'Now I think I know and understand,' I answered, and we rose and went further."

"Could it be?" wondered the curate, breaking the silence that followed.

"Not in this world," asserted the draper.

"To doubt that it *could* be," declared the gatekeeper, "would be to doubt whether the kingdom of heaven be but a foolish fancy or a divine idea."[2]

The Temple of God

In the desert by the bush,
Moses to his heart said Hush.

David on his bed did pray;
God all night went not away.

From his heap of ashes foul
Job to God did lift his soul,

God came down to see him there,
And to answer all his prayer.

On a dark hill, in the wind,
Jesus did his Father find,

But while he on earth did fare,
Every spot was place of prayer;

And where man is any day,
God cannot be far away.

But the place he loveth best,
Place where he himself can rest,

Where alone he prayer doth seek,
Is the spirit of the meek.

To the humble God doth come;
In his heart he makes his home.

THE HEIRS OF HEAVEN

And he opened his mouth, and taught them, saying, Blessed are the poor in spirit: for theirs is the kingdom of heaven.

Matthew 5:2–3

Obedience Grows the Lord's Fruit

The words of the Lord are the seed sown by the sower. Into our hearts they must fall that they may grow. Meditation and prayer must water them, and obedience keeps them in the sunlight. Thus they will bear fruit for the Lord's gathering.

Those of his disciples, that is, obedient hearers, who had any experience in trying to live would at once understand these words, at least partially. But as they obeyed and pondered further, the meaning of his teachings would keep growing within their minds and hearts.

This we see in the writings of the apostles. It will be the same with us also—we who need to understand everything Jesus said neither more nor less than they to whom he first spoke so many centuries ago. In fact, our obligation to understand is far greater than theirs at the time, inasmuch as we have had nearly two thousand years' experience of the continued coming of the kingdom he then preached: it is not yet come; it has been all the time, and is now drawing slowly nearer.

The Gospel—Different Than Expected

The Sermon on the Mount, as it is commonly called, seems to have been the Lord's first free utterance, in the presence of any large assembly, of the good news of the kingdom.

He had been teaching his disciples and messengers, and had already brought the glad tidings that his Father was their Father, to many others—to Nathanael for one, to Nicodemus, to the woman of Samaria, to every one he had cured, every one whose cry for help he had heard. His epiphany was a gradual thing, beginning, where it continues today, with the individual.

It is impossible even to guess at what number may have heard him on this occasion: he seems to have gone up the mount because of the crowd—to secure a somewhat more open position from which he could better speak. And as he went, he was followed by those who desired to be taught by him, accompanied no doubt by a good number as well in whom curiosity was the chief motive. Disciple or the merely curious, he addressed the individuality of every one who had ears to hear. Peter, Andrew, James and John are the only recognized disciples, followers, and companions we know of at this time. But while his words were addressed to such as had come to him desiring to learn of him, the things he uttered were eternal truths. The life in the words was essential for every one of his Father's children, therefore the words were for all. He who heard in order to obey was his disciple.

How different, at the first sound of it, must the good news have been from the news anxiously expected by those who waited for the Messiah! Even John the Baptist in prison lay listening for something of quite another sort. Jesus had to send him a message, by eye-witnesses of his doings, to remind him that God's thoughts are not as our thoughts, nor his ways as our ways—that the design of God is other and better than the expectation of men. His summary of the gifts he was giving to men culminated with the preaching of the good news to the poor. Even if John had known beforehand that these were to be Jesus' doings, he would probably not have recognized them as belonging to the Lord's special mission. But the Lord tells John it is not enough to have accepted him as the Messiah, he must also recognize his doings as the work he had come into the world to do, their nature so divine as to be the very business of the Son of God in whom the Father was well pleased.

The Gospel Was **Good News**

What did the goodness of the news consist of which he opened his mouth to give them? What was in the news to make the poor glad? Why was his arrival with such words in his heart and mouth, the coming of the kingdom?

All good news from heaven is of *the truth*—essential truth, involving obedient duty, and with it giving and promising help to be able to carry it out. There can be no good news for us, except of uplifting love, and no one can be lifted up who will not rise. If God himself sought to raise his little ones without their consenting effort, they would drop from his foiled endeavor. He will carry us in his arms till we are able to walk. He will carry us in his arms when we are weary from walking. But he will not carry us if we will not walk.

Very different is the good news Jesus brings us from certain prevalent representations of the gospel, founded on the pagan notion that suffering is an offset for sin. This mistaken gospel—indeed, no Gospel at all—culminates in the nonsensical assertion that the suffering of an innocent man, just because he is innocent—perfect—is a satisfaction to the holy Father for the evil deeds of his children.

As a theory concerning the atonement, nothing could be worse—either intellectually, morally, or spiritually. Announced as the Gospel itself, as the good news of the kingdom of heaven, the idea is as monstrous as any Chinese dragon. Such a so-called Gospel is no gospel, no matter how good men of certain development accept it as God-sent. It is evil news, dwarfing, enslaving, maddening—news to the child-heart of the dreariest damnation.

Doubtless some elements of the true Gospel are mixed up with this other "gospel" on most occasions of its announcement. None the more does that make it the message received from God. It can be good news only to such as are prudently willing to be delivered from a God they fear, but unable to accept the Gospel of a perfect God, in whom they must trust perfectly.

The good news of Jesus was simply the news of the thoughts and ways of the Father in the midst of his family! He told them that the way men thought for themselves and their children was not the way God thought for himself and his children. He told them that the kingdom of heaven was founded, and must at length show itself founded, on very different principles from those of the kingdoms and families of the world, meaning by the world that part of the Father's family which will not be ordered by him, will not even try to obey him.

The world's man, he who is great and successful in the world's eyes, its honorable man, is he who may have and do what he pleases, whose strength lies in money and the praise of men. Contrarily, the greatest in the kingdom of heaven is the man who is humblest and serves his fellows the most. Multitudes of men, not known as particularly ambitious or proud, still hold the proud and ambitious man in honor, and hope for themselves some shadow of his prosperity. How many men, even Christians, look for the world to come, yet seek from the powers of *this* world the deliverance from its evils, as if God were the God of the world to come only!

The oppressed of the Lord's time looked for a Messiah to set their nation free and make it rich and strong. The oppressed of our time believe in money, knowledge, and the will of a people who with power would be in their turn the oppressor.

To Whom Does God's Kingdom Belong?

Upon this occasion on the mount, the first words of the Lord were: "Blessed are the poor in spirit, for theirs is the kingdom of heaven."

It is not the proud, it is not the greedy of distinction, it is not those who gather and hoard, not those who lay down the law to their neighbors, not those that condescend, any more than those that shrug the shoulder, that have any share in the kingdom of the Father. His kingdom has no relation with or resemblance to the kingdoms of this world. It deals with not one thing that distinguishes their rulers, except to repudiate them.

The Son of God will favor no smallest ambition, even if it be in the heart of him who leans on his bosom. The kingdom of God, the refuge of the oppressed, the golden age of the new world, the real utopia, the newest yet oldest Atlantis, the home of the children, will not open its gates to the most miserable whose aim it is to rise above his equal in misery, who looks down on any one more miserable than himself.

The kingdom of God is the home of perfect brotherhood. The poor, the beggars in spirit, the men of humble heart, the unambitious for selfish gain, the unselfish, those who never despise men and never seek their praises, the lowly who see nothing to admire in themselves and therefore who cannot seek to be admired of others, the men who give themselves and what they have away—*these* are the free men of the kingdom, *these* are the citizens of the new Jerusalem.

The men and women who are aware of their own essential poverty are the ones of whom Jesus spoke. Not those who are poor in friends, poor in influence, poor in acquirements, poor in money, but those who are poor "in spirit"—who *feel themselves poor creatures*—upon them the blessing rests. Those who know nothing for which to be pleased with themselves for, and desire nothing to make them think well of themselves, who know that they need little to make their life worth living, to make their existence a good thing, to make them fit to live—*these* humble ones are the poor whom the Lord calls blessed.

When a man says, "I am low and unworthy," then the gate of the kingdom begins to open to him. For at that gate enter the true, and this man has begun to know the truth concerning himself. Whatever such a man has attained to, he straightaway forgets; it is part of him and behind him, not something of which to be proud. His concern is with what he is not, with the things that lie above and before him. The man who is proud of any accomplishment has not reached it. He is only proud of himself, and imagining a cause for his pride. If he had truly reached something worthwhile, he would already have begun to forget, for he who delights in contemplating what he has attained is not merely sliding back, but is already in the dust of self-satisfaction. The gate of the kingdom is closed to him, and he is outside.

The child who, clinging to his Father, dares not think he has in any sense attained while he is not yet as his Father—his Father's heart, his Father's heaven is his natural home. To find himself thinking of himself as above his fellows would be to that child a shuddering terror. His universe would contract around him. The least motion of self-satisfaction, the first thought of placing himself in the forefront of estimation, would be to him as a flash of dread.

God is his Life and his Lord. That his Father should be content with him is his only concern. To his closest friends, he does not compare himself. Which is the greater is of no account to him. He would not choose to be less than his friend or neighbor; he would choose rather for the other to be greater than he. He looks up to everyone. Otherwise gifted than he, his neighbor is more than he. All come from the one mighty Father: shall he judge the thoughts of God, which is greater and which is less?

In thus denying, thus turning his back on himself, the man has no thought of saintliness, no thought but of his Father and his brothers. To such a child of God heaven's best secrets are open. He clambers about the throne of the Father unrebuked. His back is ready for the smallest heavenly playmate. His arms are an open refuge for any little lost black sheep of the Father's flock. He will toil with it up the heavenly stair, up the very steps of the great white throne, to lay it on the Father's knees. For the glory of that Father is not in knowing himself God, but in giving himself away—in creating and redeeming and glorifying his children.

Becoming Our Real Self

The man who does not house self has room to be his *real* self—God's eternal idea of him. He lives eternally. In virtue of the creative power present in him with moment by moment unimpeded creation, he *is*.

How should there be in him one thought of ruling or commanding or surpassing! He can imagine no bliss, no good in being greater than someone else. He is unable to wish himself other than he is, except more what God made him for, which is indeed the highest willing of the will of God.

His brother's well-being is essential to his bliss. The thought of standing higher in the favor of God than his brother would make him miserable. He would lift every brother and sister to the embrace of the Father.

Blessed are the poor in spirit, for they are of the same spirit as God, and by nature the kingdom of heaven is theirs.[1]

Finding Our True Self

A Fictional Selection from *Sir Gibbie*

Gibbie never thought about himself, therefore was there wide room for the entrance of the Spirit. Does the questioning thought arise to any reader: How could a man be conscious of bliss without the thought of himself? I answer the doubt: when a man turns to look at himself, that moment the glow of the loftiest bliss begins to fade: the pulsing fireflies throb paler in the passionate night; an unseen vapor steams up from the marsh and dims the star-crowded sky and the azure sea; and the next moment the very bliss itself looks as if it had never been more than a phosphorescent gleam—the summer lightning of the brain. For then the man sees himself but in his own dim mirror, whereas ere he turned to look in that, he knew himself in the absolute clarity of God's present thought around him. The shoots of glad consciousness that come to the obedient man surpass in bliss whole days and years of such ravined rapture as he gains whose weariness is ever spurring the sides of his intent towards the ever retreating goal of his desires. I am a traitor even to myself if I would live without my life.

But I withhold my pen; for vain were the fancy, by treatise, sermon, poem, or tale, to persuade a man to forget himself. He cannot, if he would. Sooner will he forget the presence of a raging toothache. There is no forgetting of ourselves but in the finding of our deeper, our true self—God's idea of us when he devised us—the Christ in us. Nothing but that self can displace the false, greedy, whining self, of which most of us are so fond and proud. And that true self no man can find for himself: seeing of himself he does not even know what to search for. "But as many as received him, to them gave he power to become the sons of God." [2]

Christmas Day and Every Day

Star high,
Baby low:
'Twixt the two
Wise men go;
Find the baby,
Grasp the star—
Heirs of all things
Near and far!

Knowing God Through the World's Suffering

A Fictional Selection from *The Marquis' Secret*

"But," said Lady Clementina, "is not generosity something more than duty—something higher, something beyond it?"

"Yes," answered Malcolm, "so long as it does not go against duty, but keeps in the same direction—is in harmony with it. I imagine as we grow, we shall come to see that generosity is but our duty. The man who chooses generosity at the expense of justice, even if he gives up everything of his own, is nothing beside the man who for the sake of right will even appear selfish in the eyes of men and may even, at times, go against his own heart. How two men may look—from the outside—is nothing."

Florimel made a neat little yawn over her work. Clementina's hands rested a moment in her lap, and she looked thoughtful. "Then you are taking the side of duty against generosity?" she said after a moment.

"Think, my lady," said Malcolm. "The essence of wrong is injustice. To help another by wrong is to do injustice to somebody else. What honest man could think of that twice?"

"Might not what he did be wrong in the abstract, without having reference to any person?"

"There is no wrong man can do but against the living Right. Surely you believe, my lady, that there is a living Power of right, who *will* have right done?"

"In plain language, I suppose you mean, do I believe in a God?"

"That is what I mean, if by a God you mean a being who cares about us and loves justice—that is, fair play—one whom, therefore, we wrong to the very heart when we do a thing that is not just."

"I would gladly believe in such a being if things were so that I could. As they are, I confess it seems to be the best thing to doubt it. How can I help doubting it when I see so much suffering, oppression and cruelty in the world?"

"I used to find that a difficulty. Indeed, it troubled me sorely, until Mr. Graham helped me see that ease and prosperity and comfort—indeed, the absence of those things you mentioned— are far from what God intends us to have. What if these things, or the lack of them, should be but the means of our gaining something in its very nature so much better that—"

"But why should a being have to suffer for that 'something better' you speak of? What kind of a God would make that 'the means' for our betterment? Your theory is so frightful!"

"But suppose he knows that the barest beginnings of the good he intends would reconcile us to those difficult means and even cause us to choose his will at any expense of suffering?"

Clementina said nothing for a moment. Religious people, she found, could think as boldly as she.

"I tell you, Lady Clementina," said Malcolm, rising and approaching her a step or two, "if I had not the hope of one day being good like God himself, if I thought there was no escape out of the wrong and badness I feel within me, not all the wealth and honors of the world could reconcile me to life."

"I have read of saints," said Clementina with yet a cool dissatisfaction in her tone, "uttering such sentiments, and I do not doubt such were imagined by them. But I fail to understand how, even supposing these things true, a young man like yourself should, in the midst of a busy world and with an occupation which, to say the least. . . ."

Here she paused. After a moment, Malcolm ventured to help her: " '. . . is so far from an ideal one,' would you say, my lady?

"Something like that," answered Clementina and concluded, "I wonder how *you* can have arrived at such ideas."

"There is nothing so unusual about it, my lady," returned Malcolm. "Why should not a youth, a boy, a child desire with all his might that his heart and mind should be clean, his will strong, his thoughts just, his head clear, his soul dwelling in the place of life? Why should I not desire that my life should be a complete thing and an outgoing of life to my neighbor?"

"Still, how did you come to begin so much earlier than others?"

"All I know, my lady, is that I had the best man in the world to teach me."

"And why did not I have such a man to teach me? I could have learned of such, too."

"If you are able now, my lady, it does not follow that it would have been the best thing for you sooner. Some learn far better for not having begun early and will get on faster than others who have been at it for years. As you grow ready for it, somewhere or other you will find what is needful for you in a book or a friend, or best of all, in your own thoughts."

"But I still want you to explain to me how the God in whom you profess to believe can make use of such cruelties?"

"My lady," remonstrated Malcolm, "I never pretended to explain. All I say is that if I had reasons for hoping there was a God and I found from my observations of life that suffering often was able to lead to a valued good, then there would be nothing unreasonable about his using suffering for the highest, purest, and kindest of motives. If a man would lay claim to being a lover of truth, he ought to give the idea—the mere idea—of God fair play, lest there should be a good God after all and he all his life has done him the injustice of refusing Him his trust and obedience."

"And how are we to give the mere idea of him fair play?" asked Clementina, by this time fighting with her emotions, confused and troublesome.

"By looking at the heart of whatever claims to be a revelation of him."

"It would take a lifetime to read the half of such."

All this time Florimel was working away at her embroidery, a little smile of satisfaction flickering on her face. She was pleased to hear her clever friend talking so with her strange vassal. As to what they were saying, she had no idea. Probably it was all right, but to her it was not interesting. She was mildly debating with herself whether she should tell her friend about Lenorme.

Clementina's work now lay on her lap and her hands on her work, while her eyes at one time gazed on the grass at her feet, at another searched Malcolm's face with a troubled look. The light of Malcolm's candle was beginning to penetrate into her dusky room, the power of his faith to tell upon the weakness of her unbelief. For there is no strength in unbelief.

But whatever the nature of Malcolm's influence upon lady Clementina, she resented it. Something in her did not like him, or was it his confidence. She knew he did not approve of her, and she did not like being disapproved of. Neither did she approve of him. He was far too good for an honest and brave youth.

Not that she could say she had seen dishonesty or cowardice in him, or that she could have told which vice she would prefer to season his goodness and thus bring him to the level of her ideal. And then, for all her theories of equality, he was a groom! Therefore, to a lady, he ought to be repulsive, at least when she found him intruding into the chamber of her thoughts!

For a time her eyes had been fixed on her work, and there had been silence in the little group.

"My lady," said Malcolm, and drew a step nearer to Clementina.

She looked up. How lovely she was with the trouble in her eyes! "If only she were what she might be!" he thought. "If the form were but filled with the Spirit, the body with life!"

"My lady" he repeated, a little embarrassed, "I fear you will never arrive at an understanding of God so long as you cannot bring yourself to see the good that often comes as a result of pain. For there is nothing, from the lowest, weakest tone of suffering to the loftiest acme of pain, to which God does not respond. There is nothing in all the universe which does not in some way vibrate within the heart of God. No creature suffers alone; he suffers with his creatures and through it is in the process of bringing his sons and daughters through the cleansing and glorifying fires, without which the created cannot be made the very children of God, partakers of the divine nature and peace."

"I cannot bring myself to see the right of it."

"Nor will you, my lady, so long as you cannot bring yourself to see the good they get by it. My lady, when I was trying my best with poor Kelpie, you would not listen to me."

"You are ungenerous," said Clementina, flushing.

"My lady," persisted Malcolm, "you would not understand me. You denied me a heart because of what seemed in your eyes cruelty. I knew I was saving her from death at least, probably from a life of torture. There is but one way God cares to govern—the way of the Father-King. Poor parable though it be, my relation to Kelpie must somehow parallel God's dealing with us. The temporary suffering is for a greater good."

After a few moments of silence, Clementina took up her work. Malcolm walked slowly away.[2]

Blessed Are the Meek, For They Shall Inherit the Earth

A quiet heart, submissive, meek,
  Father, do thou bestow,
Which more than granted, will not seek
  To have, or give, or know.

Each little hill then holds its gift
  Forth to my joying eyes;
Each mighty mountain then doth lift
  My spirit to the skies.

Lo, then the running water sounds
  With gladsome, secret things!
The silent water more abounds,
  And more the hidden springs.

Live murmurs then the trees will blend
  With all the feathered song;
The waving grass low tribute lend
  Earth's music to prolong.

The sun will cast great crowns of light
  On waves that anthems roar;
The dusky billows break at night
  In flashes on the shore.

Each harebell, each white lily's cup,
  The hum of hidden bee,
Yea, every odour floating up,
  The insect revelry—

Each hue, each harmony divine
  The holy world about.
Its soul will send forth into mine,
  My soul to widen out.

And thus the great earth I shall hold,
  A perfect gift of thine;
Richer by these, a thousandfold,
  Than if broad lands were mine.

The Heirs of the Earth

Blessed are the meek: for they shall inherit the earth.

Matthew 5:5

As the poor in spirit are of the kingdom of heaven, the meek shall inherit the earth. The same principle applies. The same law holds in the earth as in the kingdom of heaven.

How should it be otherwise? Has the Creator of the ends of the earth ceased to rule it after his fashion, because his rebellious children have so long, to their own hurt, vainly endeavored to rule it after theirs?

The kingdom of heaven belongs to the poor; the meek shall inherit the earth. The earth as God sees it, as those to whom the kingdom of heaven belongs also see it, is good, all good, very good, fit for the meek to inherit. And one day they shall inherit it—not indeed as men of the world count inheritance, but as the Maker and owner of the world has from the first counted it.

So different are the two ways of inheriting, that one of the meek may be heartily enjoying his possession, while one of the proud is selfishly crowding him out from the place in it that he loves best.

Who Are the Meek?

The meek are those who do not assert themselves, do not defend themselves, never dream of avenging themselves, or of returning anything but good for evil. They do not imagine it their business to take care of themselves.

The meek man may indeed take much thought, but it will not be for himself. He never builds an exclusive wall, shutting an honest neighbor out. He will not always serve the desire, but always the good of his neighbor. His service must be true service. Self shall be no umpire in his affairs.

Man's consciousness of himself is but a shadow: the meek man's self always vanishes in the light of a real presence. His nature lies open to the Father, and to every good impulse is, as it were, empty. No bristling importance, no vain attendance of fancied rights and wrongs guards his door or crowds the passages of his house; they are for angels to come and go.

Abandoned thus to the truth, as the sparks from the gleaming river dip into the flowers of Dante's unperfected vision, so the many souls of the visible world, lights from the Father of lights, enter his heart freely. And by them he inherits the earth he was created to inherit— possesses it as his Father made him capable of possessing, and the earth of being possessed.

Because the man is meek, his eye is single. He sees things as God sees them, as God would have his child see them: to confront creation with pure eyes is to possess it.

How little is the man able to make his own, who would ravish all! The man who would grasp any portion of the earth as his own, by the exclusion of others from the space he calls his, only fools himself in the attempt. The very bread he has swallowed cannot, thus, in any real sense be his. There does not exist such a power of possessing as he would demand. There is not such a sense of having as that which he has conceived the mere shadow of in his degenerate and lapsing imagination. The real owner of his domain might be that very peddler passing his gate. True possession is received with sweetness by the divine souls of the earth. And not all the greed of the so-counted possessor can keep it locked up within his walls, for the meek are ever growing in their power of possessing.

In no way will such inheritance interfere with the claim of the man who *calls* them his. Each possessor has his own inheritance, as much as each in his own way is capable of possessing it. For possession is determined by the kind and scope of the power of possessing, and the earth has a fourth dimension of which the mere owner of its soil knows nothing.

The child of the maker or builder is naturally the inheritor of his father's things. But if the child try to possess as a house the thing his father has made an organ, will he truly succeed in possessing it? If he nestles down in a corner of the organ case, will he by any means benefit from the organ's multiplex harmony? Will he not by using it for a house render its value as an organ useless? The poverty of such a child belongs to all those who think to have and to hold after the corrupt fancies of a greedy self.

True Vision Reserved for the Meek

We cannot see the world as God means it, except in proportion as our souls are meek.

Only in meekness are we the world's inheritors. Meekness alone makes the spiritual retina pure to receive God's things as they are, mingling with them neither imperfection nor impurity of its own.

A thing so beheld that it conveys to me the divine thought inherent in its very form, that thing is truly mine. Nothing can be mine in any way but through its mediation between God and my life. The man so dull as to insist that a thing is his because he has bought and paid for it had better consider that not all the combined forces of law, justice, and goodwill can keep it his, while even death cannot take the world from the man who possesses it as alone the Maker of him and it cares that he should possess it.

The one man leaves it but carries it with him. The other carries with him only its loss. He passes, unable to close hand or mouth upon any portion of it. Its *ownership* to him was only the changes he could make in it, and the nearness to which he could bring it to the body he lived in. That body the earth in its turn now possesses, and it lies very still, changing nothing, but being changed. Is this the fine of the great buyer of land, to have his fine face full of fine dirt?

In the soul of the meek, the earth remains an endless possession—his because God, who made it, is his—his because nothing but his Maker could ever truly belong to the creature. He has the earth by his divine relation to him who sent it forth from him as a tree sends out its leaves. To inherit the earth is to grow ever more alive to the presence, in it and in all its parts, of him who is the life of men.

How far one may advance in such inheritance while yet in the body will simply depend upon the meekness he attains while yet in the body. But it may be, as some servants of God think, that the new heavens and the new earth are the same in which we now live, righteously inhabited by the meek, with their more deeply opened eyes.

What if the meek among the dead be thus possessing it even now! But I do not care to speculate. It is enough that the man who refuses to assert himself, seeking no recognition by men, leaving the care of his life to the Father, and occupying himself with the will of the Father, shall find himself, by and by, at home in his Father's house, with all the Father's property his.[1]

GIBBIE WAS ONE OF THE MEEK AND INHERITED THE EARTH

A Fictional Selection from *Sir Gibbie*

And now indeed it was a blessed time for Gibbie. It had been pleasant down in the valley, with the cattle and Donal, and foul weather sometimes; but now it was the full glow of summer; the sweet keen air of the mountain bathed him as he ran, entered into him, filled him with life like the new wine of the kingdom of God, and the whole world rose in its glory around him. Surely it is not the outspread sea, however the sight of its storms and its laboring ships may enhance the sense of safety to the on-looker, but the outspread land of peace and plenty, with its nestling houses, its well-stocked yards, its cattle feeding in the meadows, and its men and horses at labor in the fields, that gives the deepest delight to the heart of the poet! Gibbie was one of the meek, and inherited the earth. Throned on the mountain, he beheld the multiform "goings on of life," and in love possessed the whole. He was of the poet-kind also, and now that he was a shepherd, saw everything with shepherd-eyes. One moment, to his fancy, the great sun above played the shepherd to the world, the winds were the dogs, and the men and women the sheep. The next, in higher mood, he would remember the good shepherd of whom Janet had read to him, and pat the head of the collie that lay beside him: Oscar too was a shepherd and no hireling: he fed the sheep; he turned them from danger and barrenness; and he barked well.

Gibbie was always placing what he heard by the side, as it were, of what he knew; asking himself, in this case and that, what Jesus Christ would have done, or what he would require of a disciple.

When he sank foiled from any endeavour to understand how a man was to behave in certain circumstances, these or those, he always took refuge in *doing* something—and doing it better than before; leaped the more eagerly if Robert called him, spoke the more gently to Oscar, turned the sheep more carefully not to scare them—as if by instinct he perceived that the only hope of understanding lies in doing. He would cleave to the skirt when the hand seemed withdrawn; he would run to do the thing he had learned yesterday, when as yet he could find no answer to the question of today. Thus, as the weeks of solitude and love and thought and obedience glided by, the reality of Christ grew upon him, till he saw the very rocks and heather and the faces of the sheep like him, and felt his presence everywhere, and ever coming nearer. Nor did his imagination aid only a little in the growth of his being. He would dream waking-dreams about Jesus, gloriously childlike. He fancied he came down every now and then to see how things were going in the lower part of his kingdom; and that when he did so, he made use of Glashgar and its rocks for his stairway, coming down its granite scale in the morning, and again, when he had ended his visit, going up in the evening by the same steps. Then high and fast would his heart beat at the thought that some day he might come upon his path just when he had passed, see the heather lifting its head from the trail of his garment, or more slowly out of the prints left by his feet, as he walked up the stairs of heaven, going back to his Father.[2]

This Side an' That

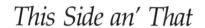

The rich man sat in his father's seat—
    Purple an' linen, an' a'thing fine!
The puir man lay at his yett i' the street—
    Sairs an' tatters, an weary pine!

To the rich man's table ilk dainty comes,
    Mony a morsel gaed frae't, or fell;
The puir man fain wud hae dined on the crumbs,
    But whether he got them I canna tell.

Servants prood, saft-fittit, an' stoot,
    Stan by the rich man's curtained doors;
Maisterless dogs 'at rin aboot
    Cam to the puir man an' lickit his sores.

The rich man deeit, an' they buried him gran',
    In linen fine his body they wrap;
But the angels tuik up the beggar man
    An' layit him doun in Abraham's lap.

The guid upo' this side, the ill upo' that—
    Sic was the rich man's waesome fa'!
But his brithers they eat, an' they drink, an' they chat,
    An' carena a strae for their Father's ha'!

The trowth's the trowth, think what ye will;
    An' some they kenna what they wad be at;
But the beggar man thoucht he did no that ill,
    Wi' the dogs o' this side, the angels o' that!

TRUE POSSESSION

When goods increase . . . what good is there to the owners thereof, saving the beholding of them with their eyes? . . . As he came forth of his mother's womb, naked shall he return to go as he came, and shall take nothing of his labor, which he may carry away in his hand.

Ecclesiastes 5:11, 15

Books, Houses, and Lands

Which is more the possessor of the world—he who has a thousand houses, or he who, without one house to call his *own*, has ten in which his knock at the door would rouse instant jubilation?

Which is the richer—the man who, his huge fortune spent, would have no refuge, or he for whose necessity a hundred would sacrifice comfort?

Which of the two possessed the earth—King Agrippa or the tentmaker Paul?

Which is the real possessor of a book—the man who has its original and every subsequent edition, and shows to many an admiring and envying visitor first one, then another characteristic binding with possessor pride; who is even able to draw forth from safekeeping and display the author's first manuscript, with the very thoughts and musings from which his thoughts came forth to the light of day—or, is it the man who cherishes one little, hollow-backed, coverless, untitled, bethumbed copy, which he takes with him on his solitary walks and broods over in his silent chamber, always finding in it some beauty or excellence or aid he had not found before, the book being to him in truth as a live companion? Which man, I say, truly possesses the book?

For what makes the thing a book? Is it not that it has a soul—the mind of him who wrote the book? Therefore only can the book itself— its soul, its mind, not its mere external body—be possessed, for life alone can be the possession of life. The dead possess their dead only to bury them.

Inheriting the Earth

Does not he who loves and understands and grows inwardly from his book possess it with such possession as is impossible to the man who is enamored with his ownership of its shell?

Just so may the world itself be possessed—either as a volume unread, or as the wine of a soul, "the precious lifeblood of a master-spirit, embalmed and treasured up on purpose to a life beyond life." It may be possessed as a book filled with words from the mouth of God, or as the mere golden-clasped covers of that book; as an embodiment or incarnation of God himself, or simply as a house built to sell. The Lord loved the world and the things of the world, not as the men of the world love them, but finding his Father in everything that came from his Father's heart.[1]

Books themselves are only things that pass and perish; and he who loves them as possessions must see them vanish from him as certainly as any other form of earthly having. Love alone lives and causes all other truth to take shape, conscious or unconscious. But God lets men have their playthings, as the children they are, that they may learn to distinguish them from true possessions. If they are not learning that, he takes them from them and tries the other way: for lack of them and its misery, they will perhaps seek the true.[2]

The same spirit, then, is required for possessing the kingdom of heaven and for inheriting the earth. How should it not be so when the one Power is the informing life of both? If we are the Lord's we possess the kingdom of heaven, and so inherit the earth. How many who call themselves by his name would have it otherwise: they would rather possess the earth and inherit the kingdom! Such as these fill our churches every Sunday: anywhere is suitable for the worship of Mammon.

Yet to be sure, earth as well as heaven may be largely possessed even now.

Two Responses to the World

Two men are walking outside together. To the one, the world yields thought after thought of delight. He sees heaven and earth embrace one another. He feels an indescribable presence over and in them.

Later, when he is alone in the solitude of his chamber, his joy will break forth into song.

To the other, oppressed with the thought of his poverty, or ruminating about how to make the much he has into more, the glory of the Lord is but a warm summer day. It enters in at no window of his soul. If offers him no gift, for, though he is walking in the very temple of God, he looks for no God in it.

Nor must there necessarily be two men to think and feel thus differently. In what diverse fashion will anyone who is subject to ever-changing moods and emotions see the same world of the same glad Creator, at different times! How sad it would be for us all if the world changed as we change, if it grew meaningless when we grow faithless! Thought for a tomorrow that may never come, dread of the dividing death which really means endless companionship, anger with one we love—all these cloud the radiant morning, and make the day dark with night.

But then at evening—having reflected with ourselves about the day, and having returned to him that feeds the ravens and watches the dying sparrow, and says to his children, "Love one another"—we find the sunset splendor glad over us, the western sky refulgent as the court of the Father, when the glad news is spread abroad that a sinner has repented.

We have mourned in the twilight of our little faith, but, having sent away our sin, the glory of God's heaven over his darkening earth has comforted us.[3]

Things Are Mere Shadows to Train Us in True Possession

Possessions are *things*. And *things* in general are very apt to prove hostile to the better life. The man who for consciousness of well-being depends upon anything but life—the life essential—is a slave. He clings to what is less than himself. He cannot be perfect until, deprived of every*thing*, he can remain calm and content, aware of a well-being untouched; for in no other way would he be possessor of all things, the child of the Eternal.

Things are given to us, this body the first such "thing," that through them we may be trained both to independence and true possession of them. We must possess them; they must not possess us.

Their use is to mediate—as earthly forms and manifestations of the things that are unseen, things in themselves unseeable, that belong not to the world of speech, but to the world of silence, not to the world of showing, but to the world of being, the world that cannot be shaken, and must remain.

These things, unseen, take form in the things of time and space—not in order that they may exist, for they exist in and from the eternal Godhead, but that their being may be known to those in training for the eternal. These unseen things the sons and daughters of God must come to possess. But often, instead of reaching out for the unseen, they grasp at the forms, regarding the things *seen* as the things to be possessed. They fall in love with the "bodies" instead of the "souls" of them.

There are good people who can hardly believe that if the rich young ruler had consented to give up his wealth, the Lord would not then have told him to keep it. They seem to think the treasure in heaven insufficient as a substitute for earthly wealth. They cannot believe he would have been better off without his wealth. The multitude of those who thus read the tale are of the same mind as the youth himself—in his worst moment, as he turned and went—with one vast difference: they are not sorrowful.[4]

Things go wrong because men have such absurd and impossible notions about *possession*. They are always trying to possess, to call their own, things which it is impossible, from their very nature, ever to possess or to make their own.[5]

All is man's *because* it is God's. The true possession of anything is to see and feel in it what God made it for; and the uplifting of the soul by that knowledge is the joy of true having. The Lord had no land of his own. He did not care to have it, any more than the twelve legions of angels he would not pray for. He had no place to lay his head—had not even a grave of his own. Once he sent a fish to fetch him money, but only to pay a tax. He even had to borrow the few loaves and little fishes with which to feed his five thousand from a boy. Things are ours that we may use them for all—sometimes that we may sacrifice them. God had but one precious thing, and he gave that![6]

In all God's works the laws of beauty are wrought out in vanishing portrayals, in birth and death. In these there is no hoarding, but an everfresh creating, an eternal flow of life from the heart of the All-beautiful. Hence, even the heart of man cannot hoard. His brain or his hand may gather into its box and hoard, but the moment the thing has passed into the box, the heart has lost it and is hungry again. If man would truly *have*, it is the Giver he must have; the eternal, the original, the ever-outpouring is then alone within his reach; the everlasting *creation* is his heritage. Therefore, all that God makes must be free to come and go through the heart of his child; the child can enjoy it only as it passes, can enjoy only its life, its soul, its vision, its meaning, not itself.[7]

To be lord of space, a man must be free of all bonds to place. To be heir of all things, his heart must have no *things* in it. He must be like him who makes things, not like one who would put everything in his pocket. He must stand on the upper, not the lower side of them. He must be as the man who makes poems, not the man who gathers books of poems. God, having made a sunset, lets it pass, and makes such a sunset no more. He has no picture gallery, no library. What if in heaven men shall be so busy growing that they have no time to write or to read![8]

The Tyranny of False Possession

Things can never really be possessed by the man or woman who cannot do without them.

Absolute divine contentment comes with the consciousness that the cause of being is within. No man can have the consciousness of God with him and not be content. The man who has not the Father, so as to be eternally content in him alone, cannot possess a sunset or a field of grass or a mine of gold or the love of a fellow-creature according to its nature—as God would have him possess it—in the eternal way of inheriting, having, and holding.

He who has God has all things, after the fashion in which he who made them has them. To man, woman, and child, I say—if you are not content, it is because God is not with you as you need him, not with you as he would be with you, as you *must* have him. For you need him as your body never needed food or air. You need him as your soul never hungered after joy or peace or pleasure. You need him far more than all these.

It is imperative that we rid ourselves of the tyranny of *things*!

See how imperative: let the young man cling with every fiber to his wealth; what God can do, he will do. His child shall not be left in the hell of possession. The angel of death will come—and now where are the things that haunted the poor soul with such manifold hindrance and obstruction! The world, and all that is in the world drops and slips from his feet, from his hands, carrying with it his body, his eyes, his ears, every purse, every safe that could delude him with the fancy of possession.

Death Helps Free Us

It is death then that thus frees and ransoms a man from the dominion of things. Then first, I presume, does the man of things become aware of their tyranny. When a man begins to abstain from anything, then for the first time he recognizes the strength of his passion. It may be that when a man has not a single thing left, he will begin to know what a necessity he had made of things. And if *then* he will begin to contend with them, to cast out of his soul what death has torn from his hands, then first will he know the full passion of possession, the slavery of prizing the worthless part of the precious.

"What good is death?" you ask. "I thought death ended our struggles. You make it sound as though then our torment begins!"

Perhaps so. But what healing there is in the torment! What healing in the falling off of those chains of possession!

Do you think it is the fetters that hurt and gall? No, the fetters of possession soothe while they eat into the soul. But when death comes, and the chains of gold are gone on which the man delighted to gaze, though they held him fast to his dungeon wall, buried from air and sunshine, *then* first he will truly begin to feel them in the soreness of their lack, in the weary indifference with which he looks on earth and sea and space and stars.

When the truth begins to dawn upon him that those chains were a horror and a disgrace, then will the good of saving death appear. Then will the man begin to understand that *having* never was, never could be well-being. Then he will know that it is not by possessing we live, but by life we possess. In this way is the loss of the things he thought he had a motion toward deliverance. It may seem to the man the first of his slavery when it is in truth the beginning of his freedom. Never a soul was set free without being made to feel its slavery. Nothing but itself can enslave a soul, nothing without itself free it.

When the drunkard, free of his body, but retaining his desire for drink yet unable to indulge it, has time at length to think, in the lack of the means of destroying thought, surely there dawns for him then at last a fearful hope! Not until, by the power of God and his own obedient effort, he is raised into such a condition that, be the temptation what it might, he would not yield for an immortality of unrequited drunkenness—all its delights and not one of its penalties—is he saved.

Thus death may give a new opportunity—with some hope for the multitude counting themselves Christians who are possessed by *things* as by a legion of devils. These are they whose standing in church is high, whose lives are regarded as stainless, who may even be kind and friendly, who give perhaps of their money, who believe in the redemption of Jesus, and talk of the salvation of the world through the church—and yet whose care all the time is to heap up, to make much into more, to add house to house and field to field, burying themselves deeper and deeper in the ash heap of *things*.

But it is not only the rich man who is under the dominion of things. They too are slaves who, having no money, are unhappy from lack of it. The man who is always digging his grave is little better than he who already lies molding in it.[9]

The Giver

*To give a thing and take again
Is counted meanness among men;
To take away what once is given
Cannot then be the way of heaven!*

*But human hearts are crumbly stuff,
And never, never love enough,
Therefore God takes and, with a smile,
Puts our best things away a while.*

*Thereon some weep, some rave, some scorn,
Some wish they never had been born;
Some humble grow at last and still,
And then God gives them what they will.*

Do We Love the Inside or the Outside?

A Fictional Selection from *The Curate's Awakening*

B ut let me tell you a strange dream I had not long ago."
Rachel's face brightened. She rose, got a little stool, and setting it down close by the chair on which her uncle was perched, seated herself at his feet to listen.

"About two years ago," related Polwarth, "a friend sent me Tauchnitz's edition of the English New Testament, which has the different readings of the three oldest known manuscripts translated at the foot of the page. I received it with such exultation that it brought on an attack of asthma, and I could scarcely open it for a week but lay with it under my pillow. Any person who loves books would understand the ecstasy I felt. Why, Mr. Wingfold, just to hold that book in my hands—I can scarcely describe the pleasure it brought me, such a prize did I consider that gift. I suppose a cherished possession of any kind would have that same effect on anyone. But for me there has never been anything quite like an old book or a revered edition of the Scriptures. In any case, such was my reaction to the New Testament I received. And when I eventually was able to study it more closely, my main surprise was to find the differences from the common version so *few* and so *small*.

"You can hardly imagine my delight in the discoveries this edition gave me. The contents within its handsome leather covers outran the anticipation I had felt as I first held it between my hands. I mention all this because it goes to account for the dream that followed and to enforce its truth. Do not, however, imagine me a believer in dreams more than any other source of mental impressions. If a dream reveals a principle, that principle is a revelation, and the dream is neither more nor less valuable than a waking thought that does the same. The truth conveyed is the revelation, not the dream.

"The dream I am now going to tell you was clearly led up to by my waking thoughts. I dreamed that I was in a desert. It was neither day nor night. I saw neither sun, moon, nor stars. A heavy yet half-luminous cloud hung over the earth. My heart was beating fast and high, for I was journeying toward an isolated Armenian convent, where I had good ground for hoping I would find the original manuscript of the fourth Gospel, the very handwriting of the Apostle John. That the old man did not actually write it himself, I never considered in my dream. The excitement mounting inside me was the same dreaming sensation as the gift from my friend had caused in my waking emotions.

"After I had walked on for a long time, I saw the level horizon before me broken by a rock, as it seemed, rising from the plain of the desert. I knew it was the monastery. It was many miles away, and as I journeyed on, it grew and grew, until it became huge as a hill against the sky. At length I came to the door, iron-clamped, deep-set in a low, thick wall. It stood wide open. I entered, crossed a court, reached the door of the monastery itself, and again entered. Every door to which I came stood open, but no guide came to meet me. I used my best judgment to get deeper and deeper into the building, for I scarce doubted that in its innermost chamber I should find the treasure I sought. At last I stood before a huge door hung with a curtain of rich workmanship, torn in the middle from top to bottom. Through the rent I passed into a stone cell. In the cell stood a table. On the table was a closed book.

"Oh! how my heart beat! Never but in that moment had I known the feeling of utter preciousness in a thing possessed. What doubts and fears would not this one lovely, oh! unutterably beloved volume, lay at rest forever! How my eyes would dwell upon every stroke of every letter formed by the hand of the dearest disciple! Nearly eighteen hundred years—and there it lay! Here was a man who actually *heard* the Master say the words and then wrote them down!

"I stood motionless and my soul seemed to wind itself among the pages, while my body stood like a pillar of salt, lost in amazement. At last, with sudden daring, I made a step toward the table. Bending with awe, I stretched out my hand to lay it on the book. But before my hand reached it, another hand, from the opposite side of the table, appeared upon it—an old, blue-veined, but powerful hand. I looked up.

"There stood the beloved disciple! His countenance was as a mirror which shone back the face of the Master. Slowly he lifted the book and turned away. Then I saw behind him as it were an altar where a fire of wood was burning, and a pang of dismay shot to my heart, for I knew what he was about to do. He laid the book on the burning wood, and regarded it with a smile as it shrank and shrivelled and smoldered to ashes. Then he turned to me and said, while a perfect heaven of peace shone in his eyes: 'Son of man, the Word of God lives and abides forever, not in the volume of the book, but in the heart of the man that in love obeys him.' And then I awoke weeping, but with the lesson of my dream."

A deep silence settled on the little company. Finally Wingfold said, "I trust I have the lesson too."

He rose, shook hands with them, and, without another word, went home.[10]

The Healer

They come to thee, the halt, the maimed, the blind,
   The devil-torn, the sick, the sore;
Thy heart their well of life they find,
   Thine ear their open door.

Ah, who can tell the joy in Palestine—
   What smiles and tears of rescued throngs!
Their lees of life were turned to wine,
   Their prayers to shouts and songs!

The story dear our wise men fable call,
   Give paltry facts the mighty range;
To me it seems just what should fall,
   And nothing very strange.

But were I deaf and lame and blind and sore,
   I scarce would care for cure to ask;
Another prayer should haunt thy door—
   Set thee a harder task.

If thou art Christ, see here this heart of mine,
   Torn, empty, moaning, and unblest!
Had ever heart more need of thine,
   If thine indeed hath rest?

Thy word, thy hand right soon did scare the bane
   That in their bodies death did breed;
If thou canst cure my deeper pain
   Then art thou Lord indeed.

To Know the Father, Obey the Son

He that hath seen me hath seen the Father . . . I am in the Father, and the Father in me . . . If ye love me, keep my commandments.

John 14:9, 10, 15

Man's Trouble

I would like to help some of my readers understand what Jesus came from the home of our Father to be to us and do for us.

Everything in the world is more or less misunderstood at first. We have to learn what it is, and come at length to see that it must be so, and that it could not be otherwise. *Then* we know it. And we never know a thing *really* until we know it thus.

I presume there is scarcely a human being who, if he was speaking openly and honestly, would not confess to something which plagued him, something from which he would like to be free, something which makes life at the moment not an altogether good or pleasant thing. Most people imagine that life would become a wonderful and altogether satisfying thing if they could only be free of such troubles and problems as they have.

The causes of their discomfort are of all kinds. The degrees of it reach from simple uneasiness to absolute misery, such as makes even death a pleasant hope. Perhaps the greater part of the energy of this world's life is spent in the endeavor to rid itself of these infinite discomforts that plague us on this earth.

To escape them, some strive with strong and continuous effort to keep rising in the social scale, only to discover at every new ascent fresh trouble, as they think, awaiting them; in truth, they have brought the trouble with them. Others, making haste to be rich, are slow to find out that the poverty of their souls, even though their pocketbooks and bank accounts are filling, will yet keep them unhappy. Some seek endless change, not realizing that the only change that will set them free is the change that must come to pass within themselves. Others expand their souls with knowledge, only to find that contentment will not dwell in the great house they have built.

To number the varieties of human endeavor to escape discomfort would be to enumerate all the modes of such life as does not know how to live. Everyone is seeking the thing whose defect appears to be the *cause* of their misery, but is in reality only the variable and changing *result* of it—the cause of the shape it takes, not the misery itself. For the moment one apparent cause of misery is removed, another at once quickly takes its place.

The real cause of his trouble is something the man or woman has not perhaps recognized as even existing. And even if he does know of its existence, in any case, he is not yet acquainted with its true nature.

The Root and Only Cure

The statement may appear absurd to one who has not yet discovered the fact for himself, but the cause of every man's discomfort is evil, moral evil—first of all, evil in himself, his own sin, his own wrongness, his own unrightness.

No special sin may be recognized as having caused this or that special physical discomfort, which may indeed have originated with some ancestor. But evil in ourselves is the cause of its continuance, the source of its necessity, and the preventive of that longsuffering which would soon take from it, or at least blunt, its sting. The evil is *essentially* unnecessary, and will ultimately pass with the attainment of the object for which it is permitted—namely, the development of a pure will in man. The suffering accompanying it also is essentially unnecessary, but while the evil lasts, the suffering, whether consequent or merely accompanying it, is absolutely necessary.

Foolish are those who would set the world right by waging war on its evils, while neglecting their own inner character and conduct. The philanthropist who regards the wrong as in the race, forgetting that the race is made up of conscious and wrong individuals, forgets also that wrong is always generated in and done by an individual. Wrongness exists in the individual, and by him is passed on, as tendency toward wrong, to the entire race.

But no evil can be cured in mankind except by its being cured in individual men and women. *Tendency* is not absolute evil. The tendency is there that it may be resisted, not yielded to. There is no way of making three men right but by making right each one of the three. But a cure in one man who repents and turns is a beginning of the cure of the whole human race.

Even if a man's suffering be a fair inheritance, for the curing of which by faith and obedience this life would not be sufficiently long, faith and obedience will yet render it endurable to the man, and overflow in help to his fellow-sufferers. The groaning body, wrapped in the garment of hope, will, with outstretched neck, look for its redemption, and endure.

The one cure for any being is to be set right—to have all its parts brought into harmony with each other. The one comfort is to know that this cure is in process. Rightness alone is cure. To free a man or woman from suffering, he or she must be set right, put in health. And the health at the root of man's being, his rightness, is to be free from wrongness, that is, from sin. The wrong, the evil is *in* him. He must be set free from it. To do this for us, Jesus was born, and remains born to all the ages.

We Know the Father by Obeying the Son

It may be my reader will desire me to say *how* the Lord will save him from his sin. That is like the lawyer's question, "Who is my neighbor?" The spirit of such a mode of receiving the offer of the Lord's deliverance is the root of all the horrors of a corrupt theology, so acceptable to those who love weak and beggarly primer books of religion. Such questions spring from the passion for the fruit of the tree of knowledge, not the fruit of the tree of life.

Men would understand; they do not care to *obey*. They try to understand where it is impossible they could understand except by obeying. They would search into the work of the Lord instead of doing their part in it—thus making it impossible for the Lord to go on with his work, and for themselves to become capable of seeing and understanding what he does. Instead of immediately obeying the Lord of life, the one condition upon which he can help them, and in itself the beginning of their deliverance, they set themselves to question their unenlightened intellects as to his plans for their deliverance—and not merely how he means to carry it out, but whether he is able to carry it out. They would bind their Samson until they have scanned his limbs and muscles. They delay in setting their foot on the stair that alone can lead them to the house of wisdom until they shall have determined the material and mode of its construction.

For the sake of knowing, they postpone that which alone can enable them to know, and substitute for the true understanding that lies beyond, a false persuasion that they already understand. They will not accept, that is, act upon, their highest privilege, that of obeying the Son of God.

It is on them that do his will that the day dawns. To them the Daystar rises in their hearts. *Obedience is the soul of knowledge.*

The Folly of Trying to Know God Apart From Obeying Him

By obedience, I intend no kind of obedience to man, or submission to authority claimed by man or community of men. I mean obedience to the will of the Father, however revealed in our conscience.

God forbid I should seem to despise understanding. The New Testament is full of urgings to understand. What I cry out upon is the misunderstanding that comes of man's endeavor to understand while not obeying.

Upon obedience must our energy be spent; understanding will follow. Not anxious to know our duty, or knowing it and not doing it, how shall we understand that which only a true heart and a clean soul can ever understand? The power in us that would understand if it were free lies in the bonds of imperfection and impurity and is therefore incapable of judging the divine. It cannot see the truth. If it could see it, it would not know it, and would not have it.[1]

There is no teacher like obedience, and no obstruction like its postponement.[2] When men can *act*, can *obey*, can face a duty, life itself will *immediately* begin to gather interest. For only in duty, action, and obedience does a person begin to come into real contact with life; and only in them can he see what life is, and grow fit for it.[3] When you have a thing to do, you will do it right in proportion to your love of right. Do the truth and you will love the truth. For by doing it you will see it as it is, and no one can see the truth as it is without loving it. The more you *talk* about what is right, or even talk about doing it, the more danger you are in of turning it into unpracticed theory. Talk without action saps the very will. Something you have to do is waiting undone all the time you are talking, and getting more and more undone. The only refuge is *to do.*[4]

But it is a happy thing for us that all we really have to concern ourselves with is—what to do *next.* No man can do the second thing.

He can only do the first. If he omits that, the wheels of time roll over him and leave him powerless behind. If he does it, he keeps in front and finds room to do the next thing and so is sure to arrive at something in due time. Let a man lay hold of something—anything—and he is on the high road.[5] We do not understand the *next* page of God's lesson book; we see only the one before us; nor shall we be allowed—it is indeed impossible we should do it—to turn the leaf until we have learned the lesson of that before us: when we understand the one before us, only then are we able to turn the next. The Perfect Heart could never have created us except to make us wise, loving, obedient, honorable children of our Father in Heaven.[6]

It is a joy to think that a man may, while still unsure about God, yet be coming close to him! How else should we be saved at all? For God alone is our salvation; to know him is salvation. He is in us all the time, else we could never move to seek him. It is true that only by perfect faith in him can we be saved, for nothing but perfect faith in him is salvation. There is no good but him, and not to be one with that good by perfect obedience is to be unsaved; the poorest *desire* to draw near him *is* an approach to him.[7]

Until a man begins to obey, the light that is in him is darkness. If, instead of doing what he is told he broods, speculating on the metaphysics of him who calls him to his work, he stands leaning his back against the door by which the Lord would enter to help him. The moment he sets about putting straight the thing that is crooked—I mean doing right where he has been doing wrong, he withdraws from the entrance, and gives way for the Master to come in. He cannot make himself pure, but he can leave that which is impure. He cannot save himself, but he can let the Lord save him.[8]

MANY SPECULATE; FEW SET THEMSELVES TO DO

A Fictional Selection from *The Marquis' Secret*

A nd Malcolm?" rejoined the schoolmaster softly. "Should you say of him that he showed equal wisdom?"

"I decline to give an opinion upon the gentleman's part in the business," answered Clementina, laughing, but glad there was so little light in the room, for she was painfully conscious of the burning of her cheeks. "Beside, I have no measure to apply to Malcolm," she went on a little hurriedly. "He is like no one I have ever talked with, and I confess there is something about him I cannot understand. Indeed, he is beyond me altogether."

"Perhaps, having known him from infancy, I might be able to explain him," returned Mr. Graham in a tone that invited questioning.

"Perhaps, then," said Clementina, "I may be permitted, in jealousy for the teaching I have received of him, to confess my bewilderment that one so young should be capable of dealing with such things as he delights in. The youth of the prophet makes me doubt his prophecy."

"At least," rejoined Mr. Graham, "the phenomenon coincides with what the Master of these things said of them—that they were revealed to babes and not to the wise and prudent. As to Malcolm's wonderful facility in giving them form and utterance, that depends so immediately on the clear sight of them that, granted a little of the poetic gift developed through reading and talk, we need not wonder much at it."

"You consider your friend a genius?" asked Clementina.

"I consider him possessed of a kind of heavenly common sense. A thing not understood lies in his mind like a fretting foreign body. But there is a far more important factor concerned than this exceptional degree of insight. Understanding is the reward of obedience. Obedience is the key to every door. I am perplexed at the stupidity of the ordinary religious being. In the most practical of all matters he will talk and speculate and try to feel, but he will not set himself to *do*. It is different with Malcolm. From the first he has been trying to obey. Nor do I see why it should be strange that even a child should understand these things. If a man may not understand the things of God whence he came, what shall he understand?"

"How, then, is it that so few understand?"

"Because where they know, so few obey. This boy, I say, did. If you had seen, as I have, the almost superhuman struggles of his will to master the fierce temper his ancestors gave him, you would marvel less at what he has so early become. I have seen him white with passion, cast himself on his face on the shore and cling with his hands to the earth as if in a paroxysm of bodily suffering, then after a few moments rise and do a service to the man who had wronged him. Is it any wonder that the light should so soon spring forth in a soul like that? When I was a younger man, I used to go out with the fishing boats now and then, drawn chiefly by my love for the boy who earned his own bread that way before he was in his teens. One night we were caught in a terrible storm and had to stand out to sea in the pitch dark. He was not then fourteen. 'Can you let a boy like that steer?' I said to the captain. 'Yes, a boy like that's just the right kind,' he answered. 'Malcolm'll steer as straight as a porpoise because there's no fear of the sea in him.' When the boy was relieved, he crept over to where I sat. 'You're not afraid, Malcolm?' I asked. 'Afraid?' he rejoined with some surprise. 'I wouldn't want to hear the Lord say, *"O you of little faith!"* ' 'But,' I persisted, 'God may mean to drown you.' 'And why not?' he returned. 'If you were to tell me I might be drowned without His meaning it, then I should be frightened enough.' Believe me, my lady, the right way is simple to find, though only they that seek it can find it. But I have allowed myself," concluded the schoolmaster, "to be carried adrift in my laudation of Malcolm. You did not come to hear praises of him, my lady."

"I owe him much," said Clementina. "But tell me, Mr. Graham, how is it that you know there is a God and one fit to be trusted as you trust Him?"

"In no way that I can bring to bear on the reason of another so as to produce conviction."

"Then what is to become of me?"

"I can do for you what is far better. I can persuade you to

look for yourself to see whether or not there lies a gate, a pathway, into belief right before you. Entering by that gate, walking on that path, you shall yourself arrive at the conviction which no man could give you. The man who seeks the truth in any other manner will never find it. Listen to me a moment, my lady. I loved that boy's mother. Because she could not love me, I was very unhappy. Then I sought comfort from the unknown Source of my life. He gave me to understand His Son, and so I understood himself, came to know Him and was comforted."

"But how do you know it was not all a delusion, the product of your own fervid imagination? Do not mistake me; I want to find it true."

"It is a right and honest question, my lady. I will tell you. First of all, I have found all my difficulties and confusions clearing themselves up ever since I set out to walk in that way. Not life's difficulties, but difficulties of belief. My consciousness of life is threefold what it was: my perception of what is lovely around me, and my delight in it; my power of understanding things and of ordering my way; the same with my hope and courage, my love to my kind, my power of forgiveness. In short, I cannot but believe that my whole being and its whole world are in the process of rectification for me. And if I thus find my whole being enlightened and redeemed and know, therefore, that I fare according to the word of the Man of whom the old story tells; if I find that His word and the resulting action founded on that word correspond and agree and open a heaven in and beyond me; if the Lord of the ancient tale, I say, has thus held word with me, am I likely to doubt much or long whether there be such a Lord or no?"

"What, then, is the way that lies before me for my own door? Help me to see it."

"It is just the old way—that of obedience. If you have ever seen the Lord, if only from afar—if you have any vaguest suspicion that the Jew Jesus, who professed to have come from God, was a better man, a different man, than other men—one of your first duties must be to open your ears to His words and see whether they seem to you to be true. Then, if they do, to obey them with your whole strength and might. This is the way of life, which will lead a man out of its miseries into life indeed."

There followed a little pause and then a long talk about what the schoolmaster had called the old story, in which he spoke with such fervid delight of this and that point in the tale, removing this and that stumbling block by giving the true reading or right interpretation, showing the what and why and how, that, for the first time in her life, Clementina began to feel as if such a man must really have lived, that His feet must really have walked over the acres of Palestine, that His human heart must indeed have thought and felt, worshiped and borne, with complete humanity. Even in the presence of her new teacher and with his words in her ears, she began to desire her own chamber that she might sit down with the neglected story and read for herself.[9]

Leave Salvation to Him; You Do What He Tells You

A Fictional Selection from *Malcolm*

"Then a public assembly is not necessary for the communication of the gifts of the Spirit?"

They were silent.

"Isn't it possible that the eagerness after such assemblies may have something to do with a want of confidence in what the Lord says of his kingdom—that it spreads like the hidden leaven—grows like the buried seed? My own conviction is, that if a man would but bend his energies to *live*, if he would but try to be a true, that is, a godlike man, in all his dealings with his fellows, a genuine neighbor and not a selfish unit, he would open such channels for the flow of the Spirit as no amount of even honest and so-called successful preaching could."

"Wha but ane was ever fit to lead sic a life's that?"

"All might be trying after it. In proportion as our candle burns it will give light. No talking about light will supply the lack of its presence either to the talker or the listeners."

"There's a heap made o' the preachin' o' the word i' the buik itsel'," said Peter with emphasis.

"Undoubtedly. But just look at our Lord: he never stopped living among his people—hasn't stopped yet; but he often refused to preach, and personally has given it up altogether now."

"Aye, but ye see he kent what he was duin'."

"And so will every man in proportion as he partakes of his Spirit."

"But dinna ye believe there *is* sic a thing as gettin' a call to the preachin'?"

"I do; but even then a man's work is of worth only as it supplements his life. A network of spiritual fibers connects the two, makes one of them."

"But surely, sir, them 'at's o' the same min' oucht to meet an' stir ane anither up? 'They that feart the Lord spak aften thegither,' ye ken."

"What should prevent them? Why should not such as delight in each other's society, meet, and talk, and pray together—address each the others if they like? There is plenty of opportunity for that, without forsaking the church or calling public meetings. To continue your quotation—'The Lord hearkened and heard'; observe, the Lord is not here said to hearken to sermons or prayers, but to the *talk* of his people. This would have saved you from false relations with men that oppose themselves, caring nothing for the truth—perhaps eager to save their souls, nothing more at the very best."

"Sir! sir! what wad ye hae? Daur ye say it's no a body's first duty to save his ain sowl alive?" exclaimed Bow-o'-meal.

"I daur't—but there's little daur intill't!" said Mr. Graham, breaking into Scotch.

Bow-o'-meal rose from his chair in indignation, Blue Peter made a grasp at his bonnet, and Jeames Gentle gave a loud sigh of commiseration.

"I allow it to be a very essential piece of prudence," added the schoolmaster, resuming his quieter English—"but the first duty! No. The Catechism might have taught you better than that! To mind his chief end must surely be man's first duty; and the Catechism says—'Man's chief end is to glorify God.' "

"And to enjoy him forever," supplemented Peter.

"That's a safe consequence. There's no fear of the second if he does the first. Anyhow, he cannot enjoy him forever this moment, and he can glorify him at once."

"Aye, but hoo?" said Bow-o'-meal, ready to swoop upon the master's reply.

"Just as Jesus Christ did—by doing his will—by obedience."

"That's no faith—it's works! Ye'll never save yer sowl that gait, sir."

"No man can ever save his soul. God only can do that. You can glorify him by giving yourself up heart and soul and body and life to his Son. Then you shall *be* saved. That you must leave to *him*, and *do what he tells you*. There will be no fear of the saving then—though it's not an easy matter—even for *him*, as has been sorely proved."

"An' hoo are we to gie oorsel's up till him?—For ye see we're practical kin' o' fowk, huz fisher-fowk, Maister Graham," said Bow-o'-meal.

The tone implied that the schoolmaster was not practical.

"I say again; in doing *his* will and not your own."

"An' what may his wull be?"

"Is not he telling you himself at this moment? Do you not know what his will is? How should *I* come between him and you! For anything I know, it may be that you pay your next-door neighbor a crown you owe him, or make an apology to the one on the other side. *I* do not know; you do."

"Dinna ye think aboot savin' yer ain sowl noo, Maister Graham?" said Bow-o'-meal, returning on their track.

"No, I don't. I've forgotten all about that. I only desire and pray to do the will of my God—which is all in all to me."

"What say ye than aboot the sowls o' ither fowk? Wadna ye save them, no?"

"Gladly would I save them—but according to the will of God. If I were, even unwittingly, to attempt it in any other way, I should be casting stumbling blocks in their path, and separating myself from my God—doing that which is not of faith, and therefore is sin. It is only where a man is at one with God that he can do the right thing or take the right way. Whatever springs from any other source than the spirit that dwelt in Jesus is of sin and works to thwart the divine will. Who knows what harm may be done to a man by hurrying a spiritual process in him?"

"I doobt, sir, gien yer doctrine was to get a hearin', there wad be unco little dune for the glory o' God i' this place!" remarked Bow-o'-meal, with sententious reproof.

"But what was done would be of the right sort, and surpassingly powerful."

"Weel, to come back to the business in han'—what wad be yer advice?" said Bow-o'-meal.

"That's a thing none but a lawyer should give. I have shown you what seem to me the principles involved. I can do no more."

"Ye dinna ca' that neebourly, whan a body comes speirin' 't!"

"Are you prepared then to take my advice?"

"Ye wadna hae a body du that aforehan'! We micht as weel a' be Papists, an' believe as we're tauld."

"Precisely so. But you can exercise your judgment upon the principles whereon my opinion is founded, with far more benefit than upon my opinion itself—which I cannot well wish you to adopt, seeing I think it far better for a man to go wrong upon his own honest judgment, than to go right upon anybody else's judgment, however honest also."

"Ye hae a heap o' queer doctrines, sir."

"And yet you ask advice of me?"

"We haena ta'en muckle, ony gait," returned Bow-o'-meal rudely, and walked from the cottage.

Jeames Gentle and Blue Peter bade the master a kindly good night, and followed Bow-o'-meal.[10]

Tell Me

"Traveler, what lies over the hill?
　Traveler, tell to me:
Tip-toe-high on the windowsill
　Over I cannot see."

"My child, a valley green lies there,
　Lovely with trees, and shy;
And a tiny brook that says, 'Take care,
　Or I'll drown you by and by!' "

"And what comes next?"—"A little town,
　And a towering hill again;
More hills and valleys up and down,
　And a river now and then."

"And what comes next?"—"A lonely moor
　Without one beaten way,
And slow clouds drifting dull before
　A wind that will not stay."

"And then?"—"Dark rocks and yellow sand,
　Blue sea and a moaning tide."
"And then?"—"More sea, and then more land,
　With rivers deep and wide."

"And then?"—"Oh, rock and mountain and vale,
　Ocean and shores and men,
Over and over, a weary tale,
　And round to your home again!"

"And is that all? From day to day,
　Like one with a long chain bound,
Should I walk and walk and not get away,
　But go always round and round?"

"No, no; I have not told you the best,
　I have not told you the end:
If you want to escape, away in the west
　You will see a stair ascend,

"Built of all colours of lovely stones,
　A stair up into the sky
Where no one is weary, and no one moans,
　Or wishes to be laid by."

"Is it far away?"—"I do not know:
　You must fix your eyes thereon,
And travel, travel through thunder and snow,
　Till the weary way is gone.

"All day, though you never see it shine,
　You must travel nor turn aside,
All night you must keep as straight a line
　Through moonbeams or darkness wide."

"When I am older!"—"Nay, not so!"
　"I have hardly opened my eyes!"
"He who to the old sunset would go,
　Starts best with the young sunrise."

"Is the stair right up? is it very steep?"
　"Too steep for you to climb;
You must lie at the foot of the glorious heap
　And patient wait your time."

"How long?"—"Nay, that I cannot tell."
　"In wind, and rain, and frost?"
"It may be so; and it is well
　That you should count the cost.

"Pilgrims from near an from distant lands
　Will step on you lying there;
But a wayfaring man with wounded hands
　Will carry you up the stair."

The Way of the Commandments

If thou wilt enter into life, keep the commandments.

Matthew 19:17

Live Truth

The Lord cared neither for isolated truth nor for orphaned deed. It was truth in the inward parts, it was the good heart, the mother of good deeds, he cherished. It was the live, active, knowing, breathing good he came to further.

The Lord cared for no speculation in morals or religion. It was good people he cared about, not notions of good things, or even good actions except as the outcome of life, except as the bodies in which the primary live actions of love and will in the soul took shape and came forth.

Could he by one word have set to rest all the questionings of all the world's philosophies as to the supreme good and the absolute truth, I venture to say that he would not have uttered that word. He would make no attempt to convince men mentally concerning the truth.

But he would die to make men good and true. His whole heart would respond to the cry of the sad publican or despairing Pharisee, "How am I to be good?"

When the young man came to Jesus inquiring about eternal life, he was immediately checked on his calling the Master *good*. He then went on, with his emphasis still on goodness, to ask what good thing he should do that he may have eternal life.

When the Lord says, "Why callest thou me good? There is none good but one," we must not put the emphasis on the me, as if the Lord refused the question, as he had declined the earlier title. He was certainly the proper person to ask, only the question was not the right one. The good *thing* was a small matter, the good *Being* was everything! I think the sense of the passage is as follows: "Why do you ask me about that which is good? Why ask me about the good thing? There is one living good, in whom the good thing, and all good, is alive and ever operant. Ask me not about the good thing, but the good Person, the good Being—the origin of all good—who, because he is, can make good."

God is the one live good, ready with his life to communicate living good, the power of being, and so doing good, for he makes good itself to exist. It is not with this good thing and that good thing we have to do, but with the Power from whence comes our power even to speak the word *good*. We have to do with God, to whom no one can look without the need of being good waking up in his heart; to think about God is to begin to be good.

To do a good thing is to do a good thing; to know God is to be good. It is not to make us do all things right he cares about, but to make us hunger and thirst after righteousness. Once we possess that, we shall never need to think of what is or is not good, but shall refuse the evil and choose the good by a motion of the will that is at once necessity and choice.

Keep the Commandments

Observe, the question in the young man's mind is not about the doing or not doing of something he knows to be right. Had such been the case, the Lord would have permitted no question at all. The one thing the Lord insists upon is the *doing* of the thing we know we ought to do. In the present instance, the youth looking for some unknown good thing to do, Jesus sends him back to the doing of what he *does* know.

A man must have something to do in the matter, and may well ask such a question of any teacher. The Lord does not for a moment turn away from it, and only declines the form of it to help the youth onward to what he really needs. The Lord has, in truth, already more than hinted where the answer lies, namely, in God himself. But that truth the youth is not yet capable of receiving. So the Lord must begin with him farther back: "If you would enter into life, keep the commandments." For truly, if the commandments have nothing to do with entering into life, why were they ever given? This is the youth's task: he must keep the commandments.

Then the road to eternal life is the keeping of the commandments!

Even if the Lord had not said so, what else could the answer to the youth's question be? What person of common moral sense would say otherwise? What else can be the way into life but the doing of what the Lord of life tells the creatures he has made and whom he would have live forever, that they must do? It is clearly the beginning of the way.   .

However, if a man had kept all those commandments, he would still not therefore have in him the life eternal. Nevertheless, without the keeping of the commandments there is no entering into life. The keeping of them is the path to the gate of life. It is not life, but it is the way—so much of the way to it. The keeping of the commandments, whether consciously or unconsciously, has the closest and deepest essential relation to eternal life.

The Latter Commandments Come First

The Lord says nothing about the first table of the law. Why does he not tell this youth, as he did the lawyer, that to love God is everything?

He had already essentially done that. He had given the youth a glimpse of the essence of his own life. He had pointed him to the Heart of all—for him to think of afterwards. But he was not ready for it yet.

He wanted eternal life. To love God with all our heart, and soul, and strength, and mind, is to *know* God, and to know him *is* eternal life. That is the end of the whole saving matter. It is no human beginning; it is the grand end and eternal beginning of all things.

But the youth was not capable of it. To begin with that would have been as sensible as to say to one asking how to reach the top of some mountain, "Just set your foot on that shining snow-clad peak, high there in the blue, and you will at once be where you wish to go."

"Love God with all your heart, and eternal life is yours": such words would only have been to mock him. This youth could not yet see or believe that *that* was eternal life! He was not yet capable of looking upon true *life* even from afar! How many of today's Christians are thus capable? How many know that they are not? How many *care* that they are not? The Lord answers the youth's question directly, tells him what to do—starting at a level he can understand, with something he can do—to enter into life: he must keep the commandments. When he asks, "Which?" Jesus specifies only those that have to do with his neighbor, ending with the highest and most difficult of them.

Of course no one can perfectly keep a single commandment of the second table any more than of the first. And there is no keeping of them other than a *perfect* keeping. To keep them means to keep them perfectly. But though I hold with all my heart that no keeping of the commandments but a perfect one will satisfy God, it is not true that there is no other kind he cares for. He will not be satisfied with less, yet he will be delighted with all honest movements, however small, in that direction. What father is not pleased with the first tottering attempt of his little one to walk? Yet at the same time, what father would be satisfied with anything but the manly step of the full-grown son?

The Purpose of the Commandments

When the Lord has definitely mentioned the commandments he means, the youth replies at once that he *has* observed these from his youth up.

The Lord takes his word for it: he looked on him and loved him.

Now are we to think that the Master truly believed he had kept the commandments perfectly? To understand the love the Lord felt for the youth, I think we must allow this: There is a keeping of the commandments, which, although anything but perfect, is yet acceptable to the heart of him from whom nothing is hid. In that way the youth had kept the commandments. He had for years been putting forth something of his life-energy to keep them.

And, however he may have failed of perfection, the youth had not missed the end for which they were given him to keep. For the immediate end of the commandments never was that men should succeed in obeying them. Rather, finding they could *not* do that which yet must be done, finding the more they tried the more that was required of them, men and women are driven to the source of life and law—of their life and God's law—to seek from God such reinforcement of life as should make the fulfillment of the law both possible and natural.

This result had been wrought in the youth. His observance had given him no satisfaction. He was not at rest. But he desired eternal life—of which there was no word in the law. The keeping of the law had served to develop a hunger which no law or its keeping could fill. Must not the imperfection of his keeping of the commandments, even in the lower sense in which he read them, have helped to reveal how far they were beyond any keeping of his, how their implicit demands rose into the infinitude of God's perfection?

Beyond the Commandments

Having kept the commandments, the youth needed and was ready for a further lesson. The Lord would not leave him where he was, for the Lord had come to seek and to save. He saw in the youth a sore need of perfection—the very thing the commonplace Christian, without such hunger, thinks he can do without—the thing God's true elect hunger after with an eternal hunger.

Perfection, the perfection of the Father, is eternal life. "If you would be perfect," said the Lord. What an honor for the youth to be supposed desirous of perfection by the very Son of God! And what an enormous demand, upon that supposition, does the Lord make of him!

To gain the perfection the youth desired, the one thing lacking was that he should sell all that he had, give it to the poor, and follow the Lord!

Could this be all that lay between him and entering into life? God only knows what the victory of such an obedience might at once have wrought in him! Much, much more would be necessary before perfection was reached, but certainly the next step, to sell and follow, would have been the next step into life. Had he taken it, in the very act would have been born in him the essence and vitality of eternal life, needing but process to develop it into the glorious consciousness of oneness with The Life.

There was nothing like this in the law. Was it not hard—hard to let earth go, and take heaven instead? Hard, for eternal life, to let dead things drop? Hard to turn his back on Mammon, and follow Jesus? Hard to lose his rich friends, and be of the Master's household? Let him say it was hard who does not know the Lord, who has never thirsted after righteousness, never longed for the life eternal!

The youth had got on so far, was so pleasing in the eyes of the Master, that he would show him the highest favor he could. He would take him to be with him—to walk with him, and rest with him, and go from him only to do for him what he did for his Father in heaven—to plead with men, be a mediator between God and men. He would set him free at once, a child of the kingdom, an heir of the life eternal.

Such *life* Jesus offered the youth, as he does at some time to each one of us—a life to enter into which requires a choice. Upon that choice, when the moment comes, hinges everything.[1]

PARTAKING IN GOD'S LIFE BY FREE CHOICE

A Fictional Selection from *The Curate's Awakening*

B ut the question is not of the idea of a God, but of the existence of God. And if he exists, he must be such as the human heart could never accept as God because of the cruelty he permits."

"I grant that argument a certain amount of force, and that very thing has troubled me at times, but I am coming to see it in a different light. I heard some children the other day saying that Dr. Faber was a very cruel man, for he pulled out the nurse's tooth, and gave the poor little baby such a nasty, nasty powder."

"Is that a fair parallel?" asked Faber.

"I think it is. What you do is often unpleasant, sometimes most painful, but it does not follow that you are a cruel man, one that hurts rather than heals."

"I think there is fault in the analogy," objected Faber. "I am nothing but a slave to laws already existing, and compelled to work according to them. It is not my fault, therefore, that the remedies I have to use are unpleasant. But if there be a God, he has the matter in his own hands."

"But suppose," suggested the curate, "that the design of God involved the perfecting of men as the children of God. Suppose his grand idea could not be content with creatures perfect only by his gift, but also involved in partaking of God's individuality and free will and choice of good. And suppose that suffering were the only way through which the individual soul could be set, in separate and self-individuality, so far apart from God that it might *will* and so become a partaker of his singleness and freedom. And suppose that God saw the seed of a pure affection, say in your friend and his wife, but saw also that it was a seed so imperfect and weak that it could not encounter the coming frosts and winds of the world without loss and decay. Yet, if they were parted now for a few years, it would grow and strengthen and expand to the certainty of an infinitely higher and deeper and keener love through the endless ages to follow—so that by suffering should come, in place of contented decline, abortion, and death, a troubled birth of joyous result in health and immortality—suppose all this, what then?"

Faber was silent a moment, and then answered, "Your theory has but one fault; it is too good to be true."

"My theory leaves plenty of difficulty, but has no such fault as that. Why, what sort of a God would content you, Mr. Faber? The one idea is too bad to be true, the other too good. Must you expand and trim until you get one exactly to the measure of yourself before you can accept it as thinkable or possible? Why, a God like that would not rest your soul a week. The only possibility of believing in a God seems to me in finding an idea of God large enough, grand enough, pure enough, lovely enough to be fit to believe in."

"And have you found such, may I ask?"

"I think I am finding such," confessed Wingfold.

"Where?"

"In the man of the New Testament."[2]

The Coorse Cratur

The Lord gaed wi' a crood o' men
  Throu Jericho the bonny;
'Twas ill the Son o' Man to ken
  Mang sons o' men sae mony:

The wee bit son o' man Zacchay
  To see the Maister seekit;
He speilt a fig-tree, bauld an' shy,
  An' sae his shortness ekit.

But as he thoucht to see his back,
  Roun turnt the haill face til 'im,
Up luikit straucht, an' til 'im spak—
  His hert gaed like to kill 'im.

"Come doun, Zacchay; bestir yersel;
  This nicht I want a lodgin'."
Like a ripe aipple 'maist he fell,
  Nor needit ony nudgin.

But up amang the unco guid
  There rase a murmurin' won'er:
"This is a deemis want o' heed,
  The man's a special sinner!"

Up spak Zacchay, his hert ableeze:
  "Half mine, the puir, Lord, hae it;
Gien oucht I've taen by ony lees,
  Fourfauld again I pay it!"

Then Jesus said, "This is a man!
  His hoose I'm here to save it;
He's ane o' Abraham's ain clan,
  An' siclike has behavit!

I cam the lost to seek an' win."
  Zacchay was ane he wantit:
To ony man that left his sin
  His grace he never scantit.

To Reach the High Places

If thou wilt be perfect, go and sell that thou hast, and give to the poor, and thou shalt have treasure in heaven: and come and follow me.

Matthew 19:21

The Moment of Decision Comes to All

When Jesus confronted the young man of Matthew 19 with the key to eternal life, he was brought face to face, no doubt for the first time, with the true state of his spiritual heart. He was a good man, worthy of the Lord's love. But he was not yet hungry with the hunger that leads to righteousness.

I do not suppose that the youth was one whom ordinary people would call a lover of money. I do not believe he was covetous, or desired even the large increase of his possessions. I imagine he was just like most good men of property: he valued his possessions—looked on them as a good. I suspect that in the case of another, he would have regarded such possession almost as a merit, something deserved. Like most of my readers, he would probably have valued a man more who had some means, and valued him less who had none. Most people have no idea how entirely they will one day have to alter their judgment, or have it altered for them, in this respect. How much better for them if they alter it for themselves!

From this false way of thinking, and all the folly and unreality that accompany it, the Lord hoped to deliver the young man. As things stood, he was a slave, for a man is in bondage to whatever he cannot part with that is less than himself. The Lord could have taken his possessions from him. But there would have been little good in that.

The Lord wished to accomplish his purpose by the exercise of the young man's will. That would indeed have been a victory for both!

If only he could do as the Lord suggested, the youth would enter into freedom and life, delivered from the bondage of Mammon by the lovely will of the Lord in him, one with his own. By the putting forth of the divine energy in him, he would escape the corruption that is in the world through lust—that is, the desire or pleasure of *having*.

But the young man would not. The price was too high, and he walked away sorrowfully.

Was the Lord then premature in his demand on the youth? Was he not ready for it? Was it meant only as a test, and not as an actual word of deliverance? Did he show the child a next step on the stair too high for him to set his foot upon?

I do not believe it. He gave him the very next lesson in the divine education for which he was ready. It was possible for him to respond, to give birth, by obedience, to the redeemed and redeeming will, and so be free. It was time the demand should be made upon him.

Do you say, "But he would not respond; he would not obey."

Then it was time, I answer, that he should refuse. It was time he should know what manner of spirit he was of, and meet the confusions of soul, the sad searchings of heart that must follow.

A time comes to *every* man and woman when he must obey, or make such refusal—*and know it*.

Does God Want Our Money in His Service?

Does what I said above mean that I think the refusal of the young man was of necessity final? that he was therefore lost? that because he declined to enter into life at that moment, the door of life was closed against him?

In truth, I have not so learned Christ. And because he went away sorrowful, there seems every indication that the lesson was not lost.

The question then comes: was such sorrow, in the mind of an earnest youth, likely to grow less or to grow more? Was all he had gone through in the way of obedience to be of no good to him? Could the nature of one who had kept the commandments be so slight that, after having sought and talked with Jesus, held communion with him who is the Life, he would care less about eternal life than before?

Alas, many have indeed looked upon Christ's face, yet have never seen him, and have turned back. Some have kept company with Christ for years, and denied him. But their weakness is not the measure of the patience or the resources of God.

Perhaps this youth was never one of the Lord's disciples so long as the Lord was on the earth, but it could be that when the youth saw that the Master himself cared nothing for wealth, and that, instead of ascending the throne of his fathers, he allowed the people to do with him what they would, leaving the world still a poor man, and by its cruelest door, perhaps then the youth became one of those who sold all they had, and came and laid the money at the apostles' feet.

In the meantime, he had that in his soul which made it heavy: by the gravity of his riches the world held him and would not let him rise. He counted his weight his strength, and it was his weakness. Moneyless in God's upper air he would have had power indeed. Money is the power of this world—a power for defeat and failure to him who holds it—a weakness to be overcome before a man can be strong. Yet many decent people fancy it a power of the world to come! It is indeed a little power, as food and drink, as bodily strength, as the winds and the waves are powers. But it is no mighty thing for the redemption of men. Yea, to the redemption of those who have it, it is the saddest obstruction.

To make this youth capable of eternal life, clearly—and the more clearly that he went away sorrowful—the first thing was to make a poor man of him! He would doubtless have gladly devoted his wealth to the service of the Master. How many would eagerly go with him, *as rich men*, to spend their fortunes for him! But part with it to free him for his service—that the young man could not do . . . *yet!*

How Can We Be Made to See?

And now, how would the wealthy youth go on with his keeping of the commandments? Would he not begin to see all the more plainly his shortcomings, the larger scope of their requirements? Might he not feel the keeping of them more imperative than ever, yet impossible without something he did not have? The commandments can never be kept while there is strife to keep them: the man is overwhelmed in the weight of their broken pieces. It needs a clean heart to have pure hands, all the power of a live soul to keep the law—a power of life, not of struggle; the strength of love, not the effort of duty.

One day the truth of his conduct must dawn upon him with absolute clearness. Bitter must be the discovery. He refused the life eternal! He turned his back upon The Life! In deepest humility and shame, yet with the profound consolation of repentance, he would return to the Master and bemoan his unteachableness.

There are those who, like St. Paul, can say, "I did wrong, but I did it in ignorance. My heart was not right, and I did not know it." The remorse of such must be very different from that of one who, brought to the point of being capable of embracing the truth, turned from it and refused to be set free. To him the time will come, God only knows its hour, when he will see the nature of his deed, *with the knowledge that he knew the right even while he did it*: the alternative, the choice, had been put before him. And all those months or days or hours or moments, he might have been following the Master, hearing the words he spoke, and seeing through his eyes into the depths of God himself!

The sum of the matter in regard to the youth is this: he had begun early to climb the eternal stair. He had kept the commandments, and by every keeping had climbed. But because he was *well-to-do*—a phrase of unconscious irony—he felt "well-to-be." Felt it, that is, except for that lack of eternal life! In any case, he felt well enough that he was unwilling to sacrifice what made him well-to-do.

His possessions gave him a standing in the world—a position of consequence—of value in his eyes. He knew himself looked up to. He liked to be looked up to. He looked up to himself because of his means, forgetting that means are but tools, and poor tools at that. To part with his wealth would be to sink to the level of his inferiors! Why should he not keep it? Why not use it in the service of the Master? What wisdom could there be in throwing away such a grand advantage?

He could devote it, but he could not cast it from him! He could devote it, but he could not devote himself! He could not make himself naked as a little child and let his Father take him!

How could a rich man believe he would be of more value without his money? that the casting of it away would make him one of God's poor? that the battle of God could be better fought without its impediment? that God's work refused as an obstruction the aid of wealth?

But the Master had repudiated money that he might do the will of his Father, and the disciple must be as his Master. Had he done as the Master told him, he would soon have come to understand.

Obedience is the opener of eyes.

To Ascend the Summit We Must Throw Aside Our Shoes

There is a danger to every good person in keeping the commandments that he will probably think of himself more highly than he ought to think. He may be correct enough as to the facts, and yet in his deductions and consequent self-regard be anything but fair. He may think himself a fine fellow, when he is simply an ordinarily reasonable individual, trying to do all but the first thing necessary to the name or honor of a man. He may even be an exceptionally fine person. But the number of fools who do not yet acknowledge the first condition of manhood in no way alters the fact that he who has begun to recognize his duty toward man and God, and acknowledge the facts of his being, is but a tottering child on the path of life.

When a child does strike out on the path, he is as wise as at the time he can be. The Father's arms are stretched out to receive him. But he is not therefore a wonderful being. He is not therefore a model of wisdom. He is not at all the admirable creature he would persuade himself to think at those times he feels most satisfied with himself. He is just one of God's poor creatures. What share this besetting sin of *the good young man* may have had in the failure of the rich young ruler, we need not inquire. But it may well be that he thought the Master undervalued his work as well as his wealth, and was less than fair to him.

The youth, climbing the stair of eternal life, had come to a plateau where no more steps were visible. On the cloud-swathed platform he stood looking in vain for further ascent.

What he himself thought he wanted, I cannot tell. I cannot guess at his idea of eternal life. I hardly think it was but the poor idea of living forever, all that commonplace minds grasp at for eternal life— which is in reality only its accompanying shadow, in itself not worth thinking about. The fact of living forever was taken for granted by all devout Jews, and I cannot but think it was taken for granted by this young man also.

When a man has eternal life, that is, when he is one with God, what should he do but live forever? Without oneness with God, the continuance of existence would be to me the all but unsurpassable curse—*the* unsurpassable itself being a god other than the God I see in Jesus.

But whatever the young man's idea, it must have held in it all such notions as he had concerning God and man and a common righteous-ness. While thus he stands, then, alone on the stair from which he could not see further, helpless to continue, behold the form of the Son of Man! It is God himself come to meet the climbing youth, to take him by the hand, and lead him up his own stair, the only stair by which ascent can be made.

Jesus shows him the first step of it through the mist. But his feet are heavy; they have golden shoes. He wants to follow up the stair. But his feet will not budge. He has come as far as he can with what he is wearing.

To go up *that* stair he must throw aside his shoes. He must walk barefooted into life eternal!

But rather than doing so, rather than stride free-limbed up the everlasting stair to the bosom of the Father, he decides to keep his precious shoes! He thinks it will be better to drag them about on the earth, than part with them for a world where they are useless!

But how miserable his precious things, his golden vessels, his embroidered garments, his stately house, must have seemed when he went back to them from the face of the Lord! Surely it cannot have been long before in shame and misery he cast all from him, even as Judas cast away the thirty pieces of silver, in the agony of everyone who wakes to the fact that he has preferred money to the Master! For, although never can man be saved without being freed from his possessions, it is still only hard, but not impossible, for a rich man to enter into the kingdom of God.[1]

The Holiness of Obedience

A Fictional Selection from *The Landlady's Master*

Andrew thought for a moment, then said, "Let me attempt to answer you in this way: how many years has the world existed, do you imagine?"

"I don't know. Geologists say hundreds of thousands, maybe millions."

"And how many since Christ lived?"

"Almost two thousand."

"Then we are but in the morning of Christianity! There is plenty of time. The day is before us."

"Dangerous doctrine for the sinner!"

"Why? Time is plentiful for his misery if he will not repent, plentiful for the mercy of God that would lead him to repentance. There is plenty of time for labor and hope, but none for indifference and delay. God *will* have his creatures good. They cannot escape him."

"Then a man may put off repentance as long as he pleases."

"Certainly he may—at least as long as he can—but it is a fearful thing to try issues with God."

"I can hardly say I understand you."

Andrew paused again. This time it was a little longer before he spoke, during which interval he offered up a silent prayer—both for the heart of his listener and for humility in his own spirit. At last he opened his mouth once more.

"Mr. Crawford," he said quietly, "you have questioned me in the way of kindly anxiety and reproof; thus perhaps that has given me the right to question you. Tell me, do you think we are bound to do what our Lord requires?"

"Of course. How could any Christian man or woman do otherwise?"

"Yet it is possible for a man to say 'Lord, Lord' and still be cast out."

"And?"

"In other words, it is possible for one who seems a Christian, who calls him *Lord*, to be cast into the fire. It is one thing to say we are bound to do what the Lord tells us, and another to *do* what he tells us."

"That I would grant."

"He says, 'Seek ye *first* the kingdom of God and his righteousness.' Mr. Crawford, if you will forgive my boldness, are you seeking the kingdom of God *first*, or are you seeking money first?"

"We are sent into the world to make a living."

"Sent into the world, we have to seek a living. We are not sent into the world to make our living but to seek the kingdom and righteousness of God. And to seek a living is very different from seeking a fortune."

"If you had a little wholesome ambition, Mr. Ingram," replied George in a bit of a huff, "you would be less given to judging your neighbors."

Andrew held his peace, and George concluded that he had the best of the argument—which was all he wanted. Of the truth concerned he did not see enough to care about. Perceiving no good was to be done, Andrew was willing to appear defeated; he did not value any victory of discussion but only the victory of the truth, and George was not yet capable of being conquered by the truth.

"No," resumed George, with the regained composure of again holding the upper hand, "we must avoid judging others. There are certain things all respectable people have agreed to regard as right: he is a presumptuous man who refuses to regard them. Reflect on it, Mr. Ingram."

A curious smile hovered about the lip of the plowman. When things to say did not come to him, he did not go and try to fetch them, but held his tongue. Long before, he had learned that when one is required to meet an untruth, words are given him; when they are not, silence is best. A man who does not love the truth, but disputes for victory, is the swine before whom pearls must not be cast. Andrew's smile meant that it had been fruitless to attempt a meeting of the minds with George upon a subject so holy as obedience to the Master.[2]

I'll Believe in Jesus Tomorrow

A Fictional Selection from *Donal Grant*

O ne thing I am sure of," said Donal, "that your lordship, as well as every man, will have fair play. But there is this to be considered; at first, if you did not know what you were about, you might not be much to blame, though it is impossible to say when there may not be a glimmer of light left; but afterwards, when you knew that you were putting yourself in danger of doing you did not know what, you must have been as much to blame. . . ."

"Then let him set the thing right! Why should we have to toil to draw his plow with but one horse where there ought to be four?

"He will see to it, my lord; do not fear—though it will probably be in a way your lordship will hardly like. He is compelled to do terrible things sometimes."

"What should compel him?"

"The love that is in him, the love that he is, towards us who would have our own way to the ruin of everything he cares for!"

Then the Spirit awoke in Donal, or came upon him, and he spoke.

"My lord," he said, "if you would ever again be able to thank God, if there be one in the other world to whom you would go, if you would make up for any wrong you have ever done, if you would ever feel in your soul once more the innocence of a child, if you care to call God your Father, and Jesus Christ your Brother, if you would fall asleep in peace and wake to a new life, I conjure you to resist the devil, to give up the habit that is dragging you lower and lower every hour. It will be very hard, I know! Anything I can do, by watching with you night and day, and giving myself to your help, I am ready for. I will do all a man can do to deliver you from the weariness that must come over you, and count myself honored, believing I shall then have lived a life worth living. Resolve, my lord—in God's name resolve at once to be free. Then will you know that you have a free will, because your will will have made itself free by doing the will of God against all disinclination of your own. It will be a glorious victory, and will at once set you high on the hill whose peak is the throne of God."

"I will begin tomorrow," said the earl, with a strange look in his eyes; "but now," he went on, "you must leave me. I need solitude to strengthen my resolve. Come to me again tomorrow."[3]

Said and Did

Said the boy as he read, "I too will be bold,
  I will fight for the truth and its glory!"
He went to the playground, and soon had told
  A very cowardly story!

Said the girl as she read, "That was grand, I declare!
  What a true, what a lovely, sweet soul!"
In half-an-hour she went up the stair,
  Looking as black as a coal!

"The mean little wretch, I wish I could fling
  This book at his head!" said another;
Then he went and did the same ugly thing
  To his own little trusting brother!

Alas for him who sees a thing grand
  And does not fit himself to it!
But the meanest act, on sea or land,
  Is to find a fault, and then do it!

CHILDREN NOT SLAVES

The truth shall make you free . . . Whosoever committeth sin is the servant of sin. And the servant abideth not in the house for ever: but the Son abideth ever.

John 8:32, 34–35

A s this passage from John 8 stands, I have not been able to make sense of it. No man could be in the house of the Father by virtue of being the servant of sin; yet this man is in the house as a servant, and the house in which he serves is not the house of sin, but the house of the Father.

The utterance is confused at best and the reasoning faulty. He must be in the house of the Father on some other ground than sin. Had no help come, this would have been sufficient cause for leaving the passage alone, as one where, perhaps, the words of the Lord were misrepresented—where, at least, perceiving more than one fundamental truth involved in the passage, I failed to follow the argument.

Most difficulties of similar nature have originated, like this, I can hardly doubt, with some scribe who, desiring to explain what he did not understand, wrote his worthless gloss on the margin. The next copier took the words for an omission that ought to be replaced in the body of the text, and inserting them, falsified the utterance, and greatly obscured its intention.

In this present case, I do not see that I could ever have known where the error lay were it not for the help of modern critics who have searched the Scriptures and ancient manuscripts and found what was really written. The difference is indeed small to the eye, but is great enough to give us fine gold instead of questionable ore.

Slavery to God Not Sin

What I take for the true reading of John 8:34–46 then, I translate thus: "Every one committing sin is a slave. But the slave does not remain in the house for ever; the son remaineth for ever. If then the son shall make you free, you shall in reality be free."

The words of the Lord here are not that he who sins is the slave of sin, as utterly true as that is; but that he is a slave, and the argument shows that he means a slave *to God*. The two are perfectly consistent. No amount of slavery to sin can keep a man from being as much the slave of God as God chooses in his mercy to make him.

It is his sin that makes him a slave instead of a child. His slavery to sin is his ruin; his slavery to God his only hope. God indeed does not love slavery. He will have children, not slaves. But he may keep a slave in his house a long time in the hope of waking up the poor slavish nature to aspire to the sonship which belongs to him, which is his birthright.

But the slave is not to be in the house forever. The father is not bound to keep his son a slave because the foolish child prefers it.

Good Slaves

Whoever will not do what God desires of him is a slave whom God can compel to do it, however God may bear with him. Whoever, knowing this or fearing punishment, obeys God, is still a slave, but a slave who comes within hearing of the voice of his master. There are, however, far higher than he, who still are only slaves.

Those to whom God is not all in all are slaves. They may not commit great sins; they may even be trying to do right. But so long as they serve God, as they call it, from duty, and do not know him as their Father, the joy of their being, they are slaves—good slaves, but still slaves. If they did not try to do their duty, they would be bad slaves. They are by no means so slavish as those who serve from fear, but they are slaves. And because they are only slaves, they can fulfill no righteousness, can do no duty perfectly, but must ever be trying after it wearily and in pain, knowing well that if they stop trying, they are lost. They are slaves indeed, for they would be glad to be adopted by one who is their own Father!

Sons and Daughters

Where then are the sons and daughters?

I know none, I answer, who are yet utterly and entirely sons or daughters. There may be such—God knows. I have not known them, or, knowing them, have not been myself such as to be able to recognize them. But I do know some who are enough sons and daughters to be at war with the slave in them, who are not content to be slaves to their Father.

Nothing I have seen or known of sonship comes near the glory of the thing. But there are thousands of sons and daughters, though their number is only a remnant, who are siding with the Father of their spirits against themselves, against all that divides them from him from whom they have come, but out of whom they have never come, seeing that in him they live and move and have their being.

Such are not slaves. They are true, though not perfect, children. They are fighting along with God against the evil separation. They are breaking at the middle wall of partition. Only the rings of their chains are left, and they are struggling to take them off. They are children—with more or less of the dying slave in them. They know the slavery is there, and what it is, and they hate the slavery in them, and are trying to slay it.

The real slave is he who does not seek to be a child, who does not desire to end his slavery, who looks upon the claim of the child as presumption, who cleaves to the traditional authorized service of forms and ceremonies, and does not know the will of him who made the seven stars and Orion, much less cares to obey it, who never lifts up his heart to cry, "Father, what would you have me to do?" Such are continually betraying their slavery by their complaints. "Do we not do well to be angry?" they cry with Jonah. And truly, being slaves, I do not know how they are to help it. When they are sons and daughters, they will no longer complain of the hardships and miseries and troubles of life, no longer grumble at their aches and pains, at the pinching of their poverty, at the hunger that assails them, no longer be indignant at their rejection by what is called society. Those who believe in their own perfect Father cannot blame him for anything they do not like.

Ah, friend, it may be that you and I are slaves. But there *are* such sons and daughters as I speak of. And may we hope one day to join them when we have cast our slavery behind us!

The slaves of sin rarely grumble at that slavery. It is their slavery to God they grumble at. Of that alone they complain—of the painful messengers he sends to deliver them from their slavery both to sin and to himself.

They must be sons or slaves. They cannot rid themselves of their owner. Whether they deny God, or mock him by acknowledging and not heeding him, or treat him as an arbitrary, formal monarch, they are slaves. Whether, taking no trouble to find out what pleases him, they do dull things for his service that he cares nothing about, or try to propitiate him by assuming with strenuous effort some yoke the Son never wore and never called on them to wear, they are slaves, and no less slaves because they are slaves to God.

They are so thoroughly slaves that they do not care to get out of their slavery by becoming sons and daughters, by finding the good of life where alone it can or could lie.[1]

The Highest Ambition: To Be God's Obedient Little Son

A Poetical Selection entitled: "Willie's Question"

Willie speaks.

Is it wrong, the wish to be great,
    For I do wish it so?
I have asked already my sister Kate;
    She says she does not know.

Yestereve at the gate I stood
    Watching the sun in the west;
When I saw him look so grand and good
    It swelled up in my breast.

Next from the rising moon
    It stole like a silver dart;
In the night when the wind began his tune
    It woke with a sudden start.

This morning a trumpet blast
    Made all the cottage quake;
It came so sudden and shook so fast
    It blew me wide awake.

It told me I must make haste,
    And some great glory win,
For every day was running to waste,
    And at once I must begin.

I want to be great and strong,
    I want to begin today;
But if you think it very wrong
    I will send the wish away.

The Father answers.

Wrong to wish to be great?
    No, Willie; it is not wrong:
The child who stands at the high closed gate
    Must wish to be tall and strong!

If you did not wish to grow
    I should be a sorry man;
I should think my boy was dull and slow,
    Nor worthy of his clan.

You are bound to be great, my boy:
    Wish, and get up, and do.
Were you content to be little, my joy
    Would be little enough in you.

Willie speaks.

Papa, Papa! I'm so glad
    That what I wish is right!
I will not lose a chance to be had;
    I'll begin this very night.

I will work so hard at school!
    I will waste no time in play;
At my fingers' ends I'll have every rule,
    For knowledge is power, they say.

I *would* be a king and reign,
    But I can't be that, and so
Field-marshal I'll be, I think, and gain
    Sharp battles and sieges slow.

I shall gallop and shout and call,
    Waving my shining sword:
Artillery, cavalry, infantry, all
    Hear and obey my word.

Or admiral I will be,
    Wherever the salt wave runs,
Sailing, fighting over the sea,
    With flashing and roaring guns.

I will make myself hardy and strong;
    I will never, never give in.
I *am* so glad it is not wrong!
    At once I will begin.

The Father speaks.

Fighting and shining along,
    All for the show of the thing!
Any puppet will mimic the grand and strong
    If you pull the proper string!

Willie speaks.

But indeed I want to *be* great,
    I should despise mere show;
The thing I want is the glory-state—
    Above the rest, you know!

The Father answers.

The harder you run that race,
    The farther you tread that track,
The greatness you fancy before your face
    Is the farther behind your back.

To be up in the heavens afar,
    Miles above all the rest,
Would make a star not the greatest star,
    Only the dreariest.

That book on the highest shelf
    Is not the greatest book;
If you would be great, it must be in yourself,
    Neither by place nor look.

The Highest is not high
    By being higher than others;
To greatness you come not a step more nigh
    By getting above your brothers.

Willie speaks.

I meant the boys at school,
    I did not mean my brother.
Somebody first, is there the rule—
    It must be me or another.

The Father answers.

Oh, Willie, it's all the same!
    They are your brothers all;
For when you say, "Hallowed be thy name!"
    Whose Father is it you call?

Could you pray for such rule to *him*?
    Do you think that he would hear?
Must he favour one in a greedy whim
    Where all are his children dear?

It is right to get up and do,
    But why outstrip the rest?
Why should one of the many be one of the few?
    Why should *you* think to be best?

Willie speaks.

Then how am I to be great?
    I know no other way;
It would be folly to sit and wait,
    I must up and do, you say!

The Father answers.

I do not want you to wait,
    For few before they die
Have got so far as begin to be great,
    The lesson is so high.

I will tell you the only plan
    To climb and not to fall:
He who would rise and be greater than
    He is, must be servant of all.

Turn it each way in your mind,
    Try every other plan,
You may think yourself great, but at length you'll find
    You are not even a man.

Climb to the top of the trees,
    Climb to the top of the hill,
Get up on the crown of the sky if you please,
    You'll be a small creature still.

Be admiral, poet, or king,
    Let praises fill both your ears,

Your soul will be but a windmill thing
    Blown round by its hopes and fears.

Willie speaks.

Then put me in the way,
    For you, Papa, are a man:
What thing shall I do this very day?
    Only be sure I *can*.

I want to know—I am willing,
    Let me at least have a chance!
Shall I give the monkey-boy my shilling?
    I want to serve at once.

The Father answers.

Give all your shillings you might
    And hurt your brothers the more;
He only can serve his fellows aright
    Who goes in at the little door.

We must do the thing we *must*
    Before the thing we *may*;
We are unfit for any trust
    Till we can and do obey.

Willie speaks.

I will try more and more;
    I have nothing now to ask;
Obedience I know is the little door:
    Now set me some hard task.

The Father answers.

No, Willie; the Father of all,
    Teacher and master high,
Has set your task beyond recall,
    Nothing can set it by.

Willie speaks.

What is it, father dear,
    That he would have me do?
I'd ask himself, but he's not near,
    And so I must ask you!

The Father answers.

Me 'tis no use to ask,
    I too am one of his boys!
But he tells each boy his own plain task:
    Listen, and hear his voice.

Willie speaks.

Father, I'm listening *so*
    To hear him if I may!
His voice must either be very low,
    Or very far away!

The Father answers.

It is neither hard to hear,
    Nor hard to understand;
It is very low, but very near,
    A still, small, strong command.

Willie answers.

I do not hear it at all;
    I am only hearing you!

The Father speaks.

Think: is there nothing, great or small,
    You ought to go and do?

Willie answers.

Let me think—I ought to feed
    My rabbits. I went away
In such a hurry this morning! Indeed
    They've not had enough today!

The Father speaks.

That is his whisper low!
    That is his very word!
You had only to stop and listen, and so
    Very plainly you heard!

That duty's the little door:
    You must open it and go in;
There is nothing else to do before,
    There is nowhere else to begin.

Willie speaks.

But that's so easily done!
    It's such a trifling affair!
So nearly over as soon as begun,
    For that he can hardly care!

The Father answers.

You are turning from his call
    If you let that duty wait;
You would not think any duty small
    If you yourself were great.

The nearest is at life's core;
    With the first, you all begin:
What matter how little the little door
    If it only let you in?

————

Willie speaks.

Papa, I am come again:
    It is now three months and more
That I've tried to do the thing that was plain,
    And I feel as small as before.

The Father answers.

Your honor comes too slow?
    How much then have you done?
One foot on a mole-heap, would you crow
    As if you had reached the sun?

Willie speaks.

But I cannot help a doubt
    Whether this way be the true:
The more I do to work it out
    The more there comes to do;

And yet, were all done and past,
    I should feel just as small,
For when I had tried to the very last—
    'Twas my duty, after all!

It is only much the same
    As not being liar or thief!

The Father answers.

One who tried it found even, with shame,
    That of sinners he was the chief!
My boy, I am glad indeed
    You have been finding the truth!

Willie speaks.

But where's the good? I shall never speed—
    Be one whit greater, in sooth!

If duty itself must fail,
    And that be the only plan,
How shall my scarce begun duty prevail
    To make me a mighty man?

The Father answers.

Ah, Willie! what if it were
    Quite another way to fall?
What if the greatness itself lie there—
    In knowing that you are small?

In seeing the good so good
    That you feel poor, weak, and low;
And hungrily long for it as for food,
    With an endless need to grow?

The man who was Lord of fate,
    Born in an ox's stall,
Was great because he was much too great
    To care about greatness at all.

Ever and only he sought
    The will of his Father good;
Never of what was high he thought,
    But of what his Father would.

You long to be great; you try;
    You feel yourself smaller still:
In the name of God let ambition die;
    Let him make you what he will.

Who does the truth, is one
    With the living Truth above:
Be God's obedient little son,
    Let ambition die in love.[2]

A CHRISTIAN IS ONE WHO DOES WHAT THE LORD JESUS TELLS HIM

A Fictional Selection from *A Daughter's Devotion*

Yes, my love," he went on. "It is not that I do not think you a Christian. I do think you one. It is that I want you to be a downright real Christian, not one that is only trying to feel as a Christian ought to feel. I have lost so much precious time in that way!"

"Tell me," said Mary, clapping her other hand over his. "What would you have me do?"

"I will tell you," he replied. "At least I will try. A Christian is one that does what the Lord Jesus tells him. Neither more nor less than that makes a Christian. It is not even understanding the Lord Jesus that makes one a Christian. It is doing what he tells us that makes us Christians, and that is the only way to understand him. Peter says that the Holy Spirit is given to them that obey him: what else can that be but just actually, really doing what he says—just as if I were to tell you to go and fetch me my Bible, and you would get up and go. Did you ever do anything, my child, just because Jesus told you to do it?"

Mary did not answer immediately. She thought for a moment, then spoke.

"Yes, Father," she said, "I think so. Two nights ago, George was very rude to me—I don't mean anything bad, but you know he can be very rough."

"I know it, my child. And you must not think I don't care because I think it better not to interfere. I am with you all the time."

"Thank you, Father. I know it. Well, when I was going to bed, I was still angry with him, so it was no wonder I found that I could not pray. Then I remembered how Jesus said we must forgive or we should not be forgiven. So I forgave George in my heart, and then I found I could pray."

The father stretched out his arms and drew her to him, murmuring, "My child! My Christ's child!" After a little pause, he began to speak again.

"It is a sad thing to hear those who desire to believe themselves Christians, talking and talking about this question and that, the discussion of which makes only for strife and not for unity—not a thought among them of the one command of Christ to love one another. I fear some are hardly content with not hating those who differ from them."

"I try, Father—and I think I do love everybody who loves him."

"Well, that is much—though it is not enough, my child. We must be like Jesus, and you know that it was while we were yet sinners that Christ died for us. Therefore, we must love all men, whether they are Christians or not."

"Tell me, then, what you want me to do, Father dear. I will do whatever you tell me."

"I want you to be just like the Lord Jesus, Mary. I want you to look out for his will, and find it, and do it. I want you not only to do it, though that is the main thing, when you think of it, but to look for it, to actively seek it that you may do it. This is not a thing to be talked about much. You may think me very silent; but I do not always talk even when I am inclined to, for the fear that I might let my feelings out through talk, instead of doing something he wants of me with it. And how repulsive are those generally who talk the most. Our strength ought to go into conduct, not into talk—least of all into talk about what they call the doctrines of the gospel. The man who does what God tells him, sits at his Father's feet, and looks up in his Father's face. Such a man is a true Christian. And men had better be careful in how they criticize such a one, for he cannot greatly mistake his Father, and certainly will not displease him, when he is thus walking in obedience. Look for the lovely will of God, my child, that you may be its servant, its priest, its sister, its queen, its slave—as Paul calls himself. How that man did glory in his Master!"

"I will try, Father," returned Mary, tears spreading down her cheeks. "I do want to be one of his slaves."

"You are bound to be. You have no choice but to choose it. It is what we are made for—freedom, the divine nature, God's life, a grand, pure, open-eyed existence! It is what Christ died for. You must hardly talk about *wanting* to; it is all *must*."[3]

Songs of the Spring Nights

I

The flush of green that dyed the day
    Hath vanished in the moon
Flower-scents float stronger out, and play
    An unborn, coming tune.

One southern eve like this, the dew
    Had cooled and left the ground;
The moon hung halfway from the blue,
    No disc, but conglobed round;

Light-leaved acacias, by the door,
    Bathed in the balmy air,
Clusters of blossomed moonlight bore,
    And breathed a perfume rare;

Great gold-flakes from the starry sky
    Fell flashing on the deep—
One scent of moist earth floating by,
    Almost it made me weep.

II

Those gorgeous stars were not my own,
    They made me alien go
The mother o'er her head had thrown
    A veil I did not know!

The moon-blanched fields that seaward went,
    The palm-flung, dusky shades,
Bore flowering grasses, knotted, bent,
    No slender, spear-like blades.

I longed to see the starry host
    Afar in fainter blue;
But plenteous grass I missed the most,
    With daisies glimmering through.

The common things were not the same!
    I longed across the foam:
From dew-damp earth that odor came—
    I knew the world my home.

III

The stars are glad in gulfy space—
    Friendly the dark to them!
From day's deep mine, their hiding-place,
    Night wooeth every gem.

A thing for faith 'mid labour's jar,
    When up the day is furled,
Shines in the sky a light afar,
    Mayhap a home-filled world.

Sometimes upon the inner sky
    We catch a doubtful shine:
A mote or star? A flash in the eye
    Or jewel of God's mine?

A star to us, all glimmer and glance,
    May teem with seraphim:
A fancy to our ignorance
    May be a truth to Him.

IV

The night is damp and warm and still,
    And soft with summer dreams;
The buds are bursting at their will,
    And shy the half moon gleams.

My soul is cool, as bathed within
    By dews that silent weep—
Like child that has confessed his sin,
    And now will go to sleep.

My body ages, form and hue;
    But when the spring winds blow,
My spirit stirs and buds anew,
    Younger than long ago.

Lord, make me more a child, and more,
    Till Time his own end bring,
And out of every winter sore
    I pass into thy spring.

FREEDOM

"If the Son therefore shall make you free, ye shall be free indeed.
John 8:36

What Is Freedom?

C ould a creator make a creature whose well-being should not depend on himself? And if he could, would the creature be the greater for that? Which would be the greater—the creature he made more dependent, or less dependent?

The slave in heart, with Milton's Satan, would immediately reply that the freest would be the farthest from him who made him. The refusal of such beings to obey is their unknown protest against their own essence. *Being* itself must, for what they call liberty, be repudiated! Creation itself, to go by their lines of life, is an injustice!

God had no right, they say, to create beings less than himself. And as he could not create equal, he ought not to have created!

But they do not complain of having been created. They complain of being required to do justice. They will not obey, but, his own handiwork, ravish from his work every advantage they can! They desire to be free with another kind of freedom than that with which God is free. Unknowingly, they seek a more complete slavery.

There is, in truth, no mid-way between absolute harmony with the Father, and the condition of slaves—submissive, or rebellious. If the latter, their very rebellion is by the strength of the Father in them. Of divine essence, they thrust their existence in the face of their essence, their own nature.

It Is God in the Slave That Makes Him Able to Rebel

The very rebellion against God with which Satan has infused mankind is in some sense but the rising in men of God's spirit against their false notion of him—against the lies they hold concerning him. They do not see that, if they themselves, his work, are the chief joy to themselves, how much more might the Life that gives them breath be a glory and joy to them. It must be so, for that Life is nearer to them than they are to themselves. It is the Life that causes them to be, and extends so infinitely above and beyond them.

For nothing can come so close as that which creates. The nearest, strongest, dearest relation possible is between creator and created. Where this is denied, the schism is the widest. Where it is acknowledged and fulfilled, the closeness is unspeakable. But ever remains what cannot be said, and I sink defeated.

The very protest of the rebel against slavery comes at once of the truth of God in him, which he cannot all cast from him, and of a slavery too low to love the truth—a meanness that will take all and acknowledge nothing, as if his very being was a disgrace to him.

The liberty of the God who would have his creature free is struggling against the slavery of the creature who would cut his own stem from his root that he might call it his own and love it. Such slavery rejoices in his own consciousness, instead of the Life of that consciousness. It poises himself on the tottering wall of his own being, instead of on the Rock on which that being is built. Such a one regards his own dominion over himself—the rule of the greater by the less, inasmuch as the conscious self is less than the true self—as a freedom infinitely greater than the range of the universe of God's being.

If he says, "At least I have it my own way!" I answer, "You do not know what is your way and what is not. You know nothing of where your impulses, your desires, your tendencies, your likings, come from. They may spring now from some chance—as from nerves or emotions—now from some roar of a wandering bodiless devil, now from some infant hate in your heart, now from the greed or lawlessness of some ancestor you would be ashamed of if you knew him, or it may be now from some far-piercing chord of a heavenly orchestra. But the moment it comes up into your consciousness, you call it your own way, and glory in it!

"How little you know of what you call your *self*! Two devils amusing themselves with a duet of inspiration, one at each of your ears, might soon make that lordly *me* you are so in love with rejoice in the freedom of willing the opposite each alternate moment. At length they would drive you mad at finding that you could not, will as you would, choose between a way and its opposite simultaneously."

To Live Without the Creative Life Is Impossible

The whole question rests and turns on the relation of creative and created, of which relation few seem to have the consciousness yet developed. To live without the eternal Creative Life is an impossibility. Freedom from God can only mean an incapacity for seeing the facts of existence, an incapacity of understanding the glory of the creature who makes common cause with his Creator in his creation of him, who wills that the lovely Will calling him into life and giving him choice should finish making him, should draw him into the circle of the creative heart, to joy that he lives by no poor power of his own will, but is one with the causing Life of his life, in closest breathing and willing, vital and claimant oneness with the Life of all life.

Such a creature knows the life of the infinite Father as the very flame of his life, and joys that nothing is done or will be done in the universe in which the Father will not make him all of a sharer that it is possible for perfect generosity to make him.

If you say this is irreverent, I doubt if you have seen the God manifest in Jesus. But all will be well, for the little god of your poor content will starve your soul to misery, and the terror of the eternal death creeping upon you will compel you to seek a perfect Father.

Oh, you hide-bound Christians, the Lord is not straightened, but you are straightened in your narrow unwilling souls! Some of you need to be ashamed of yourselves. Some of you need the fire.

How Am I to Be Free

One who reads may call out, in the agony and thirst of a child waking from a dream of endless seeking and no finding, "I am bound like Lazarus in his graveclothes! What am I to do?"

Here is the answer, drawn from this parable of our Lord, for the saying is much like a parable, teaching more than it says, appealing to the conscience and heart, not to the understanding: "You are a slave. The slave has no hold on the house; only the sons and daughters have an abiding rest in the home of their Father. God cannot always have slaves about him. You must give up your slavery and be set free from it. That is what I am here for. If I make you free, you will be free indeed. For I can make you free only by making you what you were meant to be, sons like myself. That alone is how the Son can work. But it is you who must become sons. You must will it, and I am here to help you."

It is as if he said, "You shall have the freedom of my Father's universe. For, free from yourselves, you will be free of his heart. Yourselves are your slavery. That is the darkness which you have loved rather than the light. You have given honor to yourselves, and not to the Father. You have sought honor from men, and not from the Father! Therefore, even in the house of your Father, you have only been sojourning slaves. We in his family are all one. We have no party spirit. We have no self-seeking. Fall in with us, and you shall be free as we are free."

If then the poor child cry, "How, Lord?" the answer will depend on what he means by that *how*.

If he means, "What plan will you adopt? What is your scheme for cutting my bonds and setting me free?" the answer may be a deepening of the darkness, a tightening of the bonds.

But if he means, "Lord, what would you have me to do?" the answer will not be long coming. "Give yourself to me to do what I tell you, to understand what I say, to be my good, obedient little brother, and I will wake in you the heart that my Father put in you, the same kind of heart that I have, and it will grow to love the Father, altogether and absolutely, as mine does, until you are ready to be torn to pieces for him. Then you will know that you are at the heart of the universe, at the heart of every secret—at the heart of the Father. Not until then will you be free, then free indeed!"

The Center-Truth of the Universe

Christ died to save us, not from suffering, but from ourselves. Not from injustice, far less from justice, but from *being* unjust. He died that we might live—but live as he lives, by dying as he died who died to himself that he might live unto God. If we do not die to ourselves, we cannot live to God, and he that does not live to God is dead.[1] Every creature must yield himself and lie down. He was made for liberty, and must not be left a slave. Those who will not die, die many times, die constantly, keep dying deeper, never have done dying. You will be dead, so long as you refuse to die.[2]

"Ye shall know the truth," the Lord says, "and the truth shall make you free. I am the truth, and you shall be free as I am free. To be free, you must be sons like me. To be free you must *be* that which you have to be, that for which you are created. To be free you must give the answer of sons to the Father who calls you. To be free you must fear nothing but evil, care for nothing but the will of the Father, hold to him in absolute confidence and infinite expectation. He alone is to be trusted."

Jesus has shown us the Father not only by doing what the Father does, not only by loving his Father's children even as the Father loves them, but by his perfect satisfaction with him, his joy in him, his utter obedience to him. He has shown us the Father by the absolute devotion of a perfect son. He is the Son of God because the Father and he are one, have one thought, one mind, one heart.

Upon this truth—I do not mean the dogma, but the *truth* itself of Jesus to his Father—hangs the universe. And upon the recognition of this truth—that is, upon their becoming true themselves—hangs the freedom of the children, the redemption of their whole world.

"I and the Father are one is the center-truth of the universe. And the encircling truth is, "That they also may be one in us."

The only free man, then, is he who is a child of the Father. He is a servant of all, but can be made the slave of none: he is a son of the Lord of the universe. He is in himself, by virtue of his truth, *free*. He is in himself a king.

For the Son rests his claim to royalty on this, that he was born and came into the world to bear witness to the truth.[3]

To Truly Know God, the Door Is Obedient Faith

A Fictional Selection from *The Laird's Inheritance*

"You are saying a great deal more than you can possibly know, Cosmo," answered Mr. Simon. "You have had no communication you recognize, I grant. And I, who am so much older than you, must say the same. But the air around me may be full of angels and spirits—I do not know. I like to think they may somehow be with us no matter how unseen they are. But so long as I am able to believe and hope in the one great Spirit, the Holy Spirit that fills all, it really does not matter, for he is all in all and fills all things, and all is well."

"But why might not something show itself once—just for once, if only to give one a start in the right direction?" asked Cosmo.

"I will tell you one reason," returned Mr. Simon, "—the same reason everything is as it is, and neither this nor that nor any other way. Things are the way they are because it is best for us it should be so. Suppose you saw a strange sign or wonder. One of two things would likely follow: you would either come to doubt it after it had vanished, or it would grow common to you as you remembered it. No doubt, if visions would make us sure about God, he does not care about the kind of sureness they can give. Or he does not care about our being made sure in that way.

"A thing, Cosmo, might be of little value gained in one way; while gained in another might be a vital, invaluable part of the process of life. God wants us to be sure of a thing by knowing the heart from which it comes. That is the only worthy assurance. To truly *know*, he will have us go in at the great door of obedient faith; and faith, as you know, has to do with things *not* seen. If anybody thinks he has found a back stair into the house of the knowledge of God, he will find it lands him at a doorless wall. It is the assurance that comes inside one's heart of beholding himself, of seeing what he is, that God wants to produce in us. And he would not have us think we know him before we do, for in that error many thousands walk in a vain show.

"And yet, if I do so humbly as his child, I am free to imagine, for God has given us our imaginations as well as our wills for his glory. And I imagine space full of life invisible. As I came just now through the fields, I lost myself for a time in the feeling that I was walking in the midst of lovely people of God that I have known, some in person, some by their books. Perhaps they were with me—are with me—now. For who can distinguish the many ways in which God speaks to us by his Spirit? The moment a thought is given me, whether directly from God, or through something I may have just read, or by a conversation with another, that same instant my own thought rushes to mingle with it, and I can no more tell them apart. Some stray hints from the world beyond may mingle even with the folly and stupidity of my dreams. The Bible speaks many times of God's guiding his people through them."

"But if you cannot distinguish, where is the good?" Cosmo asked.

"It is the quality of a thing, not how it arrived, that is the point. And for anything I know, true things may often be mingled with things not originating with God at all. God's spirit may be taking advantage of the door set ajar by sleep to whisper a message of love or repentance, and the troubled brain or heart or stomach may be sending forth fumes that cloud the vision, causing evil echoes to mingle with the hearing. When you look at any bright thing for a time and then close your eyes, you still see the shape of it, but in different colors. This figure has come to you from the outside world, but the brain has altered it. Even the shape itself is reproduced with but partial accuracy.

"But it is well I should remind you again that the things around us are just as full of marvel as those into which you are so anxious to look from the world beyond. The only thing worth a man's care is the will of God, and that will is the same whether in this world or in the next. That will has made this world ours, not the next. For nothing can be ours until God has given it to us. Curiosity is but the contemptible human shadow of the holy thing yonder. No, my son, let us make the best we can of this life that we may become able to make the best of the next also."

"And how do you make the best of this one?" asked Cosmo.

"Simply by falling in with God's design in the making of you, and allowing him to work out his plan in you. That design must be worked out—cannot be worked out without you. You must walk in the front of things with the will of God—not be dragged in the sweep of his garment that makes the storm behind him! To walk with God is to go hand in hand with him, like a boy with his father. Then, as to the other world, or any world, as to the past sorrow, the vanished joy, the coming fear—all is well! For the design of the making, the loving, the pitiful, the beautiful God is marching on toward divine completion. Let your prayer, my son, be like this: 'O Maker of me, go on making me, and let me help you. Come, O Father! Here I am. Let us go on. I know that my words are those of a child, but it is your own child who prays to you. It is your dark I walk in. It is your hand I hold.' "

The words of the teacher sank into the heart of Cosmo, for his spirit was already in the lofty condition of being capable of receiving wisdom directly from another. It is a lofty condition, indeed, and they who scorn it only show that they have not reached it—nor are likely to reach it soon. Those who will not be taught through eye or ear must be taught through the skin, and that is generally a long as well as a painful process. All Cosmo's maturity came from his having faith in those who were higher than he. His childlike faith had not yet been tried. But the trials of a pure, honest, teachable youth, however severe, must be very different from those of one who is unteachable. The former are for growth, the latter for change.[4]

For Where Your Treasure Is, There Will Your Heart Be Also

The miser lay on his lonely bed;
*   Life's candle was burning dim.*
His heart in an iron chest was hid
Under heaps of gold and an iron lid;
*   And whether it were alive or dead*
*   It never troubled him.*

Slowly out of his body he crept.
*   He said, "I am just the same!*
Only I want my heart in my breast;
I will go and fetch it out of my chest!"
*   Through the dark a darker shadow he leapt,*
*   Saying "Hell is a fabled flame!"*

He opened the lid. Oh, Hell's own night!
*   His ghost-eyes saw no gold!—*
Empty and swept! Not a gleam was there!
In goes his hand, but the chest is bare!
*   Ghost-fingers, aha! have only might*
*   To close, not to clasp and hold!*

But his heart he saw, and he made a clutch
*   At the fungous puff-ball of sin:*
Eaten with moths, and fretted with rust,
He grasped a handful of rotten dust,
*   And shrieked, as ghosts may, at the crumbling touch,*
*   But hid it in his breast within.*

And some there are who see him sit
*   Under the church, apart,*
Counting out coins and coins of gold
Heap by heap on the dank death-mold:
*   Alas poor ghost and his sore lack of wit—*
*   They breed in the dust of his heart!*

Another miser has now his chest,
*   And it hoards wealth more and more;*
Like ferrets his hands go in and out,
Burrowing, tossing the gold about—
*   Nor heed the heart that, gone from his breast,*
*   Is the cold heap's bloodless core.*

Now wherein differ old ghosts that sit
*   Counting ghost-coins all day*
From the man who clings with spirit prone
To whatever can never be his own?
*   Who will leave the world with not one whit*
*   But a heart all eaten away?*

THE HEART WITH THE TREASURE

Lay not up for yourselves treasures upon earth, where moth and rust doth corrupt, and where thieves break through and steal. But lay up for yourselves treasures in heaven, where neither moth nor rust doth corrupt, and where thieves do not break through nor steal. For where your treasure is, there will your heart be also.

Matthew 6:19–21

The Words of the Word

To understand the words of our Lord is the business of life. For it is the main road to the understanding of the Word himself. And to receive him is to receive the Father, and so to have Life in ourselves. And Life, the higher, the deeper, the simpler, the original, is the business of life.

The Word is that by which we live, namely, Jesus himself. And his words represent—in part, in shadow, in suggestion—himself.

Any utterance worthy of being called a *truth* is human food. How much more the *Word*, presenting to abstract laws of reasoning, but the vital relation of soul and body, heart and will, strength and rejoicing, beauty and light, to him who first gave birth to them all!

The Son came forth to *be*, before our eyes and in our hearts, that which God had made us for, that we might behold *the truth* in him, and cry out for the living God, who, in the highest sense of all is the Truth, not as understood by the intellect, but as understanding, living, and being—doing and creating the truth. "I am the truth," said our Lord; and by those who are in some measure like him in being the truth, the Word can be understood.

Let us, therefore, now try to understand him.

Sometimes, no doubt, the Savior would have spoken in a different fashion of speech if he had come to Englishmen instead of to Jews. But

the lessons he gave would have been the same. For even when questioned about a matter of passing importance, his reply contained the
enunciation of the great human principle that lay in it—changeless in
every variation of changeful circumstance. With the light of added ages
of Christian experience, it ought to be easier for us to understand his
words than it was for those who heard him.

The Heart As God Sees It

I now ask you to examine the power of the Lord's word *for* in the
context of, "For where your treasure is, there will your heart be also."

The reason he adds it here is not obvious on the surface. It has to
be sought for because of its depth and at the same time its simplicity.
But it is so complete, so imaginatively comprehensive, so immediately
operative on the conscience through its poetic suggestiveness, that
when it is once understood, there is nothing more to be said, but
everything to be done.

Is the Lord saying that the *reason* for not laying up treasures on
earth is because of their transitory and corruptible nature—that the
moth and rust and thief will cause us to lose them?

No. He adds *for*: "For where your treasure is, there will your heart
he also." What is *with* the treasure must fare the same as the treasure.
The heart that haunts the treasure house where the moth and rust
corrupt will be exposed to the same ravages as the treasure, will itself
be rusted and moth-eaten. The *treasures* are nothing; it is the condition
of the *heart* that is everything!

Many a man, many a woman, fair and flourishing to see, is going
about with a rusty moth-eaten heart within that form of strength or
beauty!

And does not the *rust* and the *moth* mean more than mere disease?
Does not the *heart* mean more than the heart? Does it not mean a deeper
heart—the heart that is your true self—not the physical heart? The self
that suffers, not pain, but misery? The self whose end is not comfort, or
enjoyment, but blessedness, even ecstasy? A heart which is the innermost
chamber wherein springs the divine fountain of your being? A heart
which God regards, though you may never have known its existence, not
even when its writhings under the gnawings of the moth and the slow
fire of the rust have communicated a dull pain to that outer heart which
sends the blood to its appointed course through your body?

If God sees that heart corroded with the rust of cares, riddled into
caverns and films by the worms of ambition and greed, then your heart
is as God sees it, for God sees things as they are. And one day you will

be compelled to see, no, to *feel* your heart as God sees it; and to know that the cankered thing which you have within you, a prey to the vilest of diseases, is indeed the center of your being, your very heart.

All Worship of the Transitory Corrupts

This lesson does not apply only to those who worship Mammon and who give their lives and best energies to the accumulation of wealth. It applies equally to those who in any way worship the transitory, who seek the praise of men more than the praise of God, who would make a show in the world by wealth or taste or intellect or power or art or genius of any kind, and so would gather golden opinions to be treasured in a storehouse of earth.

And not only to such does it apply, but surely also to those as well whose pleasures are of a more visible, transitory nature still, such as the pleasures of the senses in every direction, even when lawfully indulged, if the joy of being is centered in them.

To all who derive their pleasure and satisfaction and joy from the transitory in all its forms, these words bear terrible warning. For the hurt lies not in the fact that these pleasures are false, or that they pass away and leave a fierce disappointment behind. The hurt lies in this— that the immortal, the infinite, created in the image of the everlasting God, is housed with the fading and corrupting.

The immortal soul clings to the heart (the seat of being), until it becomes infected and interpenetrated with all the heart's diseases of self, which assume in the immortal a form more terrible by its very superiority, so that which is mere decay in the heart becomes moral vileness in the soul; that which fits the one for the dunghill casts the other into outer darkness. Then it descends with the heart into a burrow in the earth, where its budded wings wither and mold and drop away from its shoulders, instead of haunting the open plains and the high-uplifted tablelands, spreading abroad its young pinions to the sun and air, and strengthening them in further and further flights, until at last they should become strong to bear the God-born into the presence of its Father in heaven.

Therein lies the hurt of laying up treasures on earth, that in so doing the God-life in us is corrupted and eaten away.[1]

Fling It Aside, and Enter Eternal Life Free

A Fictional Selection from *The Landlady's Master*

H e never mentioned his closet. Even in dreams his secrecy was dominant. Dawtie, who had her share in nursing him, kept hoping her opportunity would come. He did not seem to hold any resentment against her. His illness would protect him, he thought, from further intrusion of her conscience upon his. She must know better than to irritate a sick man with her meddling! Everybody could not be a saint! It was enough to be a Christian like other good and salvable Christians. It was enough for him if through the merits of his Savior he gained admission to the heavenly kingdom at last!

He never thought how, once in, he could bear to stay in. It never occurred to him that heaven would be to him the dullest place in the universe of God, more wearisome than the kingdom of darkness itself. And all the time the young woman with the savior-heart was watching by his bedside, ready to speak. But the Spirit gave her no utterance, and her silence soothed his fear of her.

One night he was more restless than usual. Waking from his troubled slumber, he called her—in the tone of one who had something important to communicate.

"Dawtie," he said with a feeble voice but glittering eye, "there is no one I can trust like you. I have been thinking of what you said ever since that night. Go to my closet and bring me the cup."

Dawtie debated with herself momentarily whether to obey him would be right. But she reflected that it made little difference whether the object of his passion was in his hand or in his chest of valuables while it was all the same deep in his heart. And his words implied that he might want to take his farewell of it. So she said, "Yes, sir," and stood waiting.

He did not speak.

"I do not know where to find it," she added.

"I will tell you," he replied, but seemed to hesitate.

"I will not touch a single thing besides," said Dawtie.

He believed her, and at once proceeded.

"Take my bunch of keys from the hook behind me."

She did so. He took them and fumbled with them a moment.

"There is the key to the closet door. And there, the commonest looking key of the whole bunch, but in reality the most cunningly devised, is the key to the cabinet I keep it in!"

Then he told her where, behind a little bookcase that moved from the wall on hinges, she would find the cabinet, and in what part of it the cup would be, wrapped up in a piece of silk that had once been a sleeve worn by Madame de Genlis—which fact did not make Dawtie much wiser.

She went, found the chalice, and brought it to where the laird lay straining his ears and waiting for it as a man at the point of death might await the sacramental cup from the absolving priest.

His hands trembled as he took it, for they were the hands of a lover—strange as that love was, which not merely looked for no return but desired to give neither pleasure nor good to the thing loved. It was not a love of the merely dead, but a love of the unliving!

He pressed the thing to his bosom. Then, as if rebuked by the presence of Dawtie, he put it a little away from him and began to pore over every stone, every repoussé figure between, and every engraved ornament around the gems, each of which he knew the shape, order, and quality of color better than ever he knew the face of wife or child. But soon his hands sank on the counterpane of silk patchwork, and he lay still, grasping tightly the precious thing.

All at once he woke with a start and a cry, but found it safe in both his hands.

"You didn't try to take the cup from me—did you, Dawtie!"

"No, sir," answered Dawtie. "I would never take it out of your hand, but I *would* be glad to take it out of your heart."

"If only they would bury it with me!" he murmured, heedless of her words.

"Oh, sir! Do you want it burning your heart to all eternity? Give it up, laird, and take instead the treasure that no thief can ever steal."

"Yes, Dawtie, yes! That is the true treasure!"

"And to get it we must sell all we have."

"He gives and withholds as he sees fit."

"No, laird. To get that treasure we must give up this world's."

"I'll not believe it!"

"And then, when you go down into the blackness, longing for the cup that you will never see again, you will complain that God would not give you the strength to fling it from you?"

He hugged the chalice as he replied. "Fling it from me!" he cried fiercely. "Girl, who are you to torment me before my time!"

"God gives every man and woman the power to do what he requires, and we are fearfully to blame for not using the strength God gives us."

"I cannot bear the strain of thinking!" gasped the laird.

"Then give up thinking, and do the thing! Or shall I take it for you?"

She put out her hand as she spoke.

"No! no!" he cried, grasping the cup tighter. "You shall not touch it! You would give it to the earl! I know you! Saints hate what is beautiful!"

"I like better to look at things in my Father's hand than in my own."

"You want to see my cup—it *is* my cup!—in the hands of that spendthrift fool, Lord Borland!"

"It is in the Father's hand, whoever has it."

"Hold your tongue, Dawtie, or I will cry out and wake the house."

"They will think you dreaming, or out of your mind, and they will come and take the cup from you. Do let me put it away. Then you will go to sleep."

"I will not! I cannot trust you with it. You have destroyed my confidence in you. I may fall asleep, but if your hand comes within a foot of the cup, it will wake me. I shall sleep with my heart in the cup, and the least touch will wake me!"

"I wish you would let Andrew Ingram come to see you, sir."

"What's the matter with *him*?"

"Nothing's the matter with him, laird. But he helps every-body to do what is right."

"Conceited rascal! Do you take me for a maniac that you talk such foolery?"

His look was so wild, his old blue faded eyes gleamed with such a light of mingled fear and determination that Dawtie was almost sorry she had spoken. With trembling hands he drew the cup under his covers and lay still. If only the morning would come and bring George Crawford! *He* would take the cup back to its place, or hide it where he should know it safe and not far from him!

Dawtie sat motionless, and the old man fell into another feverish doze. She dared not stir lest he should start awake to defend his idol. She sat like a statue, moving only her eyes.

"What are you about, Dawtie?" he said at length. "You are after some mischief, you are so quiet."

"I was telling God how good you would be if he could get you to give up your odds and ends and take him instead."

"How dare you say such a thing, sitting there by my side! Are *you* to say to *him* that any sinner would be good if he would only do so and so with him! Tremble, girl, at the vengeance of the Almighty! How are you to presume to know what is best for another, and then tell *him* what you think!"

"We are told to make prayers and intercessions for all men, and I was saying what I could for you."

The laird was silent, and the rest of the night passed quietly.[2]

Power

Power that is not of God, however great,
Is but the downward rushing and the glare
Of a swift meteor that hath lost its share
In the one impulse which doth animate
The parent mass: emblem to me of fate!
Which through vast nightly wastes doth onward fare,
Wild-eyed and headlong, rent away from prayer—
A moment brilliant, then most desolate!
And, O my brothers, shall we ever learn
From all the things we see continually
That pride is but the empty mockery
Of what is strong in man! Not so the stern
And sweet repose of soul which we can earn
Only through reverence and humility!

THE FIRST BUSINESS OF LIFE—TO OBEY THE FATHER

Then was Jesus led up of the Spirit into the wilderness to be tempted of the devil . . . And when the tempter came to him, he said . . . If thou be the Son of God, cast thyself down: for it is written, He shall give his angels charge concerning thee: and in their hands they shall bear thee up. . . . Jesus said unto him, It is written again, Thou shalt not tempt the Lord thy God.

Matthew 4:1, 3, 6–7

The Son Must Only Obey

Following Christ's first temptation in the wilderness, in which Jesus refutes Satan from the Word of God, the enemy makes a second attempt.

"Then if God is to be so trusted," he says, "try him. I would like to see the result. Show thyself his chosen one. Here are his own words: 'He shall give his angels charge concerning thee; not a stone shall hurt thee.' Take him at his Word. Throw thyself down, and convince me that thou art the Son of God. For thou knowest thou dost not look like who thou sayest thou art."

Again, with the written Word, in return, the Lord meets him. And he does not quote the Scripture for logical purposes—to confute Satan intellectually, but rather to give Satan the reason for his conduct. Satan quotes Scripture as a verbal authority; our Lord meets him with Scripture as the truth by which he regulates his conduct.

If we examine it, we find that this answer contains the same principle as the one he has just given: "It is written, 'Man shall not live by bread alone, but by every word that proceedeth out of the mouth of God.' " The principle is simply this: *To the Son of God the will of God is Life.*

It was a temptation to show the powers of the world that he was the Son of God; that to him the elements were subject; that he was above the laws of nature because he was the eternal Son; and thus stop the raging of the heathen, and the vain imaginations of the people. It would be but to show them the truth.

But he was the *Son* of God. Something even greater than showing the world the truth burned in his heart: What was his *Father's* will? Such was not the divine way of convincing the world of sin, of righteousness, of judgment.

If the Father told him to cast himself down, the next instant the pinnacle would have been empty. If the devil threw him down, let God send his angels, or, if in his Father's plan, allow him to be dashed to pieces in the valley below.

But never on his *own* would he forestall the divine will. Never would he do *anything* to please Satan, or to please himself, be it even so powerful as to convince the world that he came from heaven. Only the Father would order what came next. The Son would obey. In the path of his daily work he would turn aside for no stone. There let the angels bear him up if need be. But he would not choose the path because there was or was not a stone in it. He would not choose at all. He would go only where the Spirit leads him.

True Faith—Not Doing, Not Even Believing, But Obeying

I think this will throw some light upon the words of our Lord, "If ye have faith and doubt not, if ye shall say unto this mountain, Be thou removed, and be thou cast into the sea; it shall be done."

Good people, among them John Bunyan, have been tempted to tempt the Lord their God upon the strength of this saying, just as Satan sought to tempt our Lord on the strength of the passage he quoted from the Psalms. They think that as long as they have *faith*, and believe earnestly enough, it is possible to do and accomplish *anything* to which they might set their hand.

Happily for such, the assurance to which they would give the name of faith generally fails them in time. Faith is not the fervent setting of the mind on "believing" for such-and-such an outcome—more often than not a desire generated by the man's own soul—as if *we*, and not God, were the originators and initiators of faith by the strength of our passions, the fervor of our prayers, and the forcefulness of our mental processes. True faith, rather, is that which, knowing the Lord's will, goes and does it, or, not knowing it, stands and waits, content in ignorance as in knowledge, because God wills. Faith neither presses into the hidden future, nor is careless of the knowledge that opens the path of action. It is faith's noblest exercise to act with uncertainty of the result when the duty of obedience is certain, or even when a course seems with strong probability to be duty. Even if a man is mistaken in the honest effort to obey, though his work be burned, by that very fire he will be saved. Nothing saves a man more than the burning of his work, except the doing of work that can stand the fire.

But to put God to the question in any other way than by saying, "What will you have me to do?" is an attempt to compel God to declare himself, or to hasten his work, or to imagine it *his* work what our own soul desires to accomplish.

We Tempt God by Forcing Him to Act

This probably was the sin of Judas. It is presumption of a kind similar to the making of a stone into bread. It is, as it were, either a forcing of God to act where he has created no need for action, or the making of a case wherein he shall seem to have forfeited his word if he does not act. This is the ultimate folly, thinking we can somehow coerce God into bending his will to suit our designs.

In such an attempt, the man dissociates himself from God so far that, instead of acting by the divine will from within, he acts in God's face, as it were, to see what he will do.

Man's first business is, "What does God want me to do?" not "What will God do if I do so and so?" To tempt a human parent in such a manner would be impertinence; to tempt God so is the same vice in its highest form—a natural result of that condition of mind which is worse than all the so-called cardinal sins, namely, spiritual pride, which attributes the tenderness and love of God not to man's being and man's need, but to some distinguishing excellence in the individual himself, which causes the Father to love him better than his fellows, and so pass by his faults with a smile.

Not such did the Son of God regard his relation to his Father. The faith that will remove mountains is the confidence in God that comes from seeking nothing but his will. A man who was thus faithful would die of hunger sooner than say to the stone, "Be bread." He would meet the scoffs of the unbelieving without reply and with apparent defeat, sooner than say to the mountain, "Be cast into the sea," even if he knew that it would be torn from its foundations at the word, unless he knew first that God would have it so.[1]

The Chrysalis

Methought I floated sightless, nor did know
That I had ears until I heard the cry
As of a mighty man in agony:
"How long, Lord, shall I lie thus foul and slow?
The arrows of thy lightning through me go,
And sting and torture me—yet here I lie
A shapeless mass that scarce can mould a sigh!"
The darkness thinned; I saw a thing below
Like sheeted corpse, a knot at head and feet.
Slow clomb the sun the mountains of the dead,
And looked upon the world: the silence broke!
A blinding struggle! then the thunderous beat
Of great exulting pinions stroke on stroke!
And from that world a mighty angel fled.

Man's Business Is to Do the Will of God

Fictional Selections from *The Musician's Quest*

The next morning rose brilliant—an ideal summer day. He would not go yet; he would spend one day more in the place. He opened his valise to get some lighter clothes. His eyes fell on a New Testament. Dr. Anderson had put it there. He had never opened it yet, and now he let it lie. Its time had not yet come. He went out.

Walking up the edge of the valley he came upon a little stream whose talk he had heard for some hundred yards. It flowed through a grassy hollow, with steeply sloping sides. Water is the same all the world over; but there was more than water here to bring his childhood back to Falconer. For at the spot where the path led him down to the burn, a little crag stood out from the bank—a gray stone, like many he knew on the stream that watered the valley of Rothieden. On the top of the stone grew a little heather; and beside it, bending toward the water, was a silver birch. He sat down on the foot of the rock, shut in by the high, grassy banks from the gaze of the mighty mountains. The sole unrest was the run of the water beside him, and it sounded so homey that he began to jabber in Scotch to it. With his country's birch tree beside him and the rock crowned with its turf of heather over his head, once more the words arose in his mind, "My peace I give unto you."

Now he fell to thinking what this peace could be. And it came into his mind, as he thought, that Jesus had spoken in another place about giving rest to those that came to him, while here he spoke about "*my* peace." Could this *my* mean a certain *kind* of peace that the Lord himself possessed? He then remembered the New Testament back in his room, and, resolving to try whether he could not make something more out of it, went back to the inn quieter in heart than since he left his home. In the evening he returned to the brook, and fell to searching the story, seeking after the peace of Jesus.

He did not leave the place for six weeks. Every day he went to the burn, as he called the stream, with his New Testament; every day tried yet again to make something more of what the Savior meant. By the end of the month it had dawned on him that the peace of Jesus must have been a peace that came from doing the will of his Father. From the account he gave of the discoveries he then made, I will venture to represent them here. They were these Jesus taught:

First—That a man's business is to do the will of God.

Second—That God will care for the man.

Third—That a man, therefore, must not be afraid but be at peace; and so,

Fourth—be left free to love God with all his heart, and his neighbor as himself.

But then a new question suddenly arose, "How am I to tell for certain that there ever was such a man as this one whose words I am reading?"

All this wilderness time he did nothing but read the four gospels and ponder over them. Therefore it is not surprising that he should already have become so familiar with the gospel story that the moment this question appeared, the following words should dart to the forefront of his mind:

"If any man chooses to do his will, he shall know whether my teaching comes from God or whether I speak of myself."

Here was a word from Jesus himself, giving the surest means of arriving at a conclusion of the truth or falsehood of all that he said, namely, by doing the will of God.

The next question naturally was, "What is this will of God?"

Here he found himself in difficulty. The theology of his grandmother rushed in upon him, threatening to overwhelm him with demands. They were repulsive to him. They appeared unreal and contradictory to the nature around him. Yet that alone could be no *proof* that they were not of God. Still, they demanded what *seemed* to him unjust; these demands were founded on what *seemed* to him untruth attributed to God, on ways of thinking and feeling which were degrading in a man. Thus he realized, as long as they appeared to be such to him, that to acknowledge these demands as truth, even if it turned out later that he misunderstood them, would be to wrong God.

For two more weeks he brooded and pondered over the question, as he wandered up and down that burnside or sat at the foot of the heather-crowned stone and the silver-barked birch, until the light began to dawn upon him.

It grew plain to him that what Jesus came to do was just lead his life, rather than adhering to the list of doctrinal demands he had himself been wrestling with. That he should do the work, and much besides, that the Father had given him to do—that was the will of God concerning him. With this perception arose the conviction that to *every* man and woman God has given a work to do. Each had to lead the life God meant him to lead. The will of God was thus to be found and done in the world, not solely in theology or doctrine or demands of the church. In seeking a true relation to the world, then, he would come to find his relation to God.

The time for action was come. The will of God could only be known by doing. He rose up from the stone of his meditation, took his staff in his hand, and went down the mountain, not knowing where he went. As he descended the mountain, the one question was—what was he now to *do*? If he had had the faintest track to follow he would have concluded that his business was to set out at once and find his father. But since the day when the hand of that father smote him and Mary St. John found him bleeding on the factory floor, he had not heard one word or conjecture about him. If he were to set out to find him now, it would be to search the earth for one who might have vanished from it years ago. When the time came for him to find his father, some sign would be given him—that is, some hint which he could follow with action. Until then there was no course of action open to him. As he continued to think and think, it became gradually plainer that he must begin his obedience by getting ready for anything that God might require of him. Therefore he must go on learning till the call came. [2]

Consider the Ravens

Lord, according to thy words,
I have considered thy birds;
And I find their life good,
And better the better understood:
Sowing neither corn nor wheat
They have all that they can eat;
Reaping no more than they sow
They have more than they could stow;
Having neither barn nor store
Hungry again, they eat more.
Considering, I see too that they
Have a busy life, and plenty of play;
In the earth they dig their bills deep
And work well though they do not heap;
Then to play in the air they are not loath,
And their nests between are better than both.
But this is when there blow no storms,
When berries are plenty in winter, and worms,
When feathers are rife, with oil enough—
To keep the cold out and send the rain off;
If there come, indeed, a long hard frost
Then it looks as thy birds were lost.

But I consider further, and find
A hungry bird has a free mind;
He is hungry today, not tomorrow,
Steals no comfort, no grief doth borrow;
This moment is his, thy will hath said it,
The next is nothing till thou hast made it.

Thy bird has pain, but has no fear
Which is the worst of any gear;
When cold and hunger and harm betide him,
He does not take them and stuff inside him;
Content with the day's ill he has got,
He waits just, nor haggles with his lot;
Neither jumbles God's will
With driblets from his own still.

But next I see, in my endeavour,
Thy birds here do not live forever;
That cold or hunger, sickness or age
Finishes their earthly stage;
The rooks drop in cold nights,
Leaving all their wrongs and rights;
Birds lie here and birds lie there
With their feathers all astare;
And in thy own sermon, thou
That the sparrow falls dost allow.

It shall not cause me any alarm,
For neither so comes the bird to harm
Seeing our Father, thou hast said,
Is by the sparrow's dying bed;
Therefore it is a blessed place,
And the sparrow in high grace.

It cometh therefore to this, Lord:
I have considered thy word,
And henceforth will be thy bird.

THE PERFECT WILL OF GOD MUST BE DONE

Again, the devil taketh him up into an exceeding high mountain, and showeth him all the kingdoms of the world, and the glory of them; and saith unto him, All these things will I give thee, if thou wilt fall down and worship me. Then saith Jesus unto him, Get thee hence, Satan: for it is written, Thou shalt worship the Lord thy God, and him only shalt thou serve.

Matthew 4:8–10

Was Jesus Tempted to Save the World by Force?

The third temptation which Jesus faced in the wilderness may be regarded as the contest of the seen and the unseen, of the outer and inner, of the likely and the true, of the show and the reality. And as in the ones that had come before it, the evil lay in that it was a temptation to do good, to save his brethren, instead of doing the will of his Father.

We forget that Jesus was a man, and prone to the same ambitions that lure men's hearts. It must have been a sore temptation to think that he might, if he would, lay a righteous grasp upon the reins of government, leap into the chariot of power, and ride forth conquering and to conquer. Glad visions no doubt arose before him of the prisoner breaking jubilant from the cell of injustice; of the widow lifting up her bowed head; of weeping children bursting into shouts; of oppression and wrong shrinking and withering before the wheels of the chariot, behind which sprung the fir tree instead of the thorn, and the myrtle instead of the brier.

What glowing visions of holy vengeance, what rosy dreams of human blessedness—and all from his hand—would crowd such a brain as his! They would not be like the castles-in-the-air of the aspiring youth, who builds at random because he knows he cannot realize his dreams. Rather those of Jesus would be consistent and harmonious as well as grand, because he knew them within his reach.

Could he not mold the people at his will? He had only to speak, and the result would happen! Could he not, transfigured in his snowy garments, call aloud in the streets of Jerusalem, "Behold your King?" The fierce warriors of his nation would start at the sound. The plow-share would be beaten into the sword, and the pruning-hook into the spear. And the nation, rushing to his call, would learn war yet again—a grand, holy war against the tyrants of the race.

Ah! but when were his garments white as snow? When did the light stream through them from his glorified body, glorifying them as it passed? Not when he looked to such a conquest, but when, on a mount like this, he "spake of the decease that he should *accomplish* at Jerusalem"!

"Thou shalt worship the Lord thy God, and him only shalt thou serve." Not even thine own visions of love and truth, O Savior of the world, shall be thy guide to thy goal, but the will of thy Father in heaven.

Nothing But Obedience Will Redeem the Prisoner

But how would he, thus conquering, be a servant of Satan? Why would this be a falling down and worshiping of him (that is, an ac-knowledging of the worth of him) who was the lord of misrule and its pain?

I will not inquire whether such an enterprise could be accomplished without the worship of Satan, whether men could be managed for such a seemingly righteous end without more or less of the trickery practiced by every ambitious leader, every self-serving conqueror, without double-dealing, tact, flattery, and finesse. I will not inquire into this, because, on the most distant supposition of our Lord being the leader of his country's armies, these things drop out of sight as impossibilities. If these were necessary, such a career for him refuses to be for a moment imagined.

But I will ask whether to know better and do not so well is not a serving of Satan? Is it not a serving of Satan to lead men on in the name of God as though toward the best, when the end is not the best? Is it not a serving of Satan to flatter their pride by making them conquerors of the armies of their nation instead of their own evils? In a word, would it not have been a serving of Satan to desert the mission of God, who knew that men could not be set free in that way, and so sent him to be a man, a true man, the one man, among them, that his life might become their life, so they might be as free in prison or on the cross, as upon a hillside or on a throne? Would it not have been a serving of Satan to desert the truth, and thus to give men over to the lie of believing other than spirit and truth to be the worship of the Father, other than love the fulfilling of the law, other than the offering of their best selves the service of God, other than obedient harmony with the primal love and truth and law, freedom? Would it not have been—to desert God thus, and give men over thus—to fall down and worship the Devil?

Not all the sovereignty of God, as the theologians call it, delegated to the Son, and administered by the wisdom of the Spirit that was given to him, could have brought the kingdom of heaven to pass in one corner of our earth. Nothing but the obedience of the Son, the obedience unto the death, the absolute *doing* of the will of God because it was the truth, could redeem the prisoner, the widow, the orphan. But that obedience could and would redeem them, and it would redeem them by redeeming the conquest-ridden conqueror too, the stripe-giving jailor, the unjust judge, the devouring Pharisee himself with the insatiable moth-eaten heart.

The earth should be free because Love was stronger than Death! Therefore should fierceness and wrong and hypocrisy and God-service play out their weary play.

Not a Branch Here and There, But the Whole Tree

Jesus would not give himself to only a portion of his Father's will, but to all of it. He would not pluck the spreading branches of the tree; he would lay the axe to its root. He would not deal with the mere effect of sin; he would destroy sin altogether. It would take time, but the tree would be dead at last—dead, and cast into the lake of fire. It would take time, but his Father had time enough and to spare. It would take courage and strength and self-denial and endurance; but his Father could give him all. It would cost pain of body and mind, agony and torture, but those he was ready to take on himself. It would cost him the vision of many sad and, to all but him, hopeless sights. He would have to see tears without wiping them, hear sighs without changing them into laughter, see the dead lie, and let them lie. He would have to see Rachel weeping for her children and refusing to be comforted. He must look on his brothers and sisters crying as children over their broken toys, and must not mend them. He must go on to the grave, and none of these know that thus he was setting all things right for them. His work must be one with and completing God's creation and God's history.

The disappointment and sorrow and fear he could, and would bear. The will of God would be done. Man would be free—not merely man as he thinks of himself, but man as God thinks of him. The divine idea would be set free in the divine bosom. The man on earth would see his image face to face. He would grow into the likeness of the divine thought, free not in his own fancy, but in absolute divine fact of being, as in God's idea.

The great and beautiful and perfect will of God *would* be done. "Get thee hence, Satan: for it is written, Thou shalt worship the Lord thy God, and him only shalt thou serve!"

"Then the devil leaveth him," says Matthew, "and behold angels came and ministered unto him." They brought him the food he had waited for, walking in the strength of the Word. He would have died if it had not come now.

"And when the devil had ended all the temptation," says Luke, "he departed from him for a season."[1]

God's Continual Work— Making Us Good

A Fictional Selection from *The Vicar's Daughter*

Wouldn't you think, perhaps, that God, having gone so far to make this world a pleasant and comfortable place to live in, might not have gone farther and made it quite pleasant and comfortable for everybody?"

"Whoever could make it at all could ha' done that, grannie."

"Then, as he hasn't done it, the probability is he didn't mean to do it?"

"Of course. That's what I complain of."

"Then he meant to do something else?"

"It looks like it."

"The whole affair has an unfinished look, you think?"

"I think that."

"What if it were not meant to stand, then? What if it were

meant only for a temporary assistance in carrying out something finished and lasting, and of unspeakably more importance? Suppose God were building a palace for you, and had set up a scaffold, upon which he wanted you to help him; would it be reasonable in you to complain that you didn't find the scaffold at all a comfortable place to live in? that it was drafty and cold? This world is that scaffold; and if you were busy carrying stones and mortar for the palace, you would be glad of all the cold to cool the glow of your labor."

"I'm sure I work hard enough when I get a job as my eyesight will enable me to do," said Evans, missing the point of her illustration.

"Yes, I believe you do. But what will all the labor of a workman come to who does not fall in with the design of the builder? You may say you don't understand the design; will you say also that you are under no obligation to put so much faith in the builder, who is said to be your God and Father, as to do the thing he tells you? Instead of working away at the palace, like men, will you go on tacking bits of matting and old carpet about the corners of the scaffold to keep the wind off, while that same wind keeps tearing them away and scattering them? You keep trying to live in a scaffold, which not all you could do to all eternity would make a house of. You see what I mean, Mr. Evans?"

"Well, not exactly," replied the blind man.

"I mean that God wants to build you a house whereof the walls shall be *goodness*; you want a house whereof the walls shall be *comfort*. But God knows that such walls cannot be built, that that kind of stone crumbles away in the foolish workman's hands. He would make you comfortable; but neither is that his first object, nor can it be gained without the first, which is to make you good. He loves you so much that he would infinitely rather have you good and uncomfortable, for then he could take you to his heart as his own children, than comfortable and not good, for then he could not come near you, or give you anything he counted worth having for himself or worth giving to you."

"So," said Jarvis, "you've just brought us around, grannie, to the same thing as before."

"I believe so," returned Marion. "It comes to this, that when God would build a palace for himself to dwell in with his children, he does not want his scaffold so constructed that they shall be able to make a house of it for themselves, and live like apes instead of angels."

"But if God can do anything he please," said Evans, "he might as well *make* us good, and there would be an end of it."

"That is just what he is doing," returned Marion. "Perhaps, by giving them perfect health, and everything they wanted, with absolute good temper, and making them very fond of each other besides, God might have provided himself a people he would have had no difficulty in governing, and among whom, in consequence, there would have been no crime and no struggle or suffering. But I have known a dog with more goodness than that would come to. We cannot be good without having consented to be made good. God shows us the good and the bad; urges us to be good; wakes good thoughts and desires in us; helps our spirit with his Spirit, our thought with his thought: but we must yield; we must turn to him; we must consent, yes, try to be made good. If we could become good without trying, it would be a poor goodness: *we* should not be good, after all; at best, we should only be not bad. God wants us to choose to be good, and so be partakers of his holiness; he would have us lay hold of him. He who has given his Son to suffer for us will make us suffer too, bitterly if needful, that we may repent and turn to him. He would make us as good as good can be, that is, perfectly good; and therefore will rouse us to take the needful hand in the work ourselves—rouse us by discomforts innumerable.

"You see, then, it is not inconsistent with the apparent imperfections of the creation around us, that Jesus should have done the best possible carpenter's work; for those very imperfections are actually through their imperfection the means of carrying out the higher creation God has in view, and at which he is working all the time."[2]

Hard Times

I am weary, and very lonely,
　　And can but think—think.
If there were some water only
　　That a spirit might drink—drink,
　　　　And arise,
　　　　With light in the eyes
And a crown of hope on the brow,
　　To walk abroad in the strength of gladness,
　　Not sit in the house, benumbed with sadness—
　　　　As now!

But, Lord, thy child will be sad—
　　As sad as it pleases thee;
Will sit, not seeking to be glad,
　　Till thou bid sadness flee,
　　　　And, drawing near,
　　　　With thy good cheer
Awake thy life in me.

THE ELOI

My God, my God, why hast thou forsaken me?

Matthew 27:46

The Final Temptation

I do not know that I should dare to approach this, of all utterances into which human breath has ever been molded, most awful in import, did I not feel that—containing both germ and blossom of the final devotion—it contains therefore the deepest practical lesson the human heart has to learn.

The Lord, the revealer, hides nothing that can be revealed. He will not warn away the foot that treads in naked humility even upon the ground of that terrible conflict between him and evil, when the smoke of the battle that was fought not only with garments rolled in blood but with burning and fuel of fire, rose up between him and his Father, and for one terrible moment before he broke the bonds of life and walked weary and triumphant into his arms, hid God from the eyes of his Son.

Jesus will give us even to meditate on the one thought that slew him at last, when he could bear no more, and fled to the Father to know that he loved him, and was well-pleased with him. For Satan had come at length yet again, to urge him with his last temptation, to tell him that although he had done his part, God had forgotten his. As he hung on the cross, the tempter whispered to him that, although he had lived by the word of the Father's mouth, that mouth had no more word to speak to him; that although he had refused to tempt him, God had left him to be tempted more than he could bear; that although he had worshiped none other, in the end God did not care for that worship.

The Lord hides not his sacred sufferings, for truth is light, and would be light in the minds of men. The Holy Child, the Son of the Father, has nothing to conceal, but all the Godhead to reveal. Let us then take off our shoes, and draw near, and bow our head, and kiss those feet that bear forever the scars of our victory. In those feet we clasp the safety of our suffering, sinning brotherhood.

The Final Triumph

It is with the holiest fear that we should approach the terrible fact of the sufferings of our Lord.

Let no one think that they were less because he was more. The more delicate the nature, the more alive to all that is lovely and true, lawful and right, the more does it feel the antagonism of pain, the inroad of death upon life. The more sensitive the nature, the more dreadful is that breach of the harmony of things whose sound is untrue.

Jesus felt more than man could feel, because he had a larger feeling. He was therefore worn out even sooner than another man would have been. These sufferings were awful indeed when they began to invade the region about the will. Then did Jesus bear the weight of our sin, when the struggle to keep consciously trusting in God began to sink in darkness, when the will of the man put forth its last determined effort in that cry after the vanishing vision of the Father, "My God, my God, why hast thou forsaken me?" Never before had he been unable to see God beside him. Yet never was God nearer him than now. For never was Jesus more divine. He could not see, could not feel God near; yet it was "*My* God" that he cried. Still it was to his Father he turned in his very agony.

Thus the will of Jesus, in the very moment when his faith seemed about to yield, was finally triumphant. It had no *feeling* then to support it, no blissful vision to absorb it. It stood naked in his soul and tortured, as he stood naked and scourged before Pilate. Pure and simple and surrounded by fire, his will declared for God.

The sacrifice ascended in the cry, "*My* God." The cry came not out of happiness, out of peace, out of hope. Not even out of suffering did the cry come. It was a cry *in* desolation, but it came out of faith. It was the last voice of truth, speaking when it could only cry. The divine horror of that moment is unfathomable to the human soul. It was the blackness of darkness. And yet he believed. Yet he held fast. God was still his God.

"*My* God"—and in the cry came forth the victory, and all was over soon. Of the peace that followed that cry, the peace of a perfect soul, large as the universe, pure as light, ardent as life, victorious for God and his brethren, he alone can ever know the breadth and length, and depth and height.

In the Will Is Victory Born

Without this last trial of all, the temptations of our Master would not have been so full as the human cup could hold. Without this, there would have been one region through which we had to pass—namely, death—wherein we might call aloud upon our Captain-Brother, and yet he would not hear us for he would have avoided the fatal spot!

The temptations of the desert came to the young, strong man with his path before him and the presence of his God around him. Those earlier temptations gathered their very force from the exuberance of his conscious faith. "Dare and do, for God is with thee," said the Devil. "I know it, and therefore I will wait," returned the king of his brothers.

And then, after three years of divine action, when his course was run, when the old age of finished work was come, when the whole frame was tortured until the controlling brain fell whirling down the blue gulf of fainting, and the giving up of the ghost was at hand, when his friends had forsaken him and fled, then came again the voice of the enemy at his ear: "Despair and die, for God is not with thee. All is in vain. Death, not Life, is thy refuge. Make haste to Hades, where thy torture will be over. Thou hast deceived thyself. He never was with thee. He was the God of Abraham. Abraham is dead. Whom makest thou thyself?"

"My God, my God, why hast thou forsaken me?" the Master cried. For God was his God still, although he had forsaken him—forsaken *his vision* of him that his faith might glow out triumphant. But forsaken *him*? No! He had come nearer to him than ever; come nearer even as— but with a yet deeper, more awesome pregnancy of import—the Lord himself withdrew from the bodily eyes of his friends, that he might dwell in them in a more profound way.

I do not think it was our Lord's deepest trial when in the garden he prayed that the cup might pass from him, and prayed yet again that the will of the Father might be done. For that will was then present with him. He was living and acting in that will.

But now the foreseen horror had come. He was drinking the dread cup, and the Will was vanished from his eyes. Were that Will visible in his suffering, his will would have bowed with tearful gladness under the shelter of its grandeur. But his will was left alone to drink the cup of the Will in torture. In the sickness of this agony, the will of Jesus rose perfect at last. And of itself, unsupported, it declared—a naked consciousness of misery hanging in the waste darkness of the universe—declared for God, in defiance of pain, of death, of apathy, of self, of negation, of the blackness within and around it called aloud upon the vanished God.

This is the faith of the Son of God. God withdrew, as it were, that the perfect will of the Son might arise and go forth to find the will of the Father.

Is it possible that even then Jesus thought of the lost sheep who could not believe that God was their Father? Is it possible that for them, too, in all their loss and blindness and unlove, he cried, saying the word they might say, knowing for them that *God* means *Father* and more, and knowing then, as he had never known until then, what a fearful thing it is to be without God and without hope?

I dare not even answer the question I raise.[1]

My Heart Thy Lark

Why dost thou want to sing
  When thou has no song, my heart?
If there be in thee a hidden spring,
  Wherefore will no word start?

On its way thou hearest no song,
  Yet flutters thy unborn joy!
The years of thy life are growing long—
  Art still the heart of a boy?

Father, I am thy child!
  My heart is in thy hand!
Let it hear some echo, with gladness wild,
  Of a song in thy high land.

It will answer—but how, my God,
  Thou knowest; I cannot say:
It will spring, I know, thy lark, from thy sod—
  Thy lark to meet thy day!

PREPARATION IS NECESSARY FOR FULFILLMENT OF TRUTH

Fictional Selections from *The Seaboard Parish*

D on't you think it looks sometimes, Papa, as if God turned his back on the world, or went farther away from it for a while?"

"Tell me a little more what you mean, Connie."

"Well, this night now, this dark, frozen, lifeless night, which you have been describing to me, isn't like God at all—is it?"

"No, it is not. I see what you mean now."

"It is just as if he had gone away and said, 'Now you shall see what you can do without me.' "

"Something like that. But do you know that English people— at least I think so—enjoy the changeful weather of their country much more upon the whole than those who have fine weather constantly? You see it is not enough to satisfy God's goodness that he should give us all things richly to enjoy, but he must make us able to enjoy them as richly as he gives them. He has to consider not only the gift, but the receiver of the gift. He has to make us able to take the gift and make it our own, as well as to give us the gift. In fact, it is not real giving, with the full, that is, the divine, meaning of giving, without it. He has to give us to the gift as well as give the gift to us. Now for this to happen, a break, an interruption is good, is invaluable, for then we begin to think about the thing, and do something in the matter our-selves. The wonder of God's teaching is that, in great part, he makes us not merely learn, but teach ourselves, and that is far grander than if he only made our minds as he makes our bod-ies."

"As long as our Lord was with his disciples, they could not see him aright—he was too near them. Too much light, too many words, too much revelation, blinds or stupefies. The Lord had been with them long enough. They loved him dearly, and yet often forgot his words almost as soon as he said them. He could not get it into them, for instance, that he had not come to be a king. Whatever he said, they adapted it after their own fancy; and their minds were so full of their own worldly notions of grandeur and command, that they could not receive into their souls the gift of God present before their eyes. Therefore he was taken away, that his Spirit, which was more himself than his bodily presence, might come into them—that they might receive the gift of God into their innermost being.

After he had gone out of their sight, and they looked all around and down in the grave and up in the air, and did not see him anywhere—when they thought they had lost him, he began to come to them again from the other side—from the inside. They found that the image of him which his presence with them had printed in light upon their souls, began to revive in the darkness of his absence; and not that only, but that in looking at it without his overwhelming bodily presence, lines and forms and meanings began to dawn which they had never seen before. And his words came back to them, no longer as they had received them, but as he meant them. The Spirit of Christ filling their hearts and giving them power, made them remember, by making them able to understand, all that he had said to them. They were then always saying to each other, 'You remember how . . .' whereas before, they had been always staring at each other with astonishment and something very near incredulity while he spoke to them. So that after he had gone away, he was really nearer to them than he had been before. The meaning of anything is more than its visible presence. There is a soul in everything, and that soul is the meaning of it. The soul of the world and all its beauty has come nearer to you, my dear, just because you are separated from it for a time."[2]

From *"Concerning Jesus"*

Despised! Rejected by the priest-led roar
Of the multitude! The imperial purple flung
About the form the hissing scourge had stung,
Witnessing naked to the truth it bore!
True son of father true, I thee adore.
Even the mocking purple truthful hung
On thy true shoulders, bleeding its folds among,
For thou wast king, art king for evermore!
I know the Father: he knows me the truth.
Truth-witness, therefore the one essential king,
With thee I die, with thee live worshipping!
O human God, O brother, eldest born,
Never but thee was there a man in sooth,
Never a true crown but thy crown of thorn!

TRUSTING GOD IN THE DARKNESS

A Fictional Selection from *The Landlady's Master*

How are you, Dawtie?"

"Well enough. God is with me, but sometimes it is hard to feel him."

"I cannot always see God's eyes looking at me, Dawtie, or feel him in my heart. But when we are ready to do what he wants us to do, we can know he is with us."

"Oh, Andrew, I wish I could be sure!"

"Even if he showed himself to us in person, the sight of him would make us believe in him without knowing him. What kind of faith would that be for him or for us! We must *know* him! And we come to know him by trusting him. It is hard on God that his own children will not trust him, when his perfect love is our perfect safety. But one day we shall know and trust him, Dawtie. When we do, there will be no fear, no doubt. We shall run straight home! . . . God hasn't forgotten you . . . He's still all about you and in you, Dawtie, and this has come to you just to let you know that he is. He raised you up just to spend his glory upon!"

"But it's a sore trial, Andrew, hearing him lie about me!"

"Did Jesus deserve what he got, Dawtie?"

"Not a bit, Andrew!"

"Do you think God had forgotten him?"

"Maybe he thought it just for a minute."

"Well, you have now thought it just for a minute, and you must think it no more."

"But God couldn't forget *him*, Andrew; he got what happened to him all from doing his will!"

"Evil may come upon us from other causes than doing the will of God. But from whatever cause it comes, the thing we have to see to is that through it all, we do the will of God."

"What's his will now, Andrew?"

"That you take it quietly. Shall not the Father do with his own child what he will! Can he not shift it from one arm to the other, even though the child may cry? He has you in his arms, Dawtie! It's all right!"

"Though he slay me, yet will I trust him. Is that what you would have me remember, Andrew, like you've said to me before?" said Dawtie with a faint smile.

"Aye! We can *always* trust him!"[3]

Wha's My Neibour?

Doon frae Jerus'lem a traveler took
  The laigh road to Jericho;
It had an ill name an' mony a crook,
  It was lang an' unco how.

Oot cam the robbers, an' fell o' the man,
  An' knockit him o' the heid,
Took a' whauron they couth lay their han',
  An' left him nakit for deid.

By cam a minister o' the kirk:
  "A sair mishanter?" he cried;
"Wha kens whaur the villains may lirk!
  I s' haud to the ither side!"

By cam an elder o' the kirk;
  Like a young horse he shied:
"Fie! here's a bonnie mornin's wark!"
  An' he spangt to the ither side.

By cam ane gaed to the wrang kirk;
  Douce he trottit alang.
"Puir body!" he cried, an' wi' a yerk
  Aff o' his cuddy he sprang.

He ran to the body, an' turnt it ower:
  "There's life i' the man!" he cried.
He wasna ane to stan' an' glower,
  Nor haud to the ither side!

He doctort his oons, an' heised him then
  To the back o' the beastie douce;
An' he heild him on till, twa weary men,
  They wan to the half-way hoose.

He ten'd him a' nicht, an' o' the morn did say,
  "Lan'lord, latna him lack;
Here's auchteen pence!—an ony mair ootlay
  I'll sattle 't as I come back."

Sae take til ye, neibours; read aricht the word;
  It's a portion o' God's ain spell!
"Wha is my neibour?" speirna the Lord,
  But, "Am I a neibour?" yersel.

CHOOSING TO BE MADE IN GOD'S IMAGE

For whom he foreknew, he also foreordained to be conformed to the image of his Son, that he might be the firstborn among many brethren.

Romans 8:29 (RV)

Creeping Christians

When we gaze upon Jesus on the cross, crying out in his final moments of earthly life to his Father, what, we ask, can this alpine apex of his faith have to do with the creatures who call themselves Christians, creeping about in the valleys, hardly knowing that there are mountains above them, except that they take offense at and stumble over the pebbles washed across their path by the glacier streams?

I will tell you. We are and remain such creeping Christians, because we look at ourselves and not at Christ. We are where we are because we gaze at the marks of our own soiled feet, and at the trail of our own defiled garments, instead of up at the snows of purity, where the soul of Christ did climb.

Each of us, putting his foot in the footprint of the Master, and so defacing it, turns to examine how far his neighbor's footprint corresponds with that which he still calls the Master's, although it is but his own. Or, having committed a petty fault, I mean a fault such as only a petty creature could commit, we mourn over the defilement to ourselves, and the shame of it before our friends, children, or acquaintances, instead of hastening to make the due confession and amends to our fellow, and then, forgetting our paltry self with its well-earned disgrace, lift up our eyes to the glory which alone will quicken the true man and woman in us, and kill the peddling creature we so wrongly call our *self*. The true self is that which can look Jesus in the face, and say, "*My* Lord."

When Do We Say "My God"?

When the inward sun is shining, and the wind of thought, blowing where it lists amid the flowers and leaves of fancy and imagination, rouses glad forms and feelings, it is easy to look upward, and say, "My God." It is easy when the frosts of external failure have braced the mental nerves to healthy endurance and fresh effort after labor, it is easy then to turn to God and trust in him, in whom all honest exertion gives an ability as well as a right to trust. It is easy in pain, so long as it does not pass certain undefinable bounds, to hope in God for deliverance, or pray for strength to endure.

But what is to be done when all feeling is gone? What is to be done when a man does not know whether he believes or not, whether he loves or not? What is to be done when art, poetry, religion are nothing to him, so swallowed up is he in pain or mental depression or disappointment or temptation or he knows not what?

It seems to him then that God does not care for him, and certainly he does not care for God. If he is still humble, he thinks that he is so bad that God cannot care for him. And he then believes, for a time, that God loves us only because and when and while we love him, instead of believing that God loves us always because he is our God, and that we live only by his love. Or he does not believe in a god at all, which is better. For a man is nearer the truth to believe in no god, than to believe in a wrong god.

So long as we have nothing to say to God, nothing to do with him, except in the sunshine of the mind when we feel him near us, we are poor creatures, willed *upon*, not actively *willing* within ourselves. We are reeds, flowering reeds, it may be, and pleasant to look at, but only reeds blown about by the wind—not bad, but poor creatures.

Willing to Choose the Good

And how in such a condition do we generally act?

Do we not sit mourning over the loss of our feelings? Or worse, make frantic efforts to rouse them? Or, ten times worse, relapse into a state of temporary atheism, and yield to the pressing temptation? Or, being heartless, consent to remain careless, conscious of evil thoughts and low feelings, but too lazy, too self-content to rouse ourselves against them? We know we must get rid of them someday, but in the meantime—never mind. We do not *feel* our sins to be so bad. Of course, we do not feel anything else good. We are asleep, and even if we know it, we cannot be troubled to wake. No impulse comes to arouse us, and so we remain as we are.

God does not, by the instant gift of his Spirit, make us always feel right, desire good, love purity, aspire after him and his will. The reason he doesn't must be, therefore, either because he will not, or he cannot. If he will not, it must be because it would not be well to do so. If he cannot, then he would not if he could; otherwise a better condition than God's will is conceivable to the mind of God—clearly an impossibility.

The truth is this: He wants to make us in his own image, *choosing* the good, *refusing* the evil. How could he effect this if he were *always* moving us from within, as he does at divine intervals, towards the beauty of holiness? God gives us room *to be*. He does not oppress us with his will. He "stands away from us," that we may act from ourselves, that we may exercise the pure will for good.

Do not imagine me to therefore mean that we can do anything of ourselves without God. If we choose the right at last, it is all God's doing, and only the more his that it is ours, only in a far more marvelous way than if he had kept us filled with holy impulses precluding the need of choice. For up to this very point, for this very point, he has been educating us, leading us, pushing us, driving us, enticing us, that we may choose him and his will, and so be tenfold more his children, of his own best making. We become his in the freedom of our will, found first truly our own in its loving sacrifice to him, for which in his grand fatherhood he has been thus working from the foundation of the earth. Despite the most ecstatic worship flowing from the divinest impulse, we could never be completely his children without this *willing* sacrifice.

For God made our individuality as well as, and a greater marvel than, our dependence. He made our apartness from himself, that freedom should bind us divinely dearer to himself, with a new and inscrutable marvel of love. For the Godhead is still at the root, is the making root of our individuality, and the freer the man, the stronger the bond that binds him to him who made his freedom. He made our wills, and is striving to make them free. For only in the perfection of our individuality and the freedom of our wills can we be altogether his children. This is full of mystery, but can we not see enough in it to make us very glad and very peaceful?

The Highest Condition of the Human Will

Not in any other act than one which, in spite of impulse or of weakness, declares for the truth, for God, does the will spring into absolute freedom, into true life.

See, then, what lies within our reach every time that we are thus lapped in the folds of night, when we do not see or feel or hear God and all seems blackness in our spirit. Then, at that moment, the highest condition of the human will is in sight, is attainable. I do not say the highest condition of the human being; that surely lies in the blissful vision, in the sight of God.

But the highest condition of the human will, as distinct, not as separated from God, is when, not seeing God, not seeming to itself to grasp him at all, it yet holds him fast.

The human will cannot continue in this condition, for, not finding, not seeing God, the man would die. But when the will asserts itself, the man passes from death into life, and the vision is nigh at hand. Then first, thus free, in thus asserting its freedom, is the individual will one with the will of God. The child is finally restored to the Father. The childhood and the fatherhood meet in one. The brotherhood of the race arises from the dust, and the prayer of our Lord is answered, "I in them and thou in me, that they may be made perfect in one."

Let us then arise in God-born strength every time that we feel the darkness closing, or become aware that it has closed around us, and say, "I am of the Light and not of the darkness."

Troubled soul, you are not bound to feel, but you are bound to arise. God loves you whether you feel or not. You cannot love when you will, but you are bound to fight the hatred in you to the last. Try not to feel good when you are good, but cry to Him who is good. He does not change because you change. Rather, he has a special tenderness of love toward you when you are in the dark and have no light; and his heart is glad when you arise and say, "I will go to my Father." For he sees you through all the gloom through which you cannot see him.

Will his will. Say to him: "My God, I am very dull and low and hard. But you are wise and high and tender, and you are my God. I am your child. Do not forsake me." Then fold the arms of your faith, and wait in quietness until light comes on in your darkness. Fold the arms of your faith I say, but not of action. Think to yourself of something that you ought to do, and go and do it, if it be but the sweeping of a room, or the preparing of a meal, or a visit to a friend. Heed not your feelings: Do your work.

As God lives by his own will, and we live in him, so has he given to us power to will in ourselves. How much better should we not fare if, finding that we are standing with our heads bowed away from the good, finding that we have no feeble inclination to seek the source of our life, we should yet *will* upward toward God, rousing that essence of life in us, which he has given us from his own heart, to call again upon him who is our Life, who can fill the emptiest heart, rouse the deadest conscience, quicken the dullest feeling, and strengthen the feeblest will!

Then, if ever the time should come, as perhaps it must come to each of us, when all consciousness of well-being shall have vanished, when the earth shall be but a sterile promontory, and the heavens a dull and pestilent congregation of vapors, when no man or woman shall delight us anymore, when God himself shall be but a name and Jesus an old story, then, even then, when death is griping at our hearts, and is slaying love, hope, faith, and when all existence is an agony, then, even then, we shall be able to cry out with our Lord, "My God, my God."[1]

After Thomas Kempis

I

Who follows Jesus shall not walk
    In darksome road with danger rife;
But in his heart the Truth will talk,
    And on his way will shine the Life.

So, on the story we must pore
    Of him who lives for us, and died,
That we may see him walk before,
    And know the Father in the guide.

II

In words of truth Christ all excels,
    Leaves all his holy ones behind;
And he in whom his spirit dwells
    Their hidden manna sure shall find.

Gather wouldst thou the perfect grains,
    And Jesus fully understand?
Thou must obey him with huge pains,
    And to God's will be as Christ's hand.

III

What profits it to reason high
    And in hard questions court dispute,
When thou dost lack humility,
    Displeasing God at very root!

Profoundest words man ever spake
    Not once of blame washed any clear;
A simple life alone could make
    Nathanael to his master dear.

IV

The eye with seeing is not filled,
    The ear with hearing not at rest;
Desire with having is not stilled;
    With human praise no heart is blest.

Vanity, then, of vanities
    All things for which men grasp and grope!
The precious things in heavenly eyes
    Are love, and truth, and trust, and hope.

V

Better the clown who God doth love
    Than he that high can go
And name each little star above
    But sees not God below!

What if all things on earth I knew,
    Yea, love were all my creed,
It serveth nothing with the True;
    He goes by heart and deed.

VI

If thou dost think thy knowledge good,
    Thy intellect not slow,
Bethink thee of the multitude
    Of things thou dost not know.

Why look on any from on high
    Because thou knowest more?
Thou need'st but look abroad, to spy
    Ten thousand thee before.

Wouldst thou in knowledge true advance
    And gather learning's fruit,
In love confess thy ignorance,
    And thy self-love confute.

VII

This is the highest learning,
    The hardest and the best—
From self to keep still turning,
    And honour all the rest.

If one should break the letter,
    Yea, spirit of command,
Think not that thou art better,
    Thou may'st not always stand!

We all are weak—but weaker
  Hold no one than thou art;
Then, as thou growest meeker,
  Higher will go thy heart.

VIII

Sense and judgment oft indeed
Spy but little and mislead,
  Ground us on a shelf!
Happy he whom Truth doth teach,
Not by forms of passing speech,
  But her very self!

Why of hidden things dispute,
Mind unwise, howe'er astute,
  Making that thy task
Where the Judge will, at the last,
When disputing all is past,
  Not a question ask?

Folly great it is to brood
Over neither bad or good,
  Eyes and ears unheedful!
Ears and eyes, ah, open wide
For what may be heard or spied
  Of the one thing needful!

CHOOSING TO WILL OUR WILLS INTO GOD'S WILL

Fictional Selections from *Thomas Wingfold, Curate*;
The Minister's Restoration, and *The Landlady's Master*

He was gradually learning that his faith must be an absolute one, claiming from God everything the love a perfect Father could give, or the needs he had created in his child to desire; that he must not look to himself first for help, or imagine that the divine was only the supplement to the weakness and failure of the human; that the highest effort of the human was to lay hold of the divine. He learned that he could keep no simplest law in its loveliness until he was possessed of the same spirit whence that law sprung; that he could not even love Helen aright—simply, perfectly, unselfishly—except through the presence of the originating Love; that the one thing wherein he might imitate the free creative will of God was, to will the presence and power of that will which gave birth to his. It was the vital growth of this faith even when he was too troubled to recognize the fact, that made him strong in the midst of weakness; as when the son of man cried out, "Let this cup pass," the son of God in him could yet cry, "Thy will be done." He could "inhabit trembling," and yet be brave.

One day, with a sudden questioning hunger, he rose in hast from his knees and turned almost trembling to his Greek New Testament, to find whether the words of the Master, "If any man will do the will of the Father," meant "If any man *is willing* to do the will of the Father." Finding that to be just exactly what they did mean, he was able to be at rest sufficiently to go on asking and hoping. And it was not long thereafter before he began to feel he had something worth telling, and must tell it to anyone that would hear. Heartily he set himself to pray for that spirit of truth, which the Lord had promised to them that asked it of their Father in heaven.

"My frien's, I hae little right to stand up afore ye and say anything. For as some o' ye ken, if no afore, then at least noo frae what my frien' the soutar hae jist be tellin' ye, I was once a minister o' the kirk, but upon a time I behaved mysel' so ill that, when I came to my senses, I saw it my duty to withdraw frae it. But noo I seem to hae gotten some more light upon spiritual matters that I didna hae afore, and to ken some things I didna ken afore. Sae turnin' my back upon my past sin, and believin' God has forgiven me, and is willin' I should set my hand to his plow once more, I hae thought to make a new beginnin' here in a quiet humble fashion, tellin' ye somethin' o' what I hae begun, in the mercy o' God, to un'erstand a wee for mysel'. Sae noo, if ye'll turn, them o' ye that has brought yer books wi' ye, to the seventh chapter o' John's Gospel, and the seventeenth verse, ye'll read wi' me what the Lord says there to the fowk o' Jerusalem: 'If any man be willin' to do his will, he'll ken whether what I tell him comes frae God, or whether I say it only oot o' my ain head.' Look at it for yersel's, for that's what it says in the Greek, which is plainer than the English to them that un'erstand the auld Greek tongue. If anybody *be willin'* to do the will o' God, he'll ken whether my teachin' comes frae God, or I say it o' mysel'."

"Do you mean that God never punishes anyone for what he cannot help?"

"Assuredly. God will punish only for wrong choices we make. And then his punishment will be redemptive, not retributive: to make us capable—more than merely capable; hungry, aching, yearning to be able—to make *right* choices, so that in the end we make that one supreme right choice our wills were created to make—the joyful giving up of our wills into *his*!"

"How do you prove that?"

"I will not attempt to prove it. If you are content to think of God as a being of retribution, if it does not trouble you that your God should be so unjust, then it would be fruitless for me to try to prove otherwise to you. We could discuss the question for years and only make enemies of ourselves. As long as you are satisfied with such a god, I will not try to dissuade you. Go on thinking so until at last you are made miserable by it. Then I will pour out my heart to deliver you from the falsehoods taught you by the traditions of the elders."

"Is that not a term Jesus applied to the teaching of the Pharisees?"

"We in this modern age have hundreds of our own traditions of the elders that keep us from seeing God's face as surely as those ancient regulations kept the Pharisees from seeing."

Alexa was struck, not with any truth in all he said, but with the evident truthfulness of the man himself. Right or wrong, there was that about him—a certain radiance of conviction—which certainly was not about Mr. Rackstraw.

"The things that can be shaken," said Andrew, as if thinking to himself, "may last for a time; but they will at length be shaken to pieces, so that the things which *cannot* be shaken may emerge as what they truly are. Whatever we call religion will vanish when we see God face to face."

For a while they went brushing through the heather in silence.

"May I ask you one question, Mr. Ingram?" said Alexa at length.

"Surely. Ask anything."

"And you will answer me?"

"If I am at liberty to answer you, I will."

"What do you mean by being at liberty? Are you under some vow?"

"I am under the law of love. I am bound to do nothing to hurt. An answer that would do you no good, I will not give."

"How do you know what will or will not do me good?"

"I must use what judgment I have."

"Is it true, then, that you believe God gives you whatever you ask?"

"I believe God answers all prayer," replied Andrew, "but the form of the answer depends largely upon the heart of the person praying. Selfish prayers he must doubtless answer differently than selfless prayers. For myself, I have never asked anything of him that he did not give me."

"Would you mind telling me anything you have asked of him? Do you pray for rain for your crops or for your book to sell in great quantities?"

Andrew laughed. "Such things I do not pray for. God is not

a genie in a bottle to satisfy our earthly desires."

"What do you pray for, then?"

"I have never yet required to ask anything not included in the prayer, 'Thy will be done!' "

"That will be done without you praying for it."

"Perhaps if you view those words of Christ's as a vague general prayer that somehow or other God's will in the universe will be done, I suppose you are right. But that prayer is far more personal than most people realize. And thus I do *not* believe it will be done, to all eternity, in the place where it needs doing the most, without my praying for it."

"Where is that?"

Andrew was silent a moment, thinking. Then he continued. "Where first am I accountable that his will should be done? Is it not in myself . . . in my own heart? And how is his will to be done in *me* without *my* willing it? Does he not want me to love what he loves?—to be like himself?—to do his will with the glad effort of my will?—in a word, to will what he wills? And when I find I cannot, what am I to do but pray for help? I pray, and he helps me."

"There is nothing so strange in that!"

"Surely not. It seems to me the simplest of common sense. It is my business, the business of every man, every woman, every child, that God's will be done by their obedience to that will the moment they know it."[2]

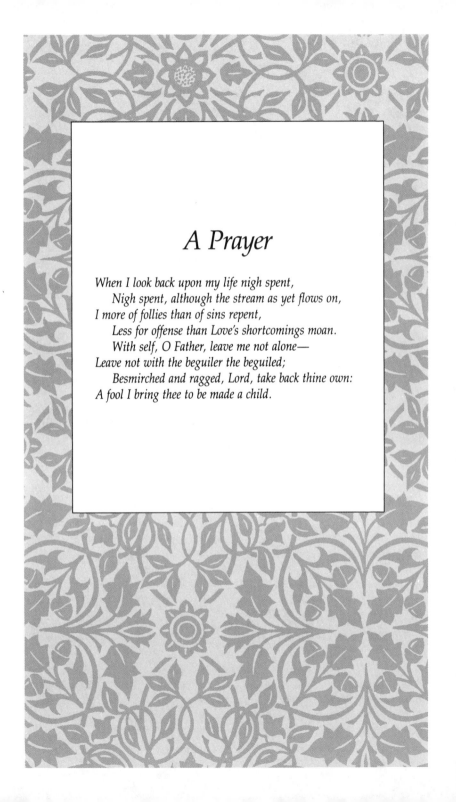

A Prayer

When I look back upon my life nigh spent,
  Nigh spent, although the stream as yet flows on,
I more of follies than of sins repent,
  Less for offense than Love's shortcomings moan.
  With self, O Father, leave me not alone—
Leave not with the beguiler the beguiled;
  Besmirched and ragged, Lord, take back thine own:
A fool I bring thee to be made a child.

LOVE IN THE LAW

Thou shalt not avenge, nor bear any grudge against the children of thy people, but thou shalt love thy neighbor as thyself: I am the Lord.

Leviticus 19:18

When Jesus told us to love our neighbor as ourself, he never thought of being original. The older the saying the better, if it uttered the truth he wanted to utter. In him it becomes fact: The *word* was made *flesh*. And so, in the wondrous meeting of extremes, the words he spoke were no mere words, but spirit and life.

The words quoted by Jesus from the words of God to Moses in Leviticus 19 are also twice quoted by St. Paul, and once by St. James—and always in a similar mode: They represent love as the fulfilling of the law.

We Are Not Made for the Law, But for Love

If love fulfills the law, is the converse then true? Is the fulfilling of the law love? The apostle Paul says: "Love worketh no ill to his neighbor, therefore love is the fulfilling of the law." Does it follow that *working no ill is love*?

Certainly not. If a man keeps the law, I know he loves his neighbor. But he is does not love his neighbor *because* he keeps the law; he keeps the law because he loves his neighbor. No heart will be content with the law in place of love. The law cannot fulfill love.

Neither can the law, as it were, even fulfill itself. I am certain that it is impossible to keep the law towards one's neighbor except one loves him. The law is infinite, reaching to such delicacies of action, that the man who tries most will be the man most aware of defeat. We are not made for law, but for love. Love is law, because it is infinitely more than law. It is of an altogether higher region than law—is, in fact, the creator of law. Had it not been for love, not one of the *shalt nots* of the law would have been uttered.

True, once uttered, they show themselves in the form of justice, even in the inferior and worldly forms of prudence and self-preservation. But it was love that spoke them first. Were there no love in us, what sense of justice could we have? Would not everyone be filled with the sense of his own wants, and be forever defeating himself? I do not say that without love in our nature justice would never be born. For I do not call that justice which consists only in a sense of our own rights. True, there are poor and withered forms of love which are immeasurably below justice now. But even now they are of speechless worth, for they will grow into that which will supersede, because it will necessitate, justice.

Why the Law?

Of what use then is the law?

To lead us to Christ, the Truth; to awaken in our minds a sense of what our deepest nature, the presence, namely, of God in us, requires of us; to let us know, in part by failure, that the purest effort of will of which we are capable cannot lift us up even to the abstaining from wrong to our neighbor. What man, for instance, who does not love his neighbor and yet wishes to keep the law, will dare be confident that never by word, look, tone, gesture, silence, will he bear false witness against that neighbor? What man can judge his neighbor aright except him whose love makes him refuse to judge him? Therefore we are told to love, and not judge. It is the sole justice of which we are capable, and that perfected will comprise all justice. Furthermore, to refuse our neighbor love, is to do him the greatest wrong.

In order to fulfill the commonest law, I repeat, we must rise into a loftier region altogether, a region that is above law, because it is spirit and life and makes the law: in order to keep the law towards our neighbor, we must love our neighbor. We are not made for law, but for grace—or for faith, to use another word so much misused. We are made on too large a scale altogether to have any pure relation to mere justice, if indeed we can say there is such a thing. It is but an abstracted idea which, in reality, will not be abstracted. The law comes to make us long for the needed grace—that is, for the divine condition in which love is all, for God is Love.

The fulfilling of the law is the practical form love will take, and the neglect of it is the conviction of an unloving spirit. The elements of the law provide the mode in which a man's will must begin at once to love his neighbor. Yet it is clear that our Lord meant far more by the love of our neighbor than the fulfilling of the law toward him. That by *love* he meant the condition of being that results in the fulfilling of the law and more is sufficiently clear from his story of the good Samaritan.

"Who is my neighbor?" asked the lawyer. And the Lord taught him that everyone to whom he could be or for whom he could do anything was his neighbor; therefore, that each of the race, as he comes within the touch of one tentacle of our nature, is our neighbor. Which of the inhibitions of the law is illustrated in the tale? Not one. The love that is more than law, rendering its breaking impossible, lives in this endless story. It expresses itself in active kindness—the recognition of kin, of *kind*, of nighness, of *neighborhood*—in tenderness and lovingkindness, the Samaritan heart akin to the Jewish heart, the Samaritan hand neighbor to the Jewish wounds.

So direct and complete is this parable of our Lord that one becomes almost ashamed of further talk about it. Suppose a man of the listening company had put the same question to our Lord that we have been considering, and had said, "But I may keep the law and yet not love my neighbor," would Jesus not have replied: "Keep the law, not in the letter, but in the spirit, that is, in the truth of action, and you will soon find, O Jew, that you do love your Samaritan"?

And yet, when thoughts and questions arise in our minds, the Lord desires that we should follow them. He will not check us with a word of heavenly wisdom scornfully uttered. He knows that not even *his* words will apply to every question of the willing soul. But we know that his Spirit will reply. When we want to know more, that more will be there for us. Not every man, for instance, finds his neighbor in need of help, and God would gladly hasten the slow results of opportunity by true thinking. Thus would we be ready for further teaching from that Spirit who is the Lord.

Upwards Toward the Center

"But how," asks the man who is willing to recognize the truth of universal brotherhood in his mind, yet finds himself unable in practical matters to fulfill the bare law even toward his wife whom he most loves, "How am I then to rise into that higher region, that divine love, in which I will be capable of fulfilling both the law and love at its core?"

And even when such a one begins to try to love his neighbor, he finds that the divine love of which he spoke is no more to be reached in itself than the law was to be reached in itself. As he cannot keep the law without first rising to love of his neighbor, so he cannot love his neighbor without first rising higher still. The whole system of the universe works upon this law—the driving of things upward toward the center. The man who will love his neighbor can do so by no immediate exercise of the will. Rather, it is done by the man fulfilled of God, from whom he came and by whom he is. In this relationship alone can he effectively love his neighbor, who also came from God and lives by God alone.

The mystery of individuality and consequent relationships is as deep as the beginnings of humanity, and the questions thence arising can be solved only by him who has, practically at least, solved the divine necessities resulting from his origin. In God alone can man meet man. In him alone the converging lines of existence touch and cross not.

When the mind of Christ, the life of the Head, pulses through every atom of man's slowly revivifying body, and he too becomes alive, then the love of his brothers is there as part of his conscious life. From Christ through the neighbors comes the life that makes man a part of the body.[1]

What Is "Serving" God?

A Fictional Selection from *The Curate's Awakening*

Later that afternoon, Wingfold took the draper to see Polwarth. The dwarf allowed Wingfold to help him in getting tea, and the conversation, as will be the case where all are in earnest, quickly found the right channel.

It is not often in life that such conversations occur. In most discussions, each man has some point to maintain, and his object is to justify his own thesis and disprove his neighbor's. He may have originally adopted his thesis because of some sign of truth in it, but his mode of supporting it is generally to block up every cranny in his soul at which more truth might enter. In the present case, unusual as it is for as many as three truth-loving men to come together on the face of this planet, here were three simply set on uttering truth they had seen, and gaining sight of truth as yet hidden from them.

I shall attempt only a general impression of the result of their evening's discussion.

"I have been trying hard to follow you, Mr. Polwarth," acknowledged the draper, after his host had for awhile had the talk to himself, "but I cannot get hold of it. Would you tell me what you mean by divine service? I think you use the phrase in some different sense from what I have been accustomed to."

"When I use the phrase *divine service*," explained Polwarth, "I mean nothing whatever about the church or its observance. I mean simply serving God. Shall I make the church a temple of idolatrous worship by supposing that it exists for the sake of supplying some need that God has, or of gratifying some taste in him, that I there listen to his Word, say prayers to him, and sing his praises for his benefit? Shall I degrade the sanctity of the closet, hallowed in the words of Jesus, by shutting myself behind its door in the vain fancy of doing something there that God requires of me as a sacred *observance*? Shall I foolishly imagine that to exercise the highest and loveliest privilege of my existence, that of pouring forth my whole heart in prayer into the heart of him who is accountable for me, who has glorified me with his own image—in my soul, gentlemen, sadly disfigured as it is in my body!—shall I call *that* serving God?"

"But," interjected Drew, "is not God pleased that a man should pour out his soul to him?"

"Yes, doubtless. But is the child who sits by his father's knee and looks up into his father's face serving that father because the heart of the father delights to look down upon the child? And shall the moment of my deepest repose, the moment when I serve myself with the life of the universe, be called serving my God? What would you think of a child who said, 'I am very useful to my father, for when I ask him for something, or tell him I love him, it gives him such pleasure'? When my child would serve me, he sees some need I have, jumps from his seat at my knee, finds that which will meet my need, and is my eager, happy servant; he has done something for his father. His seat by my knee is love, delight, well-being, peace—not service, however pleasing in my eyes. Do not talk of public worship as divine service. Search the prophets and you will find observances, fasts, sacrifices and solemn feasts of the temple were regarded by God's holy men with loathing and scorn just because by the people they were regarded as *divine service*."

"But," speculated Mr. Drew, "I can't help thinking that if the phrase ever was used in that sense, there is no meaning of that kind attached to it now: service stands merely for the forms of public worship."

"If there were no such thing as *divine service* in the true sense of the word, then it would scarcely be worthwhile to quarrel with its misapplication. But I believe that true and genuine service may be given to the living God. And for the development of the divine nature in man, it is necessary that he should do something for God. And it is not hard to discover how, for God is in every creature and in their needs. Therefore, Jesus says that whatever is done to one of his little ones is done to him. And if the soul of a believer be the temple of the Spirit, then is not the place of that man's labor—his ship, his bank, his laboratory, his school, his factory—the temple of Jesus Christ, where the spirit of the man is at work? Mr. Drew, your shop is the temple of your service where the Lord Christ ought to be throned. Your counter ought to be his altar, and everything laid on it with intent of doing as you can for your neighbor, in the name of Christ Jesus."

The little prophet's face glowed as he stopped. But neither of his companions spoke.

Polwarth went on, "You will not become a rich man, but by so doing you will be saved from growing too rich and you will be a fellow-worker with God for the salvation of his world."

"I must live; I cannot give my goods away," murmured Mr. Drew, thinking about all he had heard.

"Giving them away would be easy," added Polwarth. "No, a harder task is yours, Mr. Drew—to make your business profitable to you, and at the same time to be not only just, but interested in, and careful of, and caring for your neighbor—as a servant of the God of bounty who gives to all men liberally. Your calling is to do the best for your neighbor that you reasonably can."

"But who is to determine what is reasonable?" asked Drew.

"The man himself, thinking in the presence of Jesus Christ. There is a holy moderation which is of God, and he will gladly reveal it to you."

"There won't be many fortunes made by that rule, Mr. Polwarth."

"Very few," admitted the dwarf.

"Then do you say that no great fortunes have been righteously made?"

"I will not judge. That is for the conscience of the man himself, not for his neighbor. Why should I be judged by another man's conscience? But you see, Mr. Drew—and this is what I was driving at—you have it in your power to *serve* God through the needs of his children all the working day, from morning to night, so long as there is a customer in your shop."[2]

An Old Sermon With a New Text

My wife contrived a fleecy thing
   Her husband to infold,
For 'tis the pride of woman still
   To cover from the cold:
My daughter made it a new text
   For a sermon very old.

The child came trotting to her side,
   Ready with bootless aid:
"Lily make veckit for papa,"
   The tiny woman said:
Her mother gave the means and ways,
   And a knot upon her thread.

"Mamma, mamma!—it won't come
     through!"
   In meek dismay she cried.
Her mother cut away the knot,
   And she was satisfied,
Pulling the long thread through and through,
   In fabricating pride.

Her mother told me this: I caught
   A glimpse of something more:
Great meanings often hide behind
   The little word before!
And I brooded over my new text
   Till the seed a sermon bore.

Nannie, to you I preach it now—
   A little sermon, low:
Is it not thus a thousand times,
   As through the world we go?
Do we not tug, and fret, and cry—
   Instead of **Yes, Lord—No?**

While all the rough things that we meet
   Which will not move a jot,
The hindrances to heart and feet,
   The Crook in every Lot,
Mean plainly but that children's threads
   Have at the end a knot.

This world of life God weaves for us,
   Nor spares he pains or cost,
But we must turn the web to clothes
   And shield our hearts from frost:
Shall we, because the thread holds fast,
   Count labour vain and lost?

If he should cut away the knot,
   And yield each fancy wild,
The hidden life within our hearts—
   His life, the undefiled—
Would fare as ill as I should fare
   From the needle of my child.

As tack and sheet unto the sail,
   As to my verse the rhyme,
As mountains to the low green earth—
   So hard for feet to climb,
As call of striking clock amid
   The quiet flow of time,

As sculptor's mallet to the birth
   Of the slow-dawning face,
As knot upon my Lily's thread
   When she would work apace,
God's **Nay** is such, and worketh so
   For his children's coming grace.

Who, knowing God's intent with him,
   His birthright would refuse?
What makes us what we have to be
   Is the only thing to choose:
We understand nor end nor means,
   And yet his ways accuse!

This is my sermon. It is preached
   Against all fretful strife.
Chafe not with anything that is,
   Nor cut it with the knife.
Ah! be not angry with the knot
   That holdeth fast thy life.

LOVE THY NEIGHBOR

Thou shalt love thy neighbor as thyself.
Matthew 22:39

Is It Possible?

It *is* possible to love our neighbor as ourself.

Our Lord *never* spoke hyperbolically—although, that is the supposition on which many unconsciously interpret his words, in order to be able to persuade themselves that they believe them. We may see that it is possible before we attain to it, for our perceptions of truth are always in advance of our condition.

True, no man can see it perfectly until he has experienced it, but we must see it, that we may one day experience it. A man who knows that he does not yet love his neighbor as himself may believe in such a condition, may even see that there is no other goal of human perfection, nothing else to which the universe is speeding, propelled by the Father's will. Let him labor on, and not faint at the thought that God's day is as a thousand years: his millennium is likewise one day—even this day, for we have him, the Love, in us, working even now in our hearts to that distant end.

But while it is true that only when a man loves God with all his heart will he love his neighbor as himself, yet there are mingled processes in the attainment of this final result. Let us try to aid such operation of truth by looking farther. Let us suppose that the man who believes that our Lord both meant what he said, and knew the truth of the matter, proceeds to attempt obedience in this—of loving his neighbor as himself. He begins to think about his neighbors generally, and he tries to feel love toward them. He finds at once that they begin to classify themselves.

With some he feels no difficulty, for he loves them already. Nor indeed does he love them because they *are*, but because by friendly qualities, by showing themselves lovable—that is, loving—they have already moved his feelings as the wind moves the waters. There has been no active *willing*, no *choosing* to love, no self-generated action on his part. And he feels that this has nothing much to do with it; though, of course, he would be farther from the desired end if he had none such as these to love, and farther still if he did not love them.

Then he recalls the words of the Lord, "If ye love them who love you, what reward have ye?" His mind turns upon a second class of person, and he tries to love him. This person is not an enemy—we have not come to that class of neighbors yet—but is dull and uninteresting—in a negative way, the man thinks, unlovable. What is he to do with this person? With all his effort, he finds the goal—"Love your neighbor as yourself"—as far off as ever.

Naturally, in his failure, the question arises, "Is it my duty to love the unlovable?"

Certainly not, if he is unlovable. But that is a begging of the question. "How, then, am I to love him? *Why* should I love my neighbor as myself?"

Why Love?

It is no good to say we must love because the Lord says so. No man can love his neighbor *merely* because the Lord says so. The Lord says so because it is right and necessary and natural, and the man wants to feel it thus. Although the Lord would be pleased with any man for doing a thing because he said it, he would show his pleasure by making the man more and more dissatisfied until he knew *why* the Lord had said it. He would make him see that he could not in the deepest sense— in the way the Lord loves—obey any command until he saw the reasonableness of it.

Observe that I do not say the man ought to put off obeying the command until he sees its reasonableness: that is another thing altogether, and does not lie in the scope of my present supposition. It is a beautiful thing to obey the rightful source of a command. It is a more beautiful thing to worship the radiant source of our light, and it is for the sake of obedient vision that our Lord commands us. For then our heart meets his: we see God.

We must come back now to the question: "Why should I love my neighbor as myself? I am me. He is he. I cannot get into his consciousness, nor he into mine. I feel myself, I do not feel him. We are separate.

What have I to do with him? The world shines into my consciousness, and I am not conscious of his consciousness. I wish I could love him, but I feel nothing, and I do not see why I must. I am an individual; he is an individual. My own self must be closer to me than he could ever be. Two bodies keep me apart from him. How could I, isolated from him, ever love him as myself?"

But the mistake in such a progression of thought lies in falsely judging the individuality a separation. On the contrary, it is the sole possibility and very bond of love. Otherness is the essential ground of affection.

Yet at whatever point a person does not love, the not-loving must seem rational. For no one loves because he sees why, but because he loves. No human reason can be given for the highest necessity of divinely created existence. For reasons are always from above downward. A person must only feel the necessity, and then all questioning is over. It justifies itself.

One who has not felt love, or faith, argues about it. But he does not have the true essence of love or faith to argue about. He has but its phantom, his own ideas which he has created himself in a vain effort to understand, and which he supposes it to be. Love cannot be argued about in its absence, for there is no reflex, no symbol of it near enough to the fact of it, to admit of just treatment by the algebra of the reason or imagination. Indeed, the very talking about it raises a mist between the mind and the vision of it. But let a man once love, and all those difficulties that appeared opposed to love will just be so many arguments for loving.

Unity of Being Results From Obedient Action

Let a man once find another who has fallen among thieves, let him be a neighbor to him, pouring oil and wine into his wounds and binding them up, and setting him on his own beast, and paying for him at the inn—let him do all this merely from a sense of duty; even such will be the virtue of obeying an eternal truth even in its poor measure, of putting in actuality what he has not even seen in theory, of doing the truth even without fully believing it, that even if the truth does not after the deed give the faintest glimmer of truth to the man, he will yet be ages nearer the vital truth than before, for he will go on his way loving that Samaritan neighbor a little more than his Jewish dignity will justify. How much more, if he be a man who would love his neighbor if he could, will the higher condition unsought have been found in the action!

For man is whole. And as soon as he *unites himself* by obedient action, the truth that is in him makes itself known to him, shining from the new whole. For his action is his response to his Maker's design, his individual part in the creation of himself, his yielding to the All in all, to the tides of whose harmonious cosmopolite life all his being thenceforward lies open for interpenetration and assimilation. When the will once begins to aspire toward godliness, it will soon find that action must precede feeling, that man may know the foundation itself of feeling.

The whole system of divine education regarding the relation of man to man has for its end that a man should love his neighbor as himself. It is not a lesson that he can learn by itself, or a duty whose obligation can be shown by argument, any more than the difference between right and wrong can be defined in any other terms than their own.

It may be objected that the difference between right and wrong manifests itself to every mind: it is self-evident; whereas the loving of one's neighbor is *not* seen to be a primary truth. It is so far from being universally accepted as truth, in fact, that the greater number even of those calling themselves Christians, who hope for an eternity of blessedness through him who taught it, believe, on the contrary, that the paramount obligation of life is to take care of one's self at much risk of forgetting one's neighbor.

But the human race generally has got as far as the recognition (though most do not take it beyond mental recognition to practical obedience) of right and wrong; and therefore most men and women are born capable of making the distinction. The race has not yet lived long enough for its latest offspring to be born with the perception of the truth of love to his neighbor. It is to be seen by the present individual only after a long reception of and submission to the education of life, that is God's dealings with him in his heart. And once seen, it is believed.[1]

Ministry to One's Neighbors

A Fictional Selection from *Annals of a Quiet Neighborhood*

A m I to understand you, then, that interaction with one's neighbors ought to take the place of meditation?"

"By no means: but ought to go side by side with it, if you would have at the same time a healthy mind to judge and the means of either verifying your speculations or discovering their falsehood."

"But where am I to find such friends besides yourself with whom to hold spiritual communion?"

"It is the communion of spiritual deeds, deeds of justice, of mercy, of humility—the kind word, the cup of cold water, the visitation in sickness, the lending of money—not spiritual conversation or talk, that I refer to: the latter will come of itself where it is natural. You would soon find that it is not only to those whose spiritual windows are of the same shape as your own that you are to be a neighbor. There is one poor man in my congregation who knows more—practically, I mean, too—of spirituality of mind than any of us. Perhaps you could not teach him much, but he could teach you. In any case, our neighbors are simply those around about us. And the most ignorant man in a little place like Marshmallows, one such as you, with leisure, ought to know and understand, and have some good influence upon. He is your brother whom you are bound to care for and evaluate—I do not mean socially, but really, in himself—if it be possible. You ought at least to get into some simple human relation with him, as you would with the youngest and most ignorant of your brothers and sisters born of the same father and mother; approaching him, not with pompous lecturing or fault-finding, still less with the abomination called condescension, but with the humble service of the elder to the younger, in whatever he may be helped by you without injury to him. Never was there a more injurious mistake than the assumption that it is the business of the clergy only to have the care of souls."

"But that would be endless. It would leave me no time for myself."

"Would that be no time for yourself spent in leading a noble, Christian life; in verifying the words of our Lord by doing them; in building your house on the rock of action instead of the sands of theory; in widening your own being by entering into the nature, thoughts, feelings, even fancies of those around you? In such relationship you would find health radiating into your own bosom; healing sympathies springing up in the most barren acquaintance; channels opened for the inrush of truth into your own mind; and opportunities afforded for the exercise of that self-discipline, the lack of which led to the failures which you now bemoan. Soon, then, would you have cause to wonder how much some of your speculations had fallen into the background, simply because the truth, showing itself grandly true, had so filled and occupied your mind that it left no room for anxiety about such questions as, while secured in the interest all reality gives, were yet dwarfed by the side of it.

"Nothing, I repeat, so much as humble ministration to your neighbors, will help you to that perfect love of God which casteth out fear; nothing but the love of God—that God revealed in Christ—will make you able to love your neighbor aright. And the Spirit of God, which alone gives might for any good, will by these loves, which are life, strengthen you at last to believe in the light, even in the midst of darkness; to hold the resolution formed in health when sickness has altered the appearance of everything around you, and to feel tenderly towards your fellow, even when you yourself are plunged in dejection or racked with pain.

"But," I said, "I fear I have transgressed the bounds of all propriety by enlarging upon this matter as I have done. I can only say I have spoken in proportion to my feeling of its weight and truth."[2]

In the Night

As to her child a mother calls,
    "Come to me, child; come near!"
Calling, in silent intervals,
    The Master's voice I hear.

But does he call me verily?
    To have me does he care?
Why should he seek my poverty,
    My selfishness so bare?

The dear voice makes his gladness brim,
    But not a child can know
Why that large woman cares for him,
    Why she should love him so!

Lord, to thy call of me I bow,
    Obey like Abraham:
Thou lov'st me because thou art thou,
    And I am what I am!

Doubt whispers, Thou art such a blot
    He cannot love poor thee:
If what I am he loveth not,
    He loves what I shall be.

Nay, that which can be drawn and wooed,
    And turned away from ill,
Is what his father made for good:
    He loves me, I say still!

Learning Universal Brotherhood

He that loveth not his brother whom he hath seen, how can he love God whom he hath not seen?

1 John 4:20

Human Brothers and Sisters—Our First Neighbors

The whole constitution of human society exists for the express end of teaching the two truths by which man lives: Love to God and love to man.

I will say nothing here of the mysteries of the parental relation, because they belong to the teaching of the former truth, other than to say that we come into the world as we do, to look up to the love over us, and see in it a symbol, poor and weak, yet the best we can have or receive of the divine love. (This might be expressed in a deeper and truer fashion by saying that since God has made human affairs after his own thoughts, they are to be the best teachers of love toward him and love toward our neighbor. This is an immeasurably nobler and truer manner of regarding them than as a scheme or plan invented by the divine intellect.) How much easier would thousands find it to love God if they did not have such miserable types of him in the self-seeking, impulse-driven, purposeless, faithless beings who are all they have for father and mother.

But what I want to speak of now, with regard to the second great commandment, is the relation of brotherhood and sisterhood.

Why does my brother come of the same father and mother? Why do I behold the helplessness and confidence of his infancy? Why is the infant laid on the knee of the child? Why do we grow up with the same nurture? Why do we behold the wonder of the sunset and the mystery of the growing moon together? Why do we share one bed, join in the same games, and attempt the same exploits? Why do we quarrel, vow revenge and silence and endless enmity, and then, unable to resist the brotherhood within us, wind up arm in arm, friends again, and forget all within the hour?

Is it not that love may grow lord of all between him and me? Is it not that I may feel toward him what there are no words or forms of words to express—namely, a love in which the divine self rushes forth in utter self-forgetfulness to live in the contemplation of the brother—a love that is stronger than death—glad and proud and satisfied?

But if love stop there, what will be the result? Ruin to itself; loss of the brotherhood. He who does not love his brother for deeper reasons than those of a common parentage will cease to love him at all. Love cannot remain motionless, stagnant. It must move in one direction or the other. The love that enlarges not its borders, that is not ever-spreading and including, and deepening, will contract, shrivel, decay, and eventually die.

I have had the sons of my mother for my earthly brothers that I may learn the universal brotherhood. For there is a bond between me and the most wretched liar that ever died for the murder he would not even confess, infinitely closer than that which springs only from having one father and mother. That we are the sons and the daughters of God, born from his heart, the resulting offspring of his love, is a bond closer than all other bonds rolled into one. No man or woman ever loved his own child aright who did not love him for his humanity, for his divinity, to the complete forgetting of his origin from himself.

The son of my mother is indeed my brother by this greater and closer bond as well. But if I recognize that bond between him and me at all, I recognize it for the rest of my race. And although the first be true, I thank God that the greater does not exclude the less! It makes all the weaker bonds stronger and truer, and allows that where all are brothers, some will be closer than others.

Still my brother according to the flesh is my first neighbor, that we may be very near to each other, whether we will or not, while our hearts are tender, and so may learn *brotherhood*. For our love to each other is but the throbbing of the heart of the great brotherhood, and could come only from the eternal Father, not from our parents.

The Second Neighbor

Then my second neighbor appears, and who is this? Everyone with whom I come in contact. He or she with whom I have any transactions, any human dealings whatever. Not only the man or woman I eat with. Not only the friend with whom I share my thoughts. Not only the man or woman I love, whom my compassion would lift from some slough of despair. My neighbor is also the person who makes my clothes, the one who prints my books, the one who drives me in his cab, the one who begs from me in the street—to whom, it may be, for brotherhood's sake, I must not give as often as I might—the woman I meet in the market, and even the man who condescends to me. With all such, and hundreds more I pass through the course of a day, there is a chance of doing the part of a neighbor, if in no other way, at least by speaking truly, acting justly, and thinking kindly. Even these deeds will help move my heart toward that love which is born of righteousness.

All true action clears the springs of right feeling and lets their waters rise and flow. A man must not choose his neighbor. He must take the neighbor that God sends him. In him, whoever he or she be, lies either hidden or revealed a beautiful brother or sister. The neighbor is just the man or woman or child who is next to you at this very moment, he or she with whom *any* business, even any seeming accident of life has brought you in contact.

Thus will love spread and spread in wider and stronger pulses till the whole human race will be to you sacredly lovely. Drink-debased, vice-defeatured, pride-puffed, wealth-tainted, vanity-smeared, they will yet be brothers, yet be sisters, yet be God-born neighbors. Any rough-hewn semblance of humanity will at length be enough to move you to reverence and affection. It is harder for some to learn this than for others. There are those whose first impulse is always to repel and not to receive. But learn they may, and learn they must. Even these may grow in this grace until a countenance unknown will awake in them a yearning of affection rising to pain, because there is for it no expression, and they can only give the man to God and be still.

Does the thought of such love make your heart swell? "Ah brother, sister," do you find yourself saying to one you had hardly noticed before, "you have a soul like mine. Sights and sounds and smells visit your heart and brain as they do mine. We are not so different after all! Oh, my brother, my sister, I will love you! I cannot come very near you yet, but I will love you then all the more. It may be that you do not love your neighbor. It may be that you think only how to get from him, how to gain from him. It may be that you do not love me, or care for my love or anyone's. How lonely then must you be! How shut up in your poverty-stricken room, with the bare walls of your selfishness, and the hard couch of your unsatisfaction! I will love you for it the more. You shall not be alone with yourself. You are another life—a second self. Therefore I can, I may, and I *will* love you."

How Far Might We Dare Hope Jesus' Love Will Go?

When once to a man or woman the human face is the human face divine, and the hand of his neighbor is the hand of a brother or sister, then will he understand what St. Paul meant when he said, "I could wish that myself were accursed from Christ for my brethren."

But he will no longer understand those who, so far from feeling the love of their neighbor an essential part of their being, expect to be exempt from its law of love in the world to come. There, at least, for the glory of God, they think they may limit its expansive tendencies to the narrow circle of their own imagined heaven. On its battlements of safety, they will regard hell from afar, and say to each other, "Hark! Listen to their moans. But do not weep, for they are no longer our neighbors."

Oh, the folly of those who would place the boundaries of their own intellects around the infinity of God's redeeming love. St. Paul would be wretched before the throne of God, if he thought there was one man or woman beyond the limit of God's mercy. And he would dismiss the idea as much for God's glory as for the person's sake.

And what shall we say of the man Christ Jesus? Upheld by the love of Christ, and with a dim hope that in the distant future there might be some help for him, who that loves his brother would not arise from the company of the blessed, and walk down into the dismal regions of despair, to sit with the last, the only unredeemed, the Judas of his race, and be himself more blessed in the pains of hell than in the glories of heaven? In the midst of the golden harps and the white wings, knowing that one of his kind, one miserable brother or sister from the earthly time when men were taught to love their neighbor as themselves, was howling unheeded far below in the vaults of the creation, who would not feel that he must arise, that he had no choice, that, awful as it was, he must gird his loins and go down into the smoke and the darkness and the fire, traveling the weary and fearful road into the far country to find his brother—who, I mean, that had the mind of Christ, and the love of the Father?

But it is a wild question. God is, and shall be, All in all!

Father of our brothers and sisters! You will not be less glorious than we, taught of Christ, are able to think you. When you go into the wilderness to seek, you will not come home until you have found the lost. It is because we hope not for them in you, not knowing you, not knowing your love, that we are so hard and so heartless to the brothers and sisters whom you have given us.

Love of Others—the Inbreathing Life of God

Love of our neighbor is the only door out of the dungeon of self, where we mope and mow, striking sparks, and rubbing phosphorescence out of the walls, and blowing our own breath in our own nostrils, instead of coming out into the fair sunlight of God, the sweet winds of the universe. We think our consciousness is ourself, whereas our life consists in the inbreathing of God, and the consciousness of the universe of truth. To have ourself, to know ourself, to enjoy ourself, we call life. But in reality, if we would forget ourselves, tenfold would be our *life* in God and in our neighbors.

The region of man's life is a spiritual region. God, his friends, his neighbors, his brothers and sisters all, make up the wide world in which alone his spirit can find room. Man's dungeon is his own self. If he feels it not now, he will yet feel it one day—feel it as a living soul would feel being imprisoned in a dead body, wrapped in sevenfold graveclothes, and buried in a stone-ribbed vault within the last ripple of the sound of the chanting people in the church above.

Life is not in knowing that we are alive, but in loving all forms of life. We are made for the All, because God, who is the All, is our life. And the essential joy of our life lies abroad in the liberty of the All. Our delights, like those of the Ideal Wisdom, are with the sons of men. Our health is in the body of which the Son of Man is the head. The whole region of life is open to us—but, we must live in it or perish.

In such a life, no man shall lose the consciousness of well-being. Far deeper and more complete, God and his neighbor will flash it back upon him—pure as life. No more will he attempt to generate life in the light of his own decadence. For he shall know the glory of his own being in the light of God and of his brother.[1]

The Thank-offering

My Lily snatches not my gift;
Glad is she to be fed,
But to her mouth she will not lift
The piece of broken bread,
Till on my lips, unerring, swift,
The morsel she has laid.

This is her grace before her food,
This her libation poured;
Even thus his offering, Aaron good
Heaved up to thank the Lord,
When for the people all he stood,
And with a cake adored.

So, Father, every gift of thine
I offer at thy knee;
Else take I not the love divine
With which it comes to me;
Not else the offered grace is mine
Of sharing life with thee.

Yea, all my being I would bring,
Yielding it utterly,
Not yet a full-possessed thing
Till heaved again to thee:
Away, my self! away, and cling
To him that makes thee be!

WE BELIEVE IN HIM, NOT ABOUT HIM

A Fictional Selection from *The Musician's Quest*

"What a ladylike woman to be the matron of an asylum!" I said.

Falconer laughed. "That is no asylum. It is a private house."

"And the lady?" I asked.

"Is a lady of private means," he answered, "who prefers Bloomsbury to some of the more luxurious sections of the city, because it is easier to do noble work in it. Her heaven is on the confines of hell."

"What will she do with those children?"

"Kiss them and wash them and put them to bed."

"And after that?"

"Give them bread and milk in the morning."

"And after that?"

"Oh, there's time enough. We'll see. There's only one thing she won't do."

"What is that?"

"Turn them out again."

A pause followed. I was thinking. "Are you a society, then?" I asked at length.

"No. At least we don't use the word. And certainly no other society would acknowledge us."

"What are you, then?"

"Why should we be anything, so long as we do our work?"

"Do you lay claim to no designation of any sort?"

"We are a church if you like. There!"

"Who is your clergyman?

"Nobody."

"Where do you meet?"

"Nowhere."

"What are your rules, then?"

"We have none."

"What makes you a church?"

"Divine service."

"What do you mean by that?"

"The sort of thing you have seen tonight."

"What is your creed?"

"Jesus Christ."

"But what do you believe about him?"

"We believe in him. We consider any belief in him—however small—far better than any amount of belief about him."

"But you must have some rules," I insisted.

"None whatever. They would only cause us trouble and take us from our work. We only do as he has instructed and as he has shown us through his life."

"But who are the *we*?"

"Why, you—if you will do anything—and I and Miss St. John, and twenty others—and a great many more I don't know. It is our work that binds us together."

"But if there's nothing bigger, then when you stop, your ministry stops."

"Ah, but there is something bigger—much bigger! We are not the life of the world. God is. And when we are gone he will send out more and better laborers into the harvest fields."

"But surely the church must be constituted by more than this."

"My dear sir, you forget; I said we were *a* church, not *the* church."

"Do you belong to the Church of England?"

"Yes, some of us. She has preserved records and traditions and we owe her a great deal. And to leave her would inevitably start a quarrel, for which life is too serious in my eyes. I have no time for that."

"Then you count the Church of England *the* Church?"

"Of the universe, no; that is constituted just like ours, with the living, working Lord for the heart of it."

"Will you take me for a member?"

"No."

"Will you not, if—?"

"You may make yourself one if you will. I will not speak a word to gain you. I have shown you work. Do something, and you are of Christ's Church."[2]

Come Down

Still am I haunting
Thy door with my prayers;
Still they are panting
Up thy steep stairs!
Wouldst thou not rather
Come down to my heart,
And there, O my Father,
Be what thou art?

A Meditation of St. Eligius

Queen Mary one day Jesus sent
*   To fetch some water, legends tell;*
The little boy, obedient,
*   Drew a full pitcher from the well;*

But as he raised it to his head,
*   The water lipping with the rim,*
The handle broke, and all was shed
*   Upon the stones about the brim.*

His cloak upon the ground he laid
*   And in it gathered up the pool;**
Obedient there the water staid,
*   And home he bore it plentiful.*

Eligius said, " 'Tis fabled ill:
    The hands that all the world control,
Had here been room for miracle,
    Had made his mother's pitcher whole!

"Still, some few drops for thirsty need
    A poor invention even, when told
In love of thee the Truth indeed,
    Like broken pitcher yet may hold!

"Thy truth, alas, Lord, once I split:
    I thought to bear the pitcher high;
Upon the shining stones of guilt
    I slipped, and there the potsherds lie!

"Master, I cried, no man will drink,
*   No human thirst will e'er be stilled*
Through me, who sit upon the brink,
*   My pitcher broke, thy water spilled!*

"What will they do I waiting left?
*   They looked to me to bring thy law!*
The well is deep, and, sin-bereft,
*   I nothing have wherewith to draw!*

"But as I sat in evil plight,
    With dry parched heart and sickened brain,
Uprose in me the water bright,
    Thou gavest me thyself again!"

*Proverbs 30:4

LOVE YOUR ENEMY

Ye have heard that it hath been said, Thou shalt love thy neighbor, and hate thine enemy. But I say unto you, Love your enemies, bless them that curse you, do good to them that hate you, and pray for them which despitefully use you, and persecute you; That ye may be the children of your Father which is in heaven . . . if ye love them which love you, what reward have ye? . . . Be ye therefore perfect, even as your Father which is in heaven is perfect.

Matthew 5:43–48

Must We Really Love Perfectly?

A man may have begun to love his neighbor, with the hope of someday loving him as himself, and yet notwithstanding start back with fright at another word of our Lord. This seems to be another law yet harder than the first! In truth, it is not another at all, for without obedience to it, even the former command to love one's neighbor cannot be attained unto. The man has not yet learned to love his neighbor as himself, if his heart sinks within him at the word, "I say unto you, Love your enemies."

Surely this is at length *too* much to expect!

Will a man *ever* come to love his enemies? He may come to do good to them that hate him, but when will he pray for them that despitefully use him and persecute him? When? When he is the child of his Father in heaven. Then shall he love his neighbor as himself, even if that neighbor be his enemy. In Leviticus 19:18, quoted by our Lord and his apostles, we find the neighbor and the enemy are one.

Look at the glorious way in which Jesus interprets that scripture which went before him from the law, which ended, "I am the Lord." Jesus says, "That ye may be perfect, as your Father in heaven is perfect."

Is it then reasonable to love our enemies?

God does, therefore it must be the highest reason. But is it reasonable to expect that man should become capable of doing so? Yes, on one ground: that the divine energy is at work in man, to at length make man's actions as divine as his nature is. This is what our Lord was praying for when he said: "That they all may be one, as thou, Father, art in me, and I in thee, that they also may be one in us." Nothing could be less likely to human judgment. But our Lord knows that one day it *will* come.

Why should we love our enemies?

The deepest reason for this we cannot put into words, for it lies in the absolute reality of their being, where our enemies are of one nature with us, even of the divine nature. We cannot see into this, except into a dark abyss. But we can make out a faint shadow of something of the form of this deepest reason, if we let the thoughts of our heart move upon the face of the dim profound.

How Can We Love What We Loathe?

Humanum est errare is a truism, but it possesses, like most truisms, a latent germ of worthy truth. The very word *errare* is a sign that there is a way so truly human that, for a man to leave it, is to *wander*. If it be human to wander, still the wandering is not humanity.

The very words *humane* and *humanity* denote some shadow of that lovingkindness which, when perfected after the divine fashion, shall include even our enemies. We do not call the offering of human sacrifices, the torturing of captives, or cannibalism "humanity." But those who do these deeds are not men because they do them. Their humanity must be deeper than the deeds. It is by virtue of the divine essence which is in them, that pure essential *humanity*, that we call our enemies men and women.

It is this humanity that we are to love—a something, I would say, altogether deeper than and independent of the region of hate. It is the humanity that originates the claim of neighborhood; the neighborhood only determines the opportunity to exercise it. We *must* love this humanity, come between us and it what may.

But how can we love a man or a woman who is cruel and unjust to us? who is filled with bitter contempt, or cuts off with a harsh word every attempt of kindness we would put forth to them? who is mean, unlovely, self-righteous, complaining, self-seeking, critical, sneering, and self-admiring?

These actions or characteristics cannot be loved. The best man hates them most, and even the worst man cannot love them. But do these make up the man? Does a woman, because she does these things, bear their very form? Does there not lie within the man and the woman a divine element of brotherhood, of sisterhood, something lovely and lovable, slowly fading though it may be—dying under the fierce heat of vile passions, or the yet more fearful cold of sepulchral selfishness—but still there? Shall that divine something—which, once awakened to be its own holy self in the man, will loathe these unlovely things tenfold more than we loathe them now—go unrecognized by us?

It is the very presence of this fading humanity that makes it possible for us to hate. If it were only an animal, and not a man or a woman that hurt or harmed us, we would not hate; we would only kill. We hate the man only because we are prevented from loving him. We push over the verge of creation—*we damn*—just because we cannot embrace. For to embrace is the necessity of our deepest being. That foiled, we hate. Instead of admonishing ourselves that there is our enchained brother, that there lies our bound, disfigured, scarcely recognizable sister, captive of the devil (ready to break from their bonds all the sooner if we would but love them!)—instead, we recoil into the hate which would doom them to stay there. And the dearly lovable reality of them we sacrifice to the outer falsehood of Satan's incantations, thus leaving them to perish. Rather, we murder them to get rid of them: we *hate* them.

Yet within even those persons who are most obnoxious to our hate—deep, unseen, hidden, it may be, but just as truly lying there dormant—lies that which, could it but show itself as it is, and as it will show itself one day, would compel and draw from our hearts a devotion of love. It is not the unfriendly, the unlovely, that we are told to love, but the brother, the sister, who is unkind, who is unlovely. Shall we leave our brother to his desolate fate? Shall we not rather say, "With my love at least you shall be surrounded, for you have not your own lovingkindness to infold you. Love shall come as near you as it may, and when yours comes forth to meet mine, we shall be one in the indwelling God."

True Personhood Emerges From Love

Has this all been mere figurative speaking? I *have* been using figures, that I know. But many things which we see most vividly and certainly are more truly expressed by using a right figure, than by attempting to give them a clear outline of logical expression. My figure represents a truth.

"But look at that person," you say. "Even you cannot deny that he is completely unlovely. How can you possibly love him?"

I answer: what you say may seem to be true now, at this moment. But are we bound to let temporal conditions dictate the extent of our obedience? That very person you cannot love, when the evil thing is cast out of him, will be even more a *person*, for he will then be his *true* self. The thing that now makes you dislike him is separable from him. It is therefore not really him. In fact, it makes him all the more less his true self, for it is working death in him. At this moment he is in danger of ceasing to be a person at all. When he is clothed and in his right mind, he will be a person indeed. Then, you *could* not go on hating him, because then he will be lovely. But if you wait to love him until then, until he is easy to love, what good will have been your love? Even the publicans do as much.

Begin to love him now, and help him into the loveliness which is his. Your mind may give you many reasons to dislike him and not to love him. Do not listen to them. Do not hate him, although that is the easiest thing to do. The personality, I say, though clouded, besmeared, defiled with the wrong, lies deeper than the wrong, and indeed, so far as the wrong has reached it, is by the wrong injured, yes, it may be even destroyed. He needs your life, and mind, to help him deliver himself, to help him fight within himself against that wrong, and thus emerge into the true person he is.

Justice in Love

Some who may still not acknowledge the claim of love may yet acknowledge the claim of justice.

There are those who would shrink with horror at the idea of doing anything unjust or unfair—such is their idea of personal pride in the matter—even to the very individuals whom they would never love as Jesus meant us to love.

But if it is impossible, as I believe it is, to be just without love, how much more cannot justice coexist with hate. The pure eye for an honest perspective of another's viewpoint can only accompany the loving heart. The man who hates can hardly be delicate in doing justice to his neighbor's expressions of love, to his neighbor's preferences and peculiarities. It is hard enough to be just to our friends; how then shall our enemies fare with us? For justice demands that we shall think rightly of our neighbor as certainly as that we shall neither steal his goods nor bear false witness against him.

Man is not made for justice from his fellow, but for love, which is greater than justice. By including it, love supersedes justice. *Mere* justice is an impossibility, a fiction of analysis. It does not exist between man and man, except relatively in human *law*.

Justice to *truly* be justice must be more than justice. Love is the law of our condition, without which we can no more render justice than a man can keep a straight line walking in the dark. The eye is not single, and the body is not full of light. No man who is even indifferent to his brother can recognize the claims which that brother's humanity has upon him. In fact, the very indifference itself is an injustice.

Hence, all the law is summed up in Jesus' simple words: "Love your neighbor . . . Love your enemy."[1]

PRACTICAL FAITH

A Fictional Selection from *The Gentlewoman's Choice*

How well I understand you!" Hester exclaimed with enthusiasm. "But would you mind telling me how you first began? I started thinking of these things because I saw how miserable so many people were, and longed to do something to make life better for them."

"That was not quite the way with me," replied Christopher. "In the first place, you may suppose I could not have followed my wishes if I did not have money. I did have a good deal—left me by my grandfather. My father died when I was a child, I am glad to say."

"Glad to say!" Hester's voice revealed her shock.

"Yes. If he had lived, he may have followed in my grandfather's footsteps. Not that my grandfather was considered a bad man. On the contrary, he stood high in the world's opinion. When he died and left me his money, it was necessary that I look into his business affairs, for it was my mother's wish that I should follow the same. In the course of my investigation I came across things which I considered to be dishonest in the way the business had been run. And where there had been wrong, I felt there must be atonement, restitution. I could not look on the money that had been left me as mine, for part of it at least, I cannot say how much, ought not to be mine at all.

"Then the truth dawned on me, and I saw that my business in life must be to send the money out again into the channels of right. I could claim a workman's wages for that. The history of the business went so far back that it would have been impossible to return the sums to the same people from whom they had been taken. Therefore something else, and that a large something, must be done. Little by little it grew clearer to me that the greatest good I could do lay in doing what Christ himself did, giving the energy of my life to delivering men out of their lonely self-centeredness into the liberty of becoming sons of God. So I continued to study medicine and then, by the doctor's art, have gradually learned how God would have me spend the money upon humanity itself, repaying to mankind what had been wrongfully taken from its individuals much earlier.

"That is my story. I now try to work steadily, without haste, and have this very day gotten a new idea that may have some true possibilities in it."

"Will you tell me what it is?" asked Hester.

"I don't like talking about things before they are begun," answered Christopher.

"I know what I would do if I had money!" said Hester.

"You have given me the right to ask what—though perhaps not the right to an answer."

"I would have a house of refuge to which anyone might run for shelter or rest or warmth or food or medicine or whatever he needed. It would have no society or subscription or committee, but would be my own to use as God enabled me. It would be a refuge for the needy, those out of work, to the child with a cut finger. I would not take in drunkards or ruined speculators— at least not before they were very miserable indeed. The suffering of such is the only desirable consequence of their doing, and to save them from it would be to take away their last chance."

"It is a lovely idea," said Christopher heartily. "One of my hopes is to build a small hospital for children in some lovely place, near some sad, ugly one. But I am in no hurry. If it is to be, God will see to it. Small beginnings with slow growings have time to root themselves thoroughly. God's beginnings are always imperceptible, whether in the region of soul or of matter. How the devil would have laughed at the idea of a society or an organization for saving the world. But when he saw *one* man take it in hand, one who was in no haste even to do that, one who would only do the will of God with all his heart and soul, and cared for nothing else, then, indeed, he might tremble for his kingdom!

"It is the individual Christians forming the church by their obedient individuality that have done all the good since men for the love of Christ began to gather together. No organization, not even a religious organization, can ever accomplish anything. It is individual love alone that can combine into a larger flame. There is no true power but that which has individual roots. Neither custom nor habit nor law nor foundation is a root. The real roots are individual conscience that hates evil, individual faith that loves and obeys God, and individual heart with its kiss of charity."[2]

The Children's Heaven

The infant lies in blessed ease
  Upon his mother's breast;
No storm, no dark, the baby sees
  Invade his heaven of rest.

He nothing knows of change or death—
  Her face his holy skies;
The air he breathes, his mother's breath;
  His stars, his mother's eyes!

Yet half the soft winds wandering there
  Are sighs that come of fears;
The dew slow falling through that air—
  It is the dew of tears;
And ah, my child, thy heavenly home
  Hath storms as well as dew;
Black clouds fill sometimes all its dome,
  And quench the starry blue!

"My smile would win no smile again,
  If baby saw the things
That ache across his mother's brain
  The while to him she sings!
Thy faith in me is faith in vain—
  I am not what I seem:
O dreary day, O cruel pain,
  That wakes thee from thy dream!"

Nay, pity not his dreams so fair,
  Fear thou no waking grief;
Oh, safer he than though thou were
  Good as his vague belief!
There is a heaven that heaven above
  Whereon he gazes now;
A truer love than in thy kiss;
  A better friend than thou!

The Father's arms fold like a nest
  Both thee and him about;
His face looks down, a heaven of rest,
  Where comes no dark, no doubt.
Its mists are clouds of stars that move
  On, on, with progress rife;
Its winds, the goings of his love;
  Its dew, the dew of life.

We for our children seek thy heart,
  For them we lift our eyes:
Lord, should their faith in us depart,
  Let faith in thee arise.
When childhood's visions them forsake,
  To women grown and men,
Back to thy heart their hearts oh take,
  And bid them dream again.

THE END OF ENMITY

Love ye your enemies, and do good, and lend, hoping for nothing again; and your reward shall be great, and ye shall be the children of the Highest.

Luke 6:35

What If We Are the Enemy!

In discussing love for either neighbors or enemies, it is easy to take for granted that all barriers, all hindrances to love lie with the *other* person so considered.

But especially in consideration of the scripture regarding enemies, the question must be put to each man or woman by himself: "Is my neighbor indeed my enemy, or am I my neighbor's enemy?"

What an awful thought! Perhaps we have had the whole thing backwards all along! Even if he be mine, does not that make me his as well? Am I not thus refusing to acknowledge the child of the kingdom within his bosom, so killing the child of the kingdom within my own?

Let us claim for ourselves no more indulgence than we give to him. Such honesty will end in severity at home in our own hearts, and clemency abroad in our attitude toward others. For we are accountable for the sin in ourselves, and have to kill it. We are accountable for the good in our neighbor, and have to cherish it. But we are *not* accountable for the bad in him. He only, in the name and power of God, can kill the bad in himself. We can cherish the good in him by being good to him across all the evil fog that comes between our love and his good.

And it must not be forgotten that this fog is often the result of misapprehension and mistake, giving rise to all kinds of indignations, resentments, regrets—none of which we can accurately discern where our own selves are concerned. Scarcely anything about us is exactly as it seems. But at the core there is truth enough to dispel all falsehood and reveal life as unspeakably divine.

O brother, sister, across this weary fog, dimly lighted by the faint torches of our truth seeking, I call to the divine in you, which is mine, not to rebuke you, not to rouse you, but to say, "I love you. In God's name I love you!" And I will wait until the true self looks out of your eyes and knows the true self in me.

The Enemy—Destined to Be a Friend

In the working of divine Love upon the race, my enemy is doomed to cease to be my enemy and to become my friend. One flash of truth toward me would destroy my enmity at once. One heartfelt confession of wrong, and our enmity passes away. From each comes forth the brother who was inside the enemy all the time.

For this, Truth is at work. In the faith of this working, let us love the enemy now, accepting God's work in advance, as it were. Let us believe as though already seeing his yet invisible triumph, clasping and holding our brother fast, in defiance of the changeful wiles of the wicked one which would persuade our eyes and hearts that he is not yet our brother.

But again I must ask: what if *we* are in the wrong and do the wrong, and hate our brother and sister because *we* have injured rather than because of anything they have done to us?

What then? Then, let us cry to God as from the throat of hell! Let us cry to him, knowing the vile disease that cleaves tight to us; let us cry as though possessed of an evil spirit; let us cry as one buried alive, from the grave of our evil consciousness, that God would take pity upon us the chief of sinners, the most wretched of men, and send some help to lift us from the fearful pit and the miry clay. Nothing will help but the Spirit proceeding from the Father and the Son, the spirit of the Father and the Brother casting out and revealing. It will be with retching and foaming, with a terrible cry and a lying as one dead, that such a demon will go out of us. But what a vision will then arise in the depths of the purified soul!

"Be ye perfect, even as your father which is in heaven is perfect. . . . Love your enemies, and ye shall be the children of the highest." It is the divine glory to *forgive*.

God's Forgiveness Will Never End

Yet a time will come—say some who are steeped in the theologies of their spiritual ancestors, which Jesus called the traditions of men—

a time when even the unchangeable and almighty God will cease to forgive. At that time it will no longer belong to his perfection to love his enemies. Then will he look calmly, and have his children look calmly too, upon the ascending smoke of the everlasting torments of our strong brothers, our beautiful sisters. No, rather, the brothers are weak now; the sisters are ugly now!

O brother, believe it not! "O Christ!" the redeemed would cry, "Where are you, our strong Jesus? Come, our grand Brother. See the suffering brothers down below! See the tormented sisters! Come, Lord of Life! Monarch of Suffering! Redeem them. For us, we will go down into the burning, and see whether we cannot at least carry a drop of water through the howling flames to cool their tongues."

Believe it not, my brother, my sister, lest it quench forgiveness in you. Believe not that there is a limit, an end, to God's forgiveness, and his redeeming love and power. Believe it not, lest you justify your unforgiving heart and thus be not forgiven yourself, but go down with those your brothers to the torment, from where, if God were not better than that phantom many *call* God, you and the rest of them should *never* come out, but whence assuredly you shall come out when you have paid the uttermost farthing. Out you shall come when you have learned of God in hell what you refused to learn of him upon the gentle-toned earth, when you have learned what the sunshine and the rain could not teach you, nor the sweet compunctions of the seasons, nor the stately visits of the morning and eventide, nor the human face divine, nor the word that was nigh thee in your heart and in your mouth—the story of him who was mighty to save, because he was perfect in love.

O Father, thou art All-in-all, perfect beyond the longing of thy children, and we are all and altogether thine. Thou wilt make us pure and loving and free. We shall stand fearless in thy presence, because perfect in thy love. Then shall thy children be of good cheer, infinite in the love of each other, and eternal in thy love. Lord Jesus, let the heart of a child be given to us, in order that we may arise from the grave of our dead selves and die no more, but see the living God face to face. [1]

The Slow Waking of Conscience

A Fictional Selection from *The Marquis of Lossie*

All his life, since ever he had had business, Mr. Crathie had prided himself on his honesty, and was therefore in one of the most dangerous moral positions a man could occupy—ruinous even to the honesty itself. Asleep in the mud, he dreamed himself awake on a pedestal. At best such a man is but perched on a needle point when he thinketh he standeth.

The limited honesty of the factor clave to the interest of his employers, and let the rights he encountered take care of themselves. Those he dealt with were to him rather as enemies than friends, not enemies to be prayed for, but to be spoiled. Malcolm's doctrine of honesty in horse-dealing was to him ludicrously new. His notion of honesty in that kind was to cheat the buyer for his master if he could, proud to write in his book a large sum against the name of the animal.

That the bastard Malcolm, or the ignorant and indeed fallen fisher-girl Lizzy, should judge differently, nowise troubled him: what could they know about the rights and wrongs of business?

He said to himself, with the superior smile of arrogated common-sense, that "no mere man since the fall" could be expected to do like him; that he was divine, and had not to fight for a living; that he set us an example that we might see what sinners we were; that religion was one thing, and a very proper thing, but business was another, and a very proper thing also—with customs and indeed laws of its own far more determinate, at least definite, than those of religion, and that to mingle the one with the other was not merely absurd—it was irreverent and wrong, and certainly never intended in the Bible, which must surely be common sense. It was *the Bible* always with him— never *the will of Christ*. But although he could dispose of the question thus satisfactorily, yet, as he lay ill, supine, without any distracting occupation, the thing haunted him.

Now in his father's cottage had lain, much dabbled in by the children, a certain coverless copy of the *Pilgrim's Progress*, round in the face and hollow in the back, in which, among other pictures, was one of the Wicket-gate. This scripture of his childhood, given by inspiration of God, threw out, in one of his troubled and feverish nights, a dream-bud in the brain of the man. He saw the face of Jesus looking on him over the top of the Wicket-gate, at which he had been for some time knocking in vain, while the cruel dog barked loud from the enemy's yard. But that face, when at last it came, was full of sorrowful displeasure. And in his heart he knew that it was because of a certain transaction in horse-dealing, wherein he had hitherto lauded his own cunning—adroitness, he considered it—and success. One word only he heard from the lips of the Man—"Worker of iniquity,"—and awoke with a great start.

From that moment, truths *began* to be facts to him. The beginning of the change was indeed very small, but every beginning is small, and every beginning is a creation. Monad, molecule, protoplasm, whatever word may be attached to it when it becomes appreciable by men—being however many stages upon its journey—beginning is an irrepressible fact; and however far from good or humble even after many days, the man here began to grow good and humble. His dull unimaginative nature, a perfect attic-room of the world and its rusting affairs, had received a gift in a dream—a truth from the lips of the Lord . . . [to] lie in old Hector Crathie's cottage, that it might enter and lie in young Hector Crathie's brain until he grew old and had done wrong enough to heed it, when it rose upon him in a dream, and had its way. Henceforth the claims of his neighbor began to reveal themselves, and his mind to breed conscientious doubts and scruples, with which, struggle as he might against it, a certain respect for Malcolm would keep coming and mingling—a feeling which grew with its returns, until, by slow changes, he began at length to regard him as the minister of God's vengeance—for his punishment—and perhaps salvation—who could tell?[2]

NOTES

Introduction

1. Mike Mason, *The Mystery of the Word* (San Francisco: Harper & Row, 1988), pp. xii-ixv.

Chapter 1

1. *Unspoken Sermons*, Second Series, "The Truth in Jesus."
2. *The Lady's Confession*, pp. 80–81.
3. *Unspoken Sermons*, op. cit.
4. *Donal Grant*, chapter 1.
5. *Unspoken Sermons*, op. cit.
6. *There and Back*, chapter 5.
7. *Unspoken Sermons*, op. cit.
8. *The Baron's Apprenticeship*, p. 69.
9. *Unspoken Sermons*, op. cit.
10. *Annals of a Quiet Neighborhood*, chapter 28.
11. *David Elginbrod*, chapter 49.
12. *Donal Grant*, chapter 6.
13. *Unspoken Sermons*, op. cit.
14. *The Baron's Apprenticeship*, pp. 114–116.
15. *A Daughter's Devotion*, pp. 279–281.

Chapter Two

1. *Unspoken Sermons*, Second Series, "The Truth in Jesus."
2. *Paul Faber, Surgeon*, chapters 18, 5.
3. *Unspoken Sermons*, op. cit.
4. *The Curate's Awakening*, pp. 82–83.
5. *The Baron's Apprenticeship*, pp. 133–135.

Chapter Three

1. *Unspoken Sermons*, Second Series, "The Truth in Jesus."
2. *Donal Grant*, chapter 20.
3. *The Landlady's Master*, pp. 44, 45, 65, 67.

Chapter 4

1. *Unspoken Sermons*, Second Series, "The Hardness of the Way."
2. *The Marquis of Lossie*, chapter 61 & *The Marquis' Secret*, pp. 179–181.

Chapter 5

1. *Unspoken Sermons*, Second Series, "The Cause of Spiritual Stupidity."
2. *Donal Grant*, chapter 5.
3. *Warlock O' Glenwarlock*, chapter 42.
4. *Sir Gibbie*, chapters 23, 31, 38.
5. *The Landlady's Master*, pp. 175–176.

Chapter 6

1. *Unspoken Sermons*, Second Series, "The Cause of Spiritual Stupidity."
2. *The Laird's Inheritance*, p. 179.
3. *Unspoken Sermons*, op. cit.
4. *The Curate's Awakening*, pp. 214–215.
5. *The Highlander's Last Song*, chapter 15.

Chapter 7

1. *Unspoken Sermons*, Third Series, "The Knowing of the Son."
2. *The Highlander's Last Song*, pp. 96–99.

Chapter 8

1. *Unspoken Sermons*, Third Series, "The Knowing of the Son."
2. *Thomas Wingfold, Curate*, chapter 57.
3. *Unspoken Sermons*, op. cit.
4. *The Baron's Apprenticeship*, pp. 154–155.
5. *The Landlady's Master*, pp. 49–53.

Chapter 9

1. *Unspoken Sermons*, Second Series, "Self Denial."
2. *The Highlander's Last Song*, pp. 121–124.
3. *The Highlander's Last Song*, pp. 148–149.

Chapter 10

1. *Unspoken Sermons*, Second Series, "Self Denial."
2. *The Curate's Awakening*, pp. 216–218.

Chapter 11

1. *Unspoken Sermons*, Second Series, "Self Denial."
2. *Donal Grant*, chapter 12.
3. *Unspoken Sermons*, op. cit.
4. *The Highlander's Last Song*, pp. 77, 82.
5. *Donal Grant*, chapter 8.
6. *Donal Grant*, chapters 3, 23, 15, 35.

Chapter 12

1. *The Hope of the Gospel*, "God's Family."
2. *The Lady's Confession*, p. 150.
3. *The Hope of the Gospel*, op. cit.

4. *Paul Faber,* Surgeon, chapter 36.
5. *The Lady's Confession,* p. 171.
6. *The Hope of the Gospel,* op. cit.
7. *The Minister's Restoration,* p. 187.
8. *The Lady's Confession,* pp. 140–141.

Chapter 13

1. *The Hope of the Gospel,* "God's Family."
2. *Donal Grant,* chapter 9.

Chapter 14

1. *The Hope of the Gospel,* "God's Family."
2. *The Curate's Awakening,* pp. 144–146.

Chapter 15

1. *The Hope of the Gospel,* "The Heirs of Heaven and Earth."
2. *Sir Gibbie,* chapter 24.
3. *The Marquis' Secret,* pp. 101–105.

Chapter 16

1. *The Hope of the Gospel,* "The Heirs of Heaven and Earth."
2. *Sir Gibbie,* chapters 24, 25.

Chapter 17

1. *The Hope of the Gospel,* "The Heirs of Heaven and Earth."
2. *Donal Grant,* chapter 1.
3. *The Hope of the Gospel,* op. cit.
4. *Unspoken Sermons,* Second Series, "The Hardness of the Way."
5. *Donal Grant,* chapter 25.
6. *What's Mine's Mine,* chapters 32, 46.
7. *The Seaboard Parish,* chapter 32.
8. *Warlock O' Glenwarlock,* chapter 51.
9. *Unspoken Sermons,* op. cit.
10. *The Curate's Awakening,* pp. 91–93.

Chapter 18

1. *The Hope of the Gospel,* "Salvation From Sin."
2. *The Elect Lady,* chapter 10.
3. *The Gentlewoman's Choice,* p. 21.
4. *The Landlady's Master,* pp. 121–122.
5. *The Tutor's First Love,* p. 165.
6. *Donal Grant,* chapter 27.
7. *The Baron's Apprenticeship,* p. 175, and *There and Back,* chapter 47.
8. *The Hope of the Gospel,* op. cit.
9. *The Marquis' Secret,* pp. 142–145.
10. *Malcolm,* chapter 53.

Chapter 19

1. *Unspoken Sermons*, Second Series, "The Way."
2. *The Curate's Awakening*, pp. 172–173.

Chapter 20

1. *Unspoken Sermons*, Second Series, "The Way."
2. *The Landlady's Master*, pp. 70–71.
3. *Donal Grant*, chapter 30.

Chapter 21

1. *Unspoken Sermons*, Third Series, "Freedom."
2. *The Poetical Works of George MacDonald.*
3. *A Daughter's Devotion*, pp. 80–82.

Chapter 22

1. *Unspoken Sermons*, Third Series, "Freedom."
2. *Lilith*, chapters 42, 44, 31.
3. *Unspoken Sermons*, op. cit.
4. *The Laird's Inheritance*, pp. 154–156.

Chapter 23

1. *Unspoken Sermons*, First Series, "The Heart With the Treasure."
2. *The Landlady's Master*, pp. 154–158.

Chapter 24

1. *Unspoken Sermons*, First Series, "The Temptation in the Wilderness."
2. *The Musician's Quest*, pp. 182–184.

Chapter 25

1. *Unspoken Sermons*, First Series, "The Temptation in the Wilderness."
2. *The Vicar's Daughter*, chapter 24.

Chapter 26

1. *Unspoken Sermons*, First Series, "The Eloi."
2. *The Seaboard Parish*, chapter 3.
3. *The Landlady's Master*, pp. 175, 185–186.

Chapter 27

1. *Unspoken Sermons*, First Series, "The Eloi."
2. *Thomas Wingfold, Curate*, chapter 86, *The Minister's Restoration*, pp. 197, 201–202, and *The Landlady's Master*, pp. 142–144.

Chapter 28

1. *Unspoken Sermons*, First Series, "Love Thy Neighbor."
2. *The Curate's Awakening*, pp. 141–143.

Chapter 29

1. *Unspoken Sermons*, First Series, "Love Thy Neighbor."
2. *Annals of a Quiet Neighborhood*, chapter 20.

Chapter 30

1. *Unspoken Sermons*, First Series, "Love Thy Neighbor."
2. *The Musician's Quest*, pp. 218–219.

Chapter 31

1. *Unspoken Sermons*, First Series, "Love Thine Enemies."
2. *The Gentlewoman's Choice*, pp. 176–178.

Chapter 32

1. *Unspoken Sermons*, First Series, "Love Thine Enemy."
2. *The Marquis of Lossie*, chapter 63.

BETHANY HOUSE PUBLISHERS

Minneapolis, Minnesota 55438

The Novels of George MacDonald Edited for Today's Reader

Edited Title	Original Title
The Fisherman's Lady	Malcolm
The Marquis' Secret	The Marquis of Lossie
The Baronet's Song	Sir Gibbie
The Shepherd's Castle	Donal Grant
The Tutor's First Love	David Elginbrod
The Musician's Quest	Robert Falconer
The Maiden's Bequest	Alec Forbes
The Curate's Awakening	Thomas Wingfold
The Lady's Confession	Paul Faber
The Baron's Apprenticeship	There and Back
The Highlander's Last Song	What's Mine's Mine
The Gentlewoman's Choice	Weighed and Wanting
The Laird's Inheritance	Warlock O'Glenwarlock
The Minister's Restoration	Salted with Fire
A Daughter's Devotion	Mary Marston
The Peasant Girl's Dream	Heather and Snow
The Landlady's Master	The Elect Lady
The Poet's Homecoming	Home Again

George MacDonald: Scotland's Beloved Storyteller by Michael Phillips
Discovering the Character of God by George MacDonald
Knowing the Heart of God by George MacDonald

SUNRISE BOOKS, PUBLISHERS
Eureka, California 95501
The Sunrise Centenary Editions of the Original Works of George MacDonald in Leatherbound Collector's Editions

Novels

Alec Forbes of Howglen
Sir Gibbie
Thomas Wingfold, Curate
Malcolm
Salted with Fire
The Elect Lady

Sermons

Unspoken Sermons I
The Hope of the Gospel

Poems

A Hidden Life & Other Poems
The Disciple and Other Poems

The Masterline Series of Studies and Essays About George MacDonald

From a Northern Window: A Personal Remembrance of George MacDonald by his son Ronald MacDonald

The Harmony Within: The Spiritual Vision of George MacDonald by Rolland Hein

George MacDonald's Fiction: A Twentieth-Century View by Richard Reis

God's Fiction: Symbolism and Allegory in the Works of George MacDonald by David Robb